Handwriting Research

Impact on the Brain and Literacy Development

critical thinking · composition · memory · fluency · spelling · vocabulary · literacy · reading acquisition · decoding

ZB **Zaner-Bloser**

Acknowledgments

"Where Does Handwriting Fit In?" by Susan M. Cahill from *Intervention in School and Clinic*, Vol. 44, No. 4, Mar., 2009, 223–228. Copyright ©2009 by Hammill Institute on Disabilities. Reprinted by Permission of SAGE Publications.

"Best Practices in Spelling and Handwriting" by Bob Schlagal in *Best Practices in Writing Instruction*, Steve Graham, Charles A. MacArthur, and Jill Fitzgerald, eds. Copyright ©2007 by Guilford Publications, Inc. Reproduced with permission of Guilford Publications, Inc. via Copyright Clearance Center.

"We Still Need to Teach and Value Handwriting" reprinted from *Literacy at the Crossroads: Crucial Talk About Reading, Writing, and Other Teaching Dilemmas* by Regie Routman. Pages 121–123. Copyright ©1996 by Regie Routman. Published by Heinemann, a division of Reed Elsevier Inc., Portsmouth, NH. Used by permission of the publisher.

Reprinted with kind permission from Springer Science + Business Media: *Annals of Dyslexia*, "Handwriting: A Neglected Cornerstone of Literacy," Vol. 46, 1996, 21–35, by Betty Sheffield, July 28, 2000.

"Sensori-Motor Experience Leads to Changes in Visual Processing in the Developing Brain" by Karin Harman James From Developmental Science 13:2 (2010), pp 279-288. Reprinted by permission of John Wiley & Sons. Copyright © 2009 The Author. Journal Compilation (c) 2010 Blackwell Publishing Ltd, 9600 Garsington Road, Oxford OX4 2DQ and 350 Main Street, Malden, MA 02148, USA.

Excerpts from "What Does Reading Have to Tell Us About Writing?" by Kenneth R. Pugh, Stephen J. Frost, Rebecca Sandak, Margie Gillis, Dina Moore, Annette R. Jenner, and W. Einar Mencl in *Handbook of Writing Research*, Steve Graham, and Jill Fitzgerald, eds. New York. Copyright 2006 by Guilford Publications, Inc. Reproduced with permission of GUILFORD PUBLICATIONS, INC. via Copyright Clearance Center.

Copyright © 2007 by the American Psychological Association. Reproduced with permission. Excerpts from "What Predicts Skill in Lecture Note Taking?" by Stephen T. Peverly, Vivek Ramaswamy, Cindy Brown, James Sumowski, Moona Alidoost, and Joanna Garner in Journal of Educational Psychology 2007, Vol. 99, No. 1, 167–180, Published by American Psychological Association. The use of this information does not imply endorsement by the publisher.

Excerpt from "Performance Components Needed for Handwriting" from "Developing a Process to Address Handwriting Concerns" in *Practical Considerations for School-Based Occupational Therapists* by Lynne Pape and Kelly Ryba, Copyright 2004 by AMERICAN OCCUPATIONAL THERAPY ASSOCIATION. Reproduced with permission of AMERICAN OCCUPATIONAL THERAPY ASSOCIATION via Copyright Clearance Center.

"Development of a Mature Pencil Grasp" from *Start to Finish: Developmentally Sequenced Fine Motor Activities for Preschool Children* by Nory Marsh. Imaginart International, Inc. ©1998.

Excerpt from "The Effects of Sensorimotor-Based Intervention Versus Therapeutic Practice on Improving Handwriting Performance in 6- to 11-Year-Old Children" by Peggy L. Denton, Steven Cope, and Christine Moser. Copyright 2006 by American Occupational Therapy Association. Reproduced with permission of The American Occupational Therapy Association via Copyright Clearance Center.

Adams, Marilyn Jager, *Beginning to Read: Thinking and Learning about Print*, 1600 word excerpt from pages 361–364, print and electronic formats, ©1990 Massachusetts Institute of Technology, by permission of The MIT Press.

Excerpt from "The Influence of Writing Practice on Letter Recognition in Preschool Children: A Comparison Between Handwriting and Typing" by Marieke Longcamp, Marie-Thérèse Zerbato-Poudou, and Jean-Luc Velay, ©2005 from Acta Psychologica 119 67–79.

Excerpt from "The Effect of Handwriting Style on Alphabet Recognition" by Debby Kuhl and Peter Dewitz. Paper presented at the Annual Meeting of the American Educational Research Association, April 1, 1994, New Orleans, LA. Reprinted by permission.

Excerpt from "Are Slanted Manuscript Alphabets Superior to the Traditional Manuscript Alphabet?" by Steve Graham (1993/94) *Childhood Education*, 70, 91–95. Copyright© 1993 by the Association of Childhood Education International. Reproduced with permission of the Association for Childhood Education International via Copyright Clearance Center.

"D'Nealian and Zaner-Bloser Manuscript Alphabets and Initial Transition to Cursive Handwriting," by Jennifer Trap-Porter, John O. Cooper, David S. Hill, Karen Swisher and Louis J. LaNunziata in The Journal of Educational Research, Vol. 77, No. 6, July/Aug., 1984. Copyright 1984 by TAYLOR & FRANCIS INFORMA UK LTD - JOURNALS. Reproduced with permission of TAYLOR & FRANCIS INFORMA UK LTD - JOURNALS via Copyright Clearance Center.

This article is reprinted from C. Christensen & D. Jones (2000) "Handwriting: An Underestimated Skill in the Development of Written Language" Handwriting Today, 2, 56–69 by kind permission from The National Handwriting Association (www.nha-handwriting.org.uk).

ISBN   978-07367-7244-0

Zaner-Bloser, Inc., 1-800-421-3018

www.zaner-bloser.com

Printed in the United States of America

13 14 15 16   19840   5 4 3

SUSTAINABLE FORESTRY INITIATIVE

Certified Chain of Custody
Promoting Sustainable Forestry
www.sfiprogram.org
SFICOC-00993

Contents

Contents

REAL LIFE ADVENTURES

The computer generation.

Handwriting in the 21st Century?

Research Shows Why Handwriting Belongs in Today's Classroom

A Summary of Research Presented at Handwriting in the 21st Century? An Educational Summit

Saperstein Associates

Introduction

In a society that values technology above all else, handwriting instruction has begun to fall by the wayside. Although completing assignments by hand remains a prevalent practice in many elementary schools,[5] an estimated 25–33% of students are struggling to achieve competency in this skill.[4] Research indicates that handwriting influences reading,[1,6] writing,[1,5] language,[8] and critical thinking abilities.[10] Yet, statistics show that not all students are being provided with adequate instruction in this foundational skill.

As students become increasingly reliant on communication via digital device, some educators have shifted their focus from handwriting instruction to teaching keyboarding instead. In the 21st century classroom, keyboarding is undoubtedly necessary, but teaching this skill in lieu of handwriting can leave students at a disadvantage. If handwriting isn't learned and practiced (especially in the earlier grades), students

> [Doubt about the value of handwriting instruction] is similar to what happened with math as calculators and computers came into vogue . . . people wondered whether students needed to learn how to do math. The answer in both cases is absolutely "yes." Writing is not obsolete.
>
> —Daniel A. Domenech, executive director of the American Association of School Administrators

are not given the opportunity to experience the related benefits of this skill that has been shown to

- increase brain activation.[6]

- impact performance across all academic subjects.[2]

- provide a foundation for higher-order skills.[1, 10]

Handwriting: A Laissez-Faire Approach

Most states have now adopted the Common Core State Standards (CCSS), which offer a framework to prepare students for 21st century success in college and career. Although research shows that handwriting increases a student's potential for academic and professional achievement, this skill is rarely mentioned in the CCSS—and cursive handwriting is excluded altogether. According to the CCSS, manuscript handwriting instruction is required only through Grade 1 (but fluency and automaticity in handwriting have been shown to develop well beyond then).[5]

Beyond Grade 1, states can choose to teach manuscript handwriting, cursive handwriting, or a combination of both by invoking the right to augment the standards with an additional 15% of content that they deem appropriate. Or they can eliminate handwriting instruction entirely. The result of this laissez-faire approach is an inconsistency in handwriting instruction, and in turn, an inequity regarding students' access to a skill that lays the groundwork for academic achievement.

What exactly does the research say about how handwriting instruction affects learning? What are the implications of including—or not including—handwriting instruction in the curriculum? "Handwriting in the 21st Century?: An Educational Summit" held on January 23, 2012 in Washington, D.C. gathered educators and handwriting researchers to explore and debate these important questions. Research presented at the summit demonstrated how handwriting skills support students' cognitive development[6] and overall academic achievement.[2] However, despite studies that demonstrate the efficacy of handwriting, the lack of consistency in its instruction remains. This pertinent issue warrants a set of benchmarked standards that can be implemented by all states. With this research summary, the education community can better codify the elements of handwriting that are most important for effectively teaching this skill, thereby contributing to the highest level of education for all students—regardless of the state in which they reside.

Research Shows Handwriting's Impact On...
Reading, Writing, and Language Abilities

The CCSS recognize the interrelationship between oral and written language and how the processes that underlie these skills are essential for effective communication.[8] According to the standards, "oral language development precedes and is the foundation for written language development."[8] Written language is comprised of receptive (reading) and expressive (writing) language skills.[8] The ability to understand words (decoding and comprehension involved in reading), as the standards note, is the precursor to a student's ability to produce them (spelling and composition involved in writing).[8] Handwriting-related research indicates that the critical skill of handwriting influences the processes associated with receptive and expressive language. However, when handwriting is not taught beyond Grade 1 (which is the highest level of instruction required in the CCSS), students are deprived of the opportunity to gain fluency and automaticity in this skill that has been shown to bolster reading and writing abilities.

> An estimated 25–33% of students are struggling to achieve competency in [handwriting].[4]

As students progress in their academic careers, the CCSS require proficiency in producing clear and coherent writing in multiple genres (argument, informative/explanatory, and narrative), under increasingly challenging time frames, and for "a range of tasks, purposes, and audiences."[7] Studies demonstrate a positive correlation between handwriting and the composing abilities called for in the CCSS. If handwriting is taught, students' writing quality, quantity, and speed have been shown to improve. Additionally, when handwriting becomes automatic, students can better focus on the planning and thought organization that is required for effective composition.[1,2]

> When handwriting becomes automatic, students can better focus on the planning and thought organization that is required for effective composition.[1,2]

Handwriting influences a student's ability to write words, thereby improving the ability to transform ideas into written language by constructing multi-word sentences.[1]

Dr. Steve Graham, Currey Ingram professor of literacy at Vanderbilt University, and Dr. Tanya Santagelo, associate professor of special education at Arcadia University, conducted a meta-analysis of research studies regarding students' handwriting proficiency.[5] After analyzing whether handwriting instruction produced greater gains than no handwriting instruction, they concluded that teaching this skill resulted in improved fluency and an increase in the quantity of students' writing.[5]

Dr. Virginia Berninger, a professor of educational psychology at the University of Washington, reports that, after studying students in Grades 2, 4, and 6, those who used handwriting wrote more words, wrote words faster, and expressed more ideas than those who used keyboarding.[1] In subsequent studies of children who were trained to find and write the letters that precede and follow other letters, results indicated that the length of compositions improved.[1] This improvement was especially notable during the transition between Grade 3 and Grade 4, when composing requirements increase.[1]

In addition to displaying writing competency, students are also required by the CCSS to proficiently and independently comprehend text of increasing complexity.[8] Research findings suggest that self-generated action, in the form of handwriting, is a crucial component in setting up brain systems for reading acquisition.[6] According to Dr. Karin Harman James, associate professor of psychological and brain sciences at Indiana University, handwriting appears to contribute to reading fluency by activating visual perception of letters and improving children's accuracy and speed for recognizing letters.[6] Also, Dr. Berninger conducted a study in which students in Grade 1 who were taught handwriting were better able to see letter forms in the "mind's eye."[1] When asked to write these letters from memory, the students exhibited improvement in word reading (as well as improved handwriting and composing).[1]

When students do not adequately develop handwriting skills, the negative implications can be lifelong.[4] Without consistent exposure to handwriting, research indicates that students can experience difficulty in certain processes required for success in reading and writing, including

- retrieving letters from memory.[1,2]

- reproducing letters on paper.[1,2]

- spelling accurately.[1]

- extracting meaning from text or lecture.[10]

- interpreting the context of words and phrases.[3]

Brain Functioning

Handwriting has not only been shown to support literacy skills (reading, writing, and oral language), but it also has been shown to impact neurological processes. When children in a research study were asked to form a new letter using the same strokes as a familiar well-practiced letter, poor handwriters engaged more brain regions than good handwriters.[1] Functional Magnetic Resonance Imaging (fMRI) showed that the brains of poor handwriters consumed more of the oxygen required to burn glucose for fuel.[1] This fuel supplies the energy the brain needs in order to complete its work.[1] Therefore, the research suggests that children who struggle with handwriting are less efficient in engaging their brains when learning to write new letters.[1]

Handwriting development begins as early as infancy, when children are first able to grasp a writing object and leave a mark on paper.[1] A child's corticospinal tract—which reaches the fingertips and impacts fine motor skills—is not fully developed until age 10.[4] This is another indicator that handwriting, a fundamental skills that strengthens fine motor processes, should continue to be taught throughout the early years of a child's life.

In addition to an evolving body of research that demonstrates a link between handwriting and brain functioning, experts suggest that handwriting lightens a student's cognitive load.[10] With consistent handwriting practice, the processes involved become less demanding and more automatic, enabling students to devote a higher amount of neurological resources to critical thinking and thought organization.[10] However, when students do not learn and practice handwriting, their struggle to achieve automaticity and fluency decreases their capacity to carry out higher-order skills.

Handwriting: A Standardized Approach

The convergence of evidence provided herein leaves little room for doubt about the efficacy of handwriting and the continuing need for this critical skill in the 21st century classroom. Though keyboarding is indeed necessary in a technological era, the need for this skill should not influence an educator's decision to minimize or eliminate handwriting instruction. When properly taught, handwriting enables students to more efficiently perform the hierarchy of skills required in other subjects, which ultimately leads to better grades, better test scores, and better academic performance.[10]

By helping to build a solid academic foundation, handwriting, as research shows, is a foundational skill that helps achieve the CCSS' primary goal of preparing students for college and career "in a 21st century, globally competitive society."[9]

The Relationship Between Letter Printing and Brain Activation

EXPERIMENT

Using fMRI (functional Magnetic Resonance Imaging), Dr. James studied how letter printing affects the brain activation of children.[6]

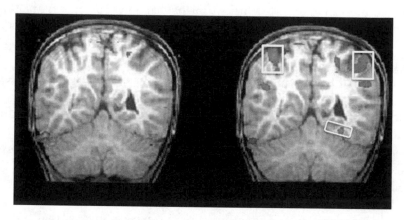

Comparison of pre-experimental (left side) and post-experimental (right side) brain scans in children[6]

(The highlighted areas indicate that there is a significant difference in conditions.)[6]

RESULTS

- After printing letters (interacting with the letters to create context, rather than simply observing letters as objects), brain activation in the children studied was significantly increased and showed similarity to that of adults.[6]

- When preschool children looked at and identified a letter, they did not exhibit the same brain activation as adults.[6]

- In the brain's visul regions, when comparing writing, typing, tracing, and visual control, much more activation was exhibited after the writing experience than any of the other experiences.[6]

IMPLICATIONS

- Neuroimaging is a sensitive marker of learning changes.[6]

- Knowing how a child's brain works should inform our educational practices.[6]

- The act of writing by hand makes a significant difference to brain activation patterns.[6]

References

[1] Berninger, V. "Evidence-Based, Developmentally Appropriate Writing Skills K–5: Teaching the Orthographic Loop of Working Memory to Write Letters So Developing Writers Can Spell Words and Express Ideas." Presented at Handwriting in the 21st Century?: An Educational Summit, Washington, D.C., January 23, 2012.

[2] Case-Smith, J. "Benefits of an OT/Teacher Model for First Grade Handwriting Instruction." Presented at Handwriting in the 21st Century?: An Educational Summit, Washington, D.C., January 23, 2012.

[3] Case-Smith, J. "21st Century Handwriting Summit." *All Sides with Ann Fisher*, January 17, 2012, http://beta.wosu.org/allsides/21st-century-handwriting-summit/

[4] Conti, G. "Handwriting Characteristics and the Prediction of Illegibility in Third and Fifth Grade Students." Presented at Handwriting in the 21st Century?: An Educational Summit, Washington, D.C., January 23, 2012.

[5] Graham, S., and Santangelo, T. "A Meta-Analysis of the Effectiveness of Teaching Handwriting." Presented at Handwriting in the 21st Century?: An Educational Summit, Washington, D.C., January 23, 2012.

[6] James, K. H. "How Printing Practice Affects Letter Perception: An Educational Cognitive Neuroscience Perspective." Presented at Handwriting in the 21st Century?: An Educational Summit, Washington, D.C., January 23, 2012.

[7] National Governors Association Center for Best Practices, Council of Chief State School Officers. "College and Career Readiness Anchor Standards for Writing." Washington D.C.: 2010.

[8] National Governors Association Center for Best Practices, Council of Chief State School Officers. "Common Core State Standards for English Language Arts," Appendix A. Washington D.C.: 2010.

[9] National Governors Association Center for Best Practices, Council of Chief State School Officers. "Common Core State Standards for English Language Arts," Introduction. Washington D.C.: 2010.

[10] Peverly, S. "The Relationship of Transcription Speed and Other Cognitive Variables to Note-Taking and Test Performance." Presented at Handwriting in the 21st Century?: An Educational Summit, Washington, D.C., January 23, 2012.

Chapter 1

Handwriting Is Important

Reprinted with permission. Ford Button, deceased.

Introduction

Handwriting is important. As the twenty-first century advances, and technology provides ever more sophisticated ways to communicate, this conclusion is being reached by educators around the world. Researchers, teachers and administrators at all levels, occupational therapists, and educational psychologists are all sounding the message. The seemingly old-fashioned skill of handwriting is proving to be more important than realized, and it must not be neglected in the curriculum.

Why focus on handwriting? Although students in the nineteenth and early twentieth centuries often spent considerable time practicing penmanship, handwriting instruction has declined in recent decades in favor of an emphasis on personal communication and self-expression. Some believe it is no longer necessary to teach handwriting in an age of electronic communication.

The authors of the articles in this chapter all comment on handwriting's lowly status. Bob Schlagal says that it is one of "the least glamorous topics in today's language arts." Betty Sheffield calls handwriting "a neglected cornerstone of literacy."

Yet as the pendulum swings away from handwriting, the gap left in students' education is revealed. As it turns out, the ability to write smoothly by hand forms a critical foundation for the development of many higher-order academic skills. Consider these facts.

Students still rely on handwriting to communicate with teachers and test evaluators. Even with the wide availability of personal computers, handwriting continues to be the primary means of communication at school. Efficient, skilled handwriting is needed for note taking, in-class writing, state proficiency tests, and standardized tests such as the SAT that require a handwritten essay. Adult professionals, from office workers to engineers and doctors, attest that legible handwriting is an important lifelong skill.

Proficient handwriting builds confidence and sets the stage for academic success. Students with legible handwriting get early praise from teachers. Those who are given the opportunity to practice and develop automatic handwriting are able to record complex thoughts quickly and write longer, higher-scoring compositions. By contrast, students who have not received handwriting instruction may develop handwriting that is slow and labored. Their illegible writing may be poorly understood and scored as incorrect. As a result, they may internalize the idea that they are not good at writing and give up trying.

Handwriting is closely linked to literacy and composition skills at all levels. Research suggests that as children learn to write letters, they also develop letter-recognition and other early language skills. Unlike pressing a key on a keyboard, handwriting promotes a deep knowledge of letters that links reading, spelling, and self-expression in children's understanding. As time goes on, from elementary school through college, proficient and automatic handwriting allows students to devote full mental capacity to the content of their writing.

Direct instruction in handwriting works to prevent writing difficulties. Although struggles with handwriting may hold students back in their development as writers, the good news is that handwriting instruction can reverse the trend and help students succeed. Having established that handwriting is important, researchers are now seeking to recommend best practices for instruction. All indications show that a traditional approach, with consistent periods of direct instruction and practice, is best for helping students acquire the essential tool of fluent handwriting.

The articles in this chapter provide many more reasons that handwriting is important. Writing from the perspective of an occupational therapist, Susan Cahill makes a plea for more handwriting instruction in the early grades. Bob Schlagal explains that handwriting, like spelling, is a foundational skill. Educator Regie Routman gives ideas why handwriting instruction should be valued in today's classroom. Finally, Betty Sheffield discusses the high costs of failing to teach our students how to write well by hand.

The Zaner-Bloser Handwriting Program

Grade Level	Instructional Focus
Preschool *On the Road to Reading and Writing*	• Directionality: top-to-bottom, left-to-right • Basic strokes for manuscript letters • Motor skills
Kindergarten	• Basic strokes for manuscript letters • Write-on guidelines • Begin letters at the top
Grade 1	• Manuscript letter formation • Introduce Keys to Legibility: Size, Shape, Slant, Spacing
Grade 2 *Choose 2M or 2C*	• 2M: Legible manuscript; applied writing • 2C: Legible manuscript; introduce cursive
Grade 3	• Legible manuscript • Introduce cursive
Grade 4	• Legible manuscript and cursive • Write for schoolwork on notebook paper
Grades 5 and 6	• Legible manuscript and cursive • Real-world practice
Middle School	• Legible manuscript and cursive with re-teaching as needed • Short, focused practice

Where Does Handwriting Fit In?

Strategies to Support Academic Achievement

Susan M. Cahill

Intervention in School and Clinic, Pages 223–228, Vol. 44, No. 4 (March, 2009), ©Hammill Institute on Disabilities.

Research suggests that handwriting is more tied to academic achievement than many educators may realize (Berninger et al., 2006; Christensen, 2005; Medwell & Wray, 2007). Still, general and special educators often push aside handwriting to focus on other areas of the curriculum (Berninger et al., 2006). In today's climate of high-stakes testing, who can blame them? However, if we continue to dismiss formal handwriting instruction, or at the very least ignore the handwriting difficulties of our students, we may miss the "writing on the wall." The purpose of this article is to provide educators with strategies to support students by teaching handwriting as well as offering supplemental opportunities for motor skill development and practice during functional tasks.

> Handwriting is closely linked to academic achievement, especially composition and literacy skills.

Handwriting is closely linked to academic achievement, especially composition and literacy skills. Children who continue to have difficulty with handwriting beyond first grade may not fully develop as writers (Graham, 1999). Research also suggests that handwriting is a predictive factor in determining the length and quality of compositions (Baker, Gersten, & Graham, 2003). Students who have difficulty with automatic text production often have difficulty switching their attention between the motor process of handwriting and what they actually want to say (Graham & Weintraub, 1996). As a result, the content and the length of the piece are compromised. Some students who are readily able to tell you the answer to a question or verbally explain a concept at length, but struggle with automatic handwriting, may give up on written assignments and experience frustration and decreased self-efficacy (Jones & Christensen, 1999). Rather than ask for help or try to explain the difficulties they are having, students avoid tasks and begin to fail. Baker et al. (2003) stated that "together with reading problems, writing problems lead to the greatest number of referrals to and placements in special and remedial education programs" (p. 110).

20

Handwriting Matters

Increased availability of computers, as well as our society's reliance on them, may cause some educators to believe that handwriting, and therefore handwriting instruction, are no longer necessary. However, research suggests that there is a high correlation between handwriting speed and typing speed; many children who struggle with automatic handwriting may also struggle with automatic keyboarding (Connelly, Gee, & Walsh, 2007). Even in this era of technological advancement, the kinesthetic process of writing letters has been found to be favorable for the development of composition skills (Berninger et al., 1997).

Unless students are fluent in keyboarding, it might actually slow down their ability to generate compositions (Preminger, Weiss, & Weintraub, 2004). Without formal keyboarding instruction, students write fewer words and less complicated pieces because they are trying to locate the correct keys. Even if keyboarding does meet the needs of some students with learning disabilities, it may not be the answer for every student. Research suggests that keyboarding should only be considered if a child's handwriting is so poor that he or she is unable to meet the demands for written communication at school and only after other strategies have been attempted to offset this functional delay (Handley-More, Deitz, Billingsley, & Coggins, 2003). Other professionals, such as school psychologists and occupational therapists, can help teachers decide which students would benefit from keyboarding instruction and when students should be encouraged to use keyboarding as their primary means of written communication.

> Current research suggests that students may learn to spell words more accurately through the process of handwriting. Direct handwriting instruction was also found to be related to improved reading at the word level for first grade students who had previously been identified as having handwriting difficulties.

Even if students do not intend to use handwriting as their primary mode of communication, instruction and practice with handwriting may support their academic achievement. Current research suggests that students may learn to spell words more accurately through the process of handwriting (Cunningham & Stanovich, 1990). Direct handwriting instruction was also found to be related to improved reading at the word level for first grade students who had previously been identified as having handwriting difficulties (Berninger et al., 2006). Some hand-writing instruction strategies that were successful with first grade students included (a) encouraging them to trace, imitate, and write letters from memory; (b) using visual cues such as arrows to consistently form letters; (c) encouraging students to visualize letter forms before writing them down; and (d) writing letters on lined paper to assist with letter placement (Berninger et al., 2006).

In addition, research suggests that when students are able to automatically use handwriting to record their thoughts and ideas, they free up cognitive resources and are able to produce more complex compositions (Baker et al., 2003; Berninger, 1992).

Handwriting and Students With Learning Disabilities

Not being able to automatically produce legible handwriting may greatly affect the learning of students with disabilities. For example, many students with processing deficits find text production as challenging as idea generation (Graham & Weintraub, 1996). Students with learning disabilities have been found to minimize the use of other writing processes and spend as much time thinking about handwriting and what their papers actually look like as they do on the content of their papers (Graham, Schwartz, & MacArthur, 1993; McCutchen, 1996).

Difficulties with orthographic-motor integration may explain the association between poor handwriting and poor learning outcomes for struggling students (Christensen, 2005; Graham, 1990). Orthographic-motor integration is the process of retrieving letter forms from memory and then producing them in written form. For example, if a student wanted to write his name, he would have to know the letters in his name, be able to recall the letter forms from memory, and then begin to write them down. In addition to fine motor skills and eye-hand coordination, orthographic-motor integration depends on the student's ability to code orthographic information. *Orthographic coding* is the term used to explain how students store and later retrieve letter forms from memory (Berninger et al., 2006). Children who have difficulty perceiving visual information and processing it may have difficulty with orthographic coding. Once children are able to discriminate between letter forms, they should be encouraged to name each letter as they write it; this strategy may assist with storage and later retrieval (Edwards, 2003).

Visual motor integration and fine motor control are two other factors that have been historically associated with handwriting difficulties (Daly, Kelley, & Krauss, 2003; Volman, van Schendel, & Jongmans, 2006). However, intervention that focuses on these two factors alone may not yield positive outcomes for students with handwriting difficulty (Denton, Cope, & Moser, 2006). Interventions geared at increasing these skills, which often combine worksheets, eye-hand coordination games, and exercises for hand strengthening and dexterity, have been found to be less effective than other methods of remediation.

Berninger et al. (2006) completed a study to evaluate the effects of different interventions on the handwriting skills of struggling students in first grade. Berninger and her colleagues found that an approach that combines orthographic training with motor training was most effective in increasing the students' handwriting skills.

She suggested that teachers and school psychologists are well equipped to address orthographic training but may require additional support from related service providers, such as occupational therapists, to address motor training and development.

Teaching Handwriting

One of the first things educators can do to ensure that students with special needs develop good writing skills, besides teaching them spelling and basic writing processes, is to provide them with formal handwriting instruction. Berninger and Fuller (1992) found that a lack of formal handwriting instruction may be especially problematic for children who have underdeveloped foundational skills and produce letter forms illegibly.

D'Nealian and Zaner-Bloser are two popular handwriting programs that are available for use in elementary schools. Researchers disagree on which program facilitates a smoother transition to cursive (see Trap-Porter, Cooper, Hill, Swisher, & LaNunziata, 1984, and Duvall, 1985). However, a common belief is that systematic instruction supports the development of handwriting skills and that instruction is essential for children who do not write instinctively (Berninger & Fuller, 1992). Students may struggle with handwriting because of different underlying causes, such as decreased visual-motor integration skills or decreased orthographic integration skills. Depending on the causes, students may benefit from additional instruction with a supplemental handwriting program that will meet their unique needs.

Several supplemental handwriting programs are available such as Callirobics, Handwriting Without Tears, Big Strokes for Little Folks, Sensible Pencil, and Loops and Other Groups. Educators may find that

> One of the first things educators can do to ensure that students with special needs develop good writing skills is to provide them with formal handwriting instruction.

many of the strategies recommended by these programs are grounded in theory or evidence.

However, an ERIC search yielded no studies that named any one of these programs in their titles or abstracts. Although it is unclear whether one program is more effective than another, educators may consider using one or more of these programs to supplement their existing handwriting curriculum.

Supplemental Opportunities for Motor Skill Development

Motor learning is a theory that looks at skill development through a dynamic systems lens. The dynamic systems approach takes into account a multitude of factors that are believed to work together to influence an individual's performance (Kamm, Thelen, & Jensen, 1990). Under this framework, a student's skill with handwriting is thought to be a result of the interaction of various intrinsic and extrinsic factors. Visual motor integration skills, hand strength, orthographic coding and integration skills, motivation to complete the task, and body position are all factors inherent to the student. The shape and size of the writing utensil, thickness of the paper and whether it is lined, size of the desk, body position and other ergonomic factors, and instructions provided for the writing assignment are considered to be inherent to the task, or extrinsic factors.

Handwriting intervention that only focuses on one factor, like visual-motor integration, is less effective than a more balanced approach that appreciates the relationship between the student's capacity, the task, and the environment. Factors related to the task and the environment, such as those listed above, should be evaluated, and accommodations and modifications should be put in place to support the development of handwriting skills. The table below provides a list of questions that teachers should consider when they notice that students are having difficulty with handwriting. Minor adjustments to the environment or the tools used during handwriting are easy to implement. These adjustments will provide some students with the necessary support to successfully complete handwriting tasks.

Questions to Consider and Suggestions to Support Handwriting Development

Questions to Consider	Suggestions to Support Handwriting
Does the student have enough space on his or her desk to complete the writing task?	Remove clutter from desks and tabletops. Children with poor posture might need space to lean or rest their elbows while writing.
Can the student place both feet squarely on the floor and still rest his or her elbows on the desk for support?	Be sure that when students sit, their ankles, knees, and hips are bent at 90° angles and they can comfortably rest their elbows on their desks. Chairs and desks that are too tall require students to expend extra energy while writing. If students are unable to comfortably rest their feet on the floor, ask the building engineer to adjust their desk and chair heights or provide students with a short stool or a stack of books to rest their feet on. These adjustments will increase students' postural stability, which will allow them to exercise greater distal control and use their writing instruments more proficiently.
Does the student switch hands or complain that his or her hand hurts during long writing tasks?	Students who have established hand dominance and continue to switch hands or complain of fatigue while writing may have decreased hand strength. Provide writing tools with a greater diameter and opportunities to develop hand muscles through activities such as cutting, playing with clay, and using manipulatives.
Does the student use excessive force when writing as evidenced by thick marks that leave deep indentations on the paper?	Excessive force when writing may indicate decreased hand strength or difficulty processing sensory information. Provide writing tools with a greater diameter and let students experiment with placing their writing papers on top of different textures, such as bubble wrap, sandpaper, and cardboard. For example, students who press too hard while writing on top of bubble wrap will rip their papers. This will cue them to reduce the force they use on their writing instruments. The other textured materials will provide them with varied sensory feedback. This may help to build muscle memory and increase automatic letter writing.

(continued)

Questions to Consider	Suggestions to Support Handwriting
Does the student use a mature pencil grip?	Some students hold their pencils incorrectly or develop inefficient habits. If students are still learning to hold writing utensils, instruct them how to hold their pencils correctly and see whether a pencil gripper helps them to maintain this position. If students already have an established pencil grip, consult with an occupational therapist to determine whether the grip is efficient and will promote writing speed.
Does the student consistently rest his or her head on the desk, rub his or her eyes, squint, or close one eye when reading or writing?	Students who demonstrate any of these characteristics may have difficulty with vision. Refer these students to the school nurse for a vision screening. Remind students who have glasses to wear them as prescribed.
Does the student appear distracted by the amount of visual information presented on a worksheet?	Reduce the amount of visual stimulation by removing unnecessary pictures, using large fonts, reducing the amount of information on a single page, and providing well-defined spaces or lines for answers.

Practice is also considered to be a key component of motor learning (Asher, 2006). Children with handwriting difficulties require blocked and constant practice to master letter formation without the pressure of worrying about content and grammar. Blocked practice provides children with the opportunity to work on emerging skills during a task that follows a predictable sequence (Poole, 1991). Blocked practice can take the form of writing different letters until the formation is consistent or even writing common sight words. Blocked handwriting practice may lead to automaticity and increased writing speed. Automatic handwriting allows students to spend all of their energy on writing content instead of having to divide their attention between content and text production.

Christensen (2005) evaluated the effects of a handwriting intervention that provided students with blocked practice and found that this intervention was more effective than journal writing in helping students to write longer and more complex compositions. The intervention was tested with 50 children who struggled with handwriting but were not learning it for the first time. The intervention took place 20 minutes per day for 8 weeks and consisted of letter, word, and sentence writing that followed a predictable sequence. Children mastered writing each letter of the alphabet and then moved on to writing 60 letters per minute. After this was completed, children were able to progress to word writing and then sentence writing. Besides focusing on writing letters, words, and sentences, educators may embed blocked handwriting practice into daily routine activities. For example, asking students to consistently write a heading that includes their name, the date, and the subject area on all the assignments they turn in is a way to offer blocked practice. Other examples include asking students to write the days of the week, months of the year, and the first and last names of their family members. Additional examples of blocked practice are included in the table below.

> **Practice is also considered to be a key component of motor learning.**

Examples of Blocked Practice

Write the list of subjects in an assignment notebook every day.

Sign in and out when leaving the room to go to the bathroom or to the office.

Write spelling words five times each.

Write the lunch order every morning.

Copy definitions of vocabulary words.

Write the alphabet daily.

Write numbers in sequence daily.

Copy homework assignments from the chalkboard.

Constant practice provides students with an opportunity to develop emerging skills under relatively stable conditions (Poole, 1991). If a teacher wants to provide constant practice, he or she would make sure that the students had approximately the same amount of time to write their headings and that they were allowed to use materials that were familiar and found to be effective, such as a sharpened pencil and lined, loose-leaf paper.

In keeping with motor learning, once students master basic skills, teachers introduce a challenge point (Guadagnoli & Lee, 2004). This concept represents the "just right" challenge or the point just beyond the student's level of proficiency. Any one of the variables involved in the previous practice examples can be altered to increase the task's level of difficulty. However, teachers should consider altering only one variable at a time. For example, the teacher may decrease the number of minutes that students have available to write their headings or might provide unlined paper instead of lined loose leaf. Challenge points should provide opportunities to refine skills while still allowing students to feel efficacious.

Teachers who challenge students to practice legible handwriting during composition writing should do so with caution. Energy spent on proper letter formation could detract from the length and quality of the student's composition. Rather, teachers should encourage students to work through the composition process first and then focus on legibly rewriting their pieces before turning them in as final products.

Practice During Functional Tasks

Concepts from motor learning combined with traditional handwriting curricula and practice during functional tasks have been found to increase skills in children with poor handwriting (Denton et al., 2006). Students who are provided with formal handwriting instruction and supplemental writing activities may increase their proficiency. For example, besides completing class assignments, teachers might consider offering students the opportunity to write birthday wish lists, Web sites they would like to explore, thank-you notes, or plans for the weekend. Students may be more apt to write for an extended period of time if they are interested, find value in the activity, and are not worried about receiving grades. In addition, students may approach the task of handwriting more conscientiously if they know they are writing for real audiences and not just for practice.

> Students who are provided with formal handwriting instruction and supplemental writing activities may increase their proficiency.

Another strategy that has been shown to be effective is to allow students to write with and on various media (Denton et al., 2006). For example, a teacher might provide students with a variety of writing utensils to use during journal time, such as markers, mechanical pencils, and gel pens. In addition, teachers might consider ordering small dry erase boards or slate boards for the classroom. These tools can easily be incorporated into daily instruction. Although these specific strategies lack evidence to support them, they have the potential to inspire some reluctant writers.

Conclusion

Some students perceive handwriting as a nuisance. However, research indicates that poor handwriting affects learning outcomes for students with delayed skills (Graham, 1999; Graham & Weintraub, 1996). Students who struggle with handwriting benefit from extra support early in their school careers.

Educators who want to support struggling writers may start by helping them to improve their handwriting. Systematic handwriting instruction, supplemental skill development, and practice with functional tasks can help increase handwriting skills. By incorporating these strategies in their repertoires, teachers can provide students with opportunities to develop handwriting skills, free up cognitive energy to better focus on writing content, and potentially increase their academic achievement.

> Educators who want to support struggling writers may start by helping them to improve their handwriting.

About the Author

Susan M. Cahill, MAEA, OTR/L, is a clinical assistant professor of occupational therapy at the University of Illinois at Chicago. Her current interests include students' perceptions of learning strategies and prereferral services.

References

Asher, A. (2006). Handwriting instruction in elementary schools. *American Journal of Occupational Therapy, 60,* 461-471.

Baker, S., Gersten, R., & Graham, S. (2003). Teaching expressive writing to children with learning disabilities: Research based applications and examples. *Journal of Learning Disabilities, 36,* 109-123.

Berninger, V., & Fuller, F. (1992). Gender differences in orthographic, verbal, and compositional fluency: Implications for assessing writing disabilities in primary grade children. *Journal of School Psychology, 30,* 363-382.

Berninger, V., Rutberg, J., Abbott, R., Garcia, N., Anderson-Youngstrom, M., Brooks, A., et al. (2006). Tier 1 and tier 2 early intervention for handwriting and composing. *Journal of School Psychology, 44,* 3-30.

Berninger, V., Vaughan, K., Abbott, R., Abbott, S., Rogan, L., Brooks, A., et al. (1997). Treatment of handwriting problems in beginning writers: Transfer from handwriting to composition. *Journal of Educational Psychology, 89,* 652-666.

Christensen, C. (2005). The role of orthographic-motor integration in the production of creative and well-structured written text for students in secondary school. *Educational Psychology, 25,* 441-453.

Connelly, V., Gee, D., & Walsh, E. (2007). A comparison of keyboarded and handwritten compositions and the relationship with transcription speed. *British Journal of Educational Psychology, 77,* 479-492.

Cunningham, A., & Stanovich, K. (1990). Early spelling acquisition: Writing beats the computer. *Journal of Educational Psychology, 82,* 159-162.

Daly, C., Kelley, G., & Krauss, A. (2003). Brief report—Relationship between visual-motor integration and handwriting skills of children in kindergarten: A modified replication study. *American Journal of Occupational Therapy, 5,* 459-462.

Denton, P., Cope, S., & Moser, C. (2006). The effects of sensorimotor-based intervention versus therapeutic practice on improving handwriting performance in 6- to 11-year-old children. *American Journal of Occupational Therapy, 60,* 16-27.

Duvall, B. (1985). Evaluating the difficulty of four handwriting styles used for instruction. *Spectrum, 3,* 13-20.

Edwards, L. (2003). Writing instruction in kindergarten: Examining an emerging area of research for children with writing and reading difficulties. *Journal of Learning Disabilities, 36,* 136-148.

Graham, S. (1990). The role of production factors in learning disabled students' compositions. *Journal of Educational Psychology, 82,* 781-791.

Graham, S. (1999). The role of text production in writing development. *Learning Disability Quarterly, 22,* 75-77.

Graham, S., Schwartz, S., & MacArthur, C. (1993). Knowledge of writing and composing process, attitude toward writing, and self-efficacy for students with and without learning disabilities. *Journal of Learning Disabilities, 26,* 237-249.

Graham, S., & Weintraub, N. (1996). A review of handwriting research: Progress and prospects from 1980-1994. *Educational Psychology Review, 8,* 7-87.

Guadagnoli, M., & Lee, T. (2004). Challenge point: A framework for conceptualizing the effects of various practice conditions in motor learning. *Journal of Motor Behavior, 36,* 212-224.

Handley-More, D., Deitz, J., Billingsley, F., & Coggins, T. (2003). Facilitating written work using computer word processing and word prediction. *American Journal of Occupational Therapy, 57,* 139-151.

Jones, D., & Christensen, C. (1999). Relationship between automaticity in handwriting and student's ability to generate written text. *Journal of Educational Psychology, 91,* 44-49.

Kamm, K., Thelen, E., & Jensen J. (1990). A dynamical systems approach to motor development. *Physical Therapy, 70,* 763-775.

McCutchen, D. (1996). A capacity theory of writing: Working memory in composition. *Educational Psychology Review, 8,* 299-325.

Medwell, J., & Wray, D. (2007). Handwriting: What do we know and what do we need to know? *Literacy, 41,* 10-15.

Poole, J. (1991). Application of motor principles in occupational therapy. *American Journal of Occupational Therapy, 45,* 531-537.

Preminger, F., Weiss, P., & Weintraub, N. (2004). Predicting occupational performance: Handwriting versus keyboarding. *American Journal of Occupational Therapy, 58,* 193-201.

Trap-Porter, J., Cooper, O., Hill, D., Swisher, K., & LaNunziata, L. (1984). D'Nealian and Zaner-Bloser manuscript alphabet and initial transition to cursive handwriting. *Journal of Educational Research, 77,* 343-345.

Volman, M., van Schendel, B., & Jongmans, M. (2006). Handwriting difficulties in primary school children: A search for underlying mechanisms. *American Journal of Occupational Therapy, 60,* 451-460.

Best Practices in Spelling and Handwriting

Bob Schlagal

Best Practices in Writing Instruction, Pages 179–201, ©2007 Guilford Publications, Inc.

Spelling and handwriting are among the least glamorous topics in today's language arts. By contrast, in the 19th and a portion of the 20th century, schooling in literacy involved heavy emphasis on penmanship and spelling along with a great deal of drill and practice.

Broadly speaking, two forces have helped push spelling and handwriting to the margins of the curriculum. The first was a shift in instructional priorities in the late 20th century that emphasized personal communication while de-emphasizing grammar, spelling, punctuation, and handwriting in composition. (These latter are sometimes regarded as unimportant surface features that have little to do with written communication itself.) The second force is a contemporary emphasis on electronic forms of communication. Word processing programs and the spell-check function have led some to believe that teaching children how to spell or write legibly is no longer necessary. This is not the case. There will continue to be many settings in which fluid, legible handwriting and correct spelling are essential.

> **There will continue to be many settings in which fluid, legible handwriting and correct spelling are essential.**

The curricular swing that pushed handwriting and spelling to the sidelines of the language arts is no different from other such trend-driven shifts. As is always the case, heavy emphasis on one aspect of the curriculum leads to neglect of others, but recognition of that fact does not mean a return to historic concepts and practices is in order. Any renewed emphasis on spelling and handwriting must take into account what we now know about the significance of these skills and the role they play in the overall picture of reading and writing. What contemporary research reveals is that although these aspects of literacy are not ends in themselves, they are nonetheless foundational. Serious deficits in one or both of these skills can undercut success in writing and reading. Indeed, these skills play a deeper role than is popularly thought, though a very different one than our ancestors conceived.

Best Practices in Handwriting

Well-developed penmanship was once a requirement for all business and professional work. Students worked hard to develop an elegant and legible hand, and penmanship was a major focus in business colleges. Beginning in the 1930s, handwriting instruction ceased being a separate school subject and was folded into spelling and writing instruction. Recent emphasis on meaning in writing (at times to the exclusion of other skills), the availability of computer-based writing technology, and an all-too-crowded school curriculum have made handwriting seem an area of little importance. Perhaps nothing speaks so directly to the reduced status of handwriting at this time than the current edition of *The Handbook of Research on Teaching the English Language Arts* (Flood, Lapp, Squire, & Jensen, 2003). Of its more than 1,000 pages of text, less than one is given to handwriting.

> **Failure to develop legible and automatic letter and word formation may interfere with content in writing.**

Despite the diminished place of handwriting in the curriculum and the broad availability of word processing programs, fluent and legible writing remains a necessary practical skill. In the academic world alone, it is needed for adequate note taking, state proficiency tests, and standardized tests requiring handwritten essays. Although elegant, well-crafted penmanship is no longer a strict requirement for academic or business success, there are consequences for sloppy and illegible work. Poor handwriting influences judgments about the quality of written work (Briggs, 1980) and even about the education or intelligence of writers. Students' perceptions of their own handwriting also affect their judgments about themselves as writers (Graham, 1992; Graham & Weintraub, 1996).

Poorly developed handwriting can affect more than judgments about written content and writing ability. In combination with poor spelling and by itself, it can contribute to disability in written expression (Graham, Harris, & Fink, 2000). Just as a failure to develop accurate and automatic decoding can impair comprehension in readers (Perfetti, 1985), failure to develop legible and automatic letter and word formation may interfere with content in writing (Jones & Christensen, 1999). Students who struggle to retrieve letters from memory, to reproduce them on the page, and to scale them to other letters have less attention available to spend on spelling, planning, and effectively expressing intended meanings. In contrast, when the component skills of writing are automatic, writers are free to devote their energy to the composition itself—although attention alone is not enough to guarantee improved content. Because of the excessive labor and unattractive results involved in such writing, students are more likely to avoid or minimize the process when possible (Graham & Weintraub, 1996).

There is evidence that direct instruction and sufficient practice in handwriting can play a significant role in preventing the development of writing disabilities among younger students (Graham et al., 2000). This important fact should be considered both from the point of view of regularly planned instruction in the primary grades and from the point of view of intervention among students who struggle with handwriting.

Issues in Handwriting

There is a long-standing controversy over the best way to teach the formation of letters. Should children be introduced to writing through a traditional manuscript alphabet and later bridged into cursive, as was common throughout most of the 20th century? Should students begin with cursive to prevent the difficulties of learning a new way to write in later grades? Or should they be taught a slanted or italic version of print that is designed to connect with cursive and so ease the difficulty of transition?

> Forming manuscript letters involves far fewer fine-motor movements than does forming cursive or slanted letters and is therefore easier for young children.

Those who favor introducing writing through manuscript argue that vertical, lower-case letters are close to what children encounter in print and that printed letters in writing are easier for them to read (Sheffield, 1996). In addition, they argue that children who come to school with letter knowledge will have learned and been exposed to basic manuscript forms. By making explicit instructional connections with what children already know, teachers avoid the problem of having to revise or correct what their students may have already learned. Further, advocates argue that forming manuscript letters involves far fewer fine-motor movements than does forming cursive or slanted letters and is therefore easier for young children.

Those who advocate beginning with cursive state that writing is more a kinesthetic than a visual act (Sheffield, 1996). Because an element of word knowledge is motor memory (Hanna et al., 1971), it is said that developing memory for spellings is easier when words are written in a continuous flow rather than when composed of physically separated letters. Although teaching cursive may make greater demands on students in the beginning, it is also said that there are immediate benefits to this approach, even for beginners. For example, because *b* and *d* are formed differently in cursive and are not mirror images of one another, reversal problems can be avoided from the outset. Also, because letters within words are connected, children are said to be able to manage the problem of spacing *between* words more easily, and, as mentioned above, children do not have to make the time-consuming and often imperfect transition from manuscript to cursive in second and/or third grade.

Most advocates of the cursive-only approach are concerned primarily with disabled readers and writers (Sheffield, 1996). Teaching these students cursive is often part of the instructional retraining process. Tutors or therapists seek to undo the fixed, imperfect, partial learning that characterizes disabled reading and writing and to rebuild them on a firmer foundation. Training students in cursive is often an integral part of this process. Whether the experience of clinicians working with disabled writers provides the best insights for general education is unclear. Despite the logic of the cursive-only claims, there is too little research at this point to verify them, especially for normal populations (Graham & Weintraub, 1996).

> The evidence appears to support the use of the traditional manuscript form with a transition to cursive later in the primary grades.

Because of the difficulty that many children experience in making the transition from manuscript to cursive, some advocate the use of a slanted initial teaching alphabet that is more like cursive than vertical manuscript. It is claimed that this promotes easier and more complete adaptation to cursive. Many schools choose to use slanted or italic letter forms in their handwriting instruction precisely because of these transitional problems.

A distinct shortcoming of a slanted or italic alphabet involves the increased number and complexity of strokes that young children must perform in order to make the letters (Graham, 1992). As a result, students are less able to produce consistently well-shaped and proportioned letters. In addition, evidence does not support the claim that slanted alphabets assist in the transition to cursive or result in quicker, more fluid, or more legible writing (Graham & Weintraub, 1996).

Due to its relative simplicity and comparative legibility, the evidence appears to support the use of the traditional manuscript form with a transition to cursive later in the primary grades. The question remains: What practices best assist students in developing good handwriting?

Handwriting Instruction

Because careful teaching and practice of handwriting can facilitate fluency in writing and may prevent writing disabilities (Graham et al., 2000), it is important to provide explicit instruction and sufficient opportunity to practice correct letter formation. Short daily practice sessions are likely to be more effective (and more interesting) than longer, less regular sessions. Although there should be time to practice handwriting as a separate skill, it should not replace time for regular writing. There should be abundant opportunity in the classroom for students to write meaningfully and purposefully so that they can apply and extend the skills they acquire through separate practice (Graham & Weintraub, 1996; Henderson, 1990).

> It is important to provide explicit instruction and sufficient opportunity to practice correct letter formation.

How the alphabet is best introduced is not a settled matter nor is the order in which letters are best taught. ABC order is not necessarily the most effective way to introduce letters, in part because the reversible letters *b* and *d* come so close to each other. (Thoroughly teaching one before teaching the other is likely to reduce confusion.) Further, if letter sounds are taught with letter names, the sounds for the vowels *a* and *e*— short sounds as in s*a*d and b*e*d—are initially confusing to young children (Read, 1975). Therefore, a teaching order in which confusable letters and sounds are carefully separated seems preferable to a strict ABC order.

> Teacher modeling of correct letter formation is an important component of instruction.

Teacher modeling of correct letter formation is an important component of instruction. For beginners, both visual and verbal modeling (i.e., the teacher demonstrates how a letter is made correctly while describing how it is formed) appears to be the most effective means of introducing a letter prior to practice (Graham & Weintraub, 1996).

Teacher explanations appear to be less effective for students in higher grades than modeling alone (Graham & Weintraub, 1996). Perhaps, already knowing the letters, older students find teacher explanations unneeded and distracting. Nonetheless, clear and correct models are an important ingredient in guiding students to effective practice.

Copying a letter from a correct model is helpful to students' practice, and it can be made more effective by adding several components. The teacher can provide a model in which numbered arrows indicate how the strokes are to be made (Berninger et al., 1997). After examining the model carefully, the student should cover it and write the letter from memory. Incorporating numbered arrows and adding a simple visual memory technique appears to be more effective than other forms of copying. This method has an interesting parallel in the helpful "look, say, cover, write, check" tradition in spelling practice (Henderson, 1990). Students can also benefit from learning to verbalize a set of rules for forming a letter so that they can guide themselves through the process, but the verbal guide should be one easily committed to memory (Graham & Weintraub, 1996).

Conclusion

More than anything else, contemporary research on spelling and handwriting tells us that these skills are not unimportant. They are not merely decorative elements of the writing process, but building blocks. Neglecting them can lead to

> **Poorly developed spelling or handwriting can affect the higher-level literacy processes in which they are embedded.**

social, educational, and personal consequences. Further, poorly developed spelling or handwriting can affect the higher-level literacy processes in which they are embedded. Although there is no reason to return the practice of these skills to the place they held in the 19th century, there is every reason to give them a more important role in the curriculum. Much that we know now can improve the quality and efficiency of spelling and handwriting instruction. By carefully considering the research, classroom teachers can find or create thoughtful programs to advance learning and increase engagement and interest in these core aspects of literacy.

References

Berninger, V., Vaughn, K., Abbott, R., Abbott, S., Rogan, L., Brooks, A., et al. (1997). Treatment of handwriting problems in beginning writers: Transfer from handwriting to composition. *Journal of Educational Psychology, 89,* 652–666.

Briggs, D. (1980). A study of the influence of handwriting upon grades using examination scripts. *Educational Review, 32,* 185–193.

Flood, J., Lapp, D., Squire, J. R., & Jensen, J.M. (Eds.). (2003). *Handbook of research on teaching the language arts.* Mahwah, NJ: Erlbaum.

Graham, S. (1992). Issues in handwriting instruction. *Focus on Exceptional Children, 25,* 1–14.

Graham, S., Harris, K.R., & Fink, B. (2000). Is handwriting causally related to learning to write? Treatment of handwriting problems in beginning writers. *Journal of Educational Psychology, 92,* 620–633.

Graham, S., & Weintraub, N. (1996). A review of handwriting research: Progress and prospects from 1980 to 1994. *Educational Psychology Review, 8,* 7–87.

Hanna, P. R., Hodges, R. E., & Hanna, J.S. (1971). *Spelling; Structure and strategies.* Boston: Houghton Mifflin.

Henderson, E. H. (1990). *Teaching spelling* (2nd ed.). Boston: Houghton Mifflin.

Jones, D., & Christensen, C.A. (1999). Relationship between automaticity in handwriting and students' ability to generate written text. *Journal of Educational Psychology, 91,* 44–49.

Perfetti, C. A. (1985). *Reading ability,* New York: Oxford University Press.

Read, C. (1975). *Children's categorization of speech sounds in English.* Urbana, IL: National Council of Teachers of English.

Sheffield, B. (1996). Handwriting: A neglected cornerstone of literacy. *Annals of Dyslexia, 46,* 21–35.

We Still Need to Teach and Value Handwriting

Regie Routman

Literacy at the Crossroads: Crucial Talk About Reading, Writing, and Other Teaching Dilemmas, Pages 121–123, ©1996 Heinemann.

Handwriting can be an emotionally charged issue. In the language arts support group in one of my district's elementary buildings, we spent several weeks talking about expectations for handwriting. Lots of issues surfaced. Should we teach lowercase letters in kindergarten? Are we asking children to write too much too soon? Is legibility enough? How much time should we spend teaching stroke formation? When should we begin teaching cursive? How much practice and repetition is necessary? Because the research on teaching handwriting is scarce and conflicting, we had difficulty resolving these issues. Nonetheless, most of us were able to agree that handwriting is important to us and to many of our students' parents and that legibility is the desired goal.

> We are sending a message to students and parents that we value legibility, attention to detail, neatness, correctness, and excellence.

When we teach and value handwriting, we are sending a message to students and parents that we value legibility, attention to detail, neatness, correctness, and excellence. To write beautifully by hand takes time, practice, and pride. It is literally a dying art. I welcome a handwritten letter. It seems to be more personal and to have more voice than a word-processed one. I love to get "h-mail—handwritten and heartwritten." I save all personal, handwritten letters and cards in a special file for future reference and rereading. (By contrast, I am much less likely to save a letter received through e-mail.) When I want to send a personal message, I always handwrite it on special paper or beautiful blank cards.

Yes, we can print out computer-generated, spell-checked material, and this is great much of the time. Indeed, for some students, word-processing has freed up the process of writing, and that has been terrific. We need to remember, though, that just because a finished piece looks professional doesn't mean that it's better written or even well written. For me, these printed pieces can lack the voice and personal style that comes through in a handwritten piece.

Let me give you an example. At the end of the school year, fourth-grade teacher Joan Servis and I worked with her students to write final-evaluation narratives. These "report cards," written by the students, were not supplementary to the teacher's report; they were the official reports.... The students went through drafts and revisions and took the project very seriously. Almost all final reports were word-processed so they would look professional. They were so well crafted, complete, and official-looking that it "looked" as if the students couldn't possibly have done them. In retrospect, Joan and I noticed that the narratives of the few late finishers, who handwrote their final reports, stood out for their uniqueness. The individual handwriting styles made those narratives look child-centered and personal. This year we are going to have all students handwrite their final narratives.

> Because the book reviews of their favorite books were going to be displayed at the local book store, the handwriting had to be polished and legible.

Or again, third-grade teacher Danny Young—who does a marvelous job with writing workshop—found out that his kids couldn't handwrite very well when they needed to. While his students were publishing pieces of excellent quality, everything that went to final copy was word-processed on the computer. When Danny and I, working together, taught the students how to write book reviews, we found out that their handwriting was sorely lacking. Because the book reviews of their favorite books were going to be displayed at the local book store, the handwriting had to be polished and legible. Therefore, Danny took the time—in a meaningful context and for a mutually valued purpose (not as a copying exercise)—to teach handwriting and to revalue it.

What We Can Do About Handwriting
Educate parents about the importance of early play in the home.
While the research on handwriting is conflicting, one thing is certain. We are seeing more kids who have difficulty with handwriting because they haven't had enough motor experience with their hands. Instead of manipulating and playing with blocks, they have been sedentary—spending excessive time in front of the television.

Make sure parents know we teach handwriting.
Parents, used to the importance of handwriting from their own schooling, expect handwriting to be taught. Use journals or daily

writing to diagnose and observe penmanship. Formally teach stroke formation in the lower grades, and give time for practice. Make the goal legibility.

Make sure parents know we value handwriting.

Do mention handwriting in newsletters; post handwritten work; expect students to handwrite some final copies—personal letters, for example. Let parents know we value and expect legibility and quality penmanship.

By permission of Johnny Hart and Creators Syndicate, Inc.

An Excerpt From

Handwriting: A Neglected Cornerstone of Literacy

Betty Sheffield

Annals of Dyslexia, Vol. 46, Pages 21–35, July 28, 2000.

As with so much else in American education, the perceived importance of teaching accurate handwriting goes in cycles. Berninger (1994) comments on "the zebra syndrome, with its either/or logic" in philosophy of teaching. She criticizes education's tendency to focus on what is stylish at the moment rather than incorporating a more global approach to training teachers and teaching students. Phelps and Stempel (1987) speak of the "shifting emphasis away from the teaching of handwriting... during the sixties," with penmanship back again in style at the time of their article. Now that whole language is often the teaching method of choice, the American school system is working its way through another wave of handwriting not being taught directly.

It is argued here that automatic legible writing is an essential basis for written expression. And yet, crowded school curricula and neglect by educational institutions and researchers often leave no room for appropriate and sufficient attention to teaching this critical skill. This is unfortunate because early consistent teaching of handwriting is crucial to success in school. Decisions about what to teach, how to teach, and when to teach handwriting need to be based on what is essential for children rather than on accepted custom, current fad, or inadequate research.

Importance of Direct Early Teaching of Handwriting

There are at least three reasons handwriting must be carefully taught to all children. First, handwriting allows access to kinesthetic memory, our earliest, strongest, and most reliable memory channel. Second, serviceable handwriting needs to be at a spontaneous level so that a student is free to concentrate on spelling, and to focus on higher-level thought and written expression. Third, teachers judge and grade students based on the appearance of their work, and the world judges adults on the quality of their handwriting.

Handwriting is important because it taps into kinesthetic learning. Our first and strongest memory system is the kinesthetic one (Zaporozhets and Elkonin 1971). Competent writing is our access to utilization of this crucial channel for school learning. Because kinesthetic learning is such a strong learning channel and so reliable, all children need to assimilate accurate formation of alphabet letters to a point that forming these letters requires no conscious effort. Dyslexic students in particular often need to use writing in order to learn to read. All students have a right to comfortable, legible, and automatic handwriting.

Handwriting provides an essential basis for higher-level written work. Competent handwriting frees a student to concentrate on a higher level of written content. Vail speaks of the "paralytic cumulative effects of handwriting problems" (Vail 1986). At an early age, a child must memorize the names, shapes, and orientation of letters, a task made more difficult by a lack of direct teaching. Emphasizing how often this automaticity is not achieved, Phelps, Stempel, and Speck (1985) studied 1372 Dallas students in grades 3 through 8. They concluded that 10% of the 3rd and 4th graders had difficulty with speed and legibility. And 20% of the 5th through 8th graders tested wrote too slowly to meet school demands. Many high school students cannot write legibly or quickly enough to deal with their school work.

> **All students have a right to comfortable, legible, and automatic handwriting. Handwriting provides an essential basis for higher-level written work.**

Handwriting is often a criterion used to judge a person's intelligence or level of education. Students and adults with poor handwriting are judged and judge themselves on their handwriting. In Great Britain, Briggs (1970) researched the effect of poor handwriting on the grading of 6th grade essays. Ten comparable essays on the subject of "the day of the big fog" were chosen from the work of 100 children. The essays were copied in a variety of excellent to terrible handwriting styles. The essays were then judged by ten different groups of teachers from ten different schools. The quality of handwriting did affect grading by experienced markers regardless of the papers' content. Alston and Taylor (1987) report on research conducted by Briggs in 1980 in which already graded exams by college seniors were copied in different handwriting styles. These copies were then graded by experienced graders. There was significant variation in grading based on the quality of handwriting. Alston and Taylor (1987) add that "problems in this mechanical skill are likely to spill over into the child's level of success and failure throughout the curriculum."

Reasons for Insufficient Attention Being Paid to Handwriting

Lack of Research

One difficulty in dealing with the subject of teaching handwriting is the scant amount of useful published research. Phelps and Stempel (1989) characterize this field of study as developing rapidly but still poorly researched. Alston and Taylor (1987) have surveyed the teaching of handwriting in the United Kingdom and to some extent in America. They speak of "fashions in teaching that...have considerable influence... despite the fact that there is little empirical foundation for their promotion." Peck, Askov, and Fairchild (1980), in their survey of research in handwriting, mention a lack of research concerning production and legibility of writing. They also complain of the lack of statistical studies measuring the value of manuscript versus cursive writing for initial teaching of primary children with specific learning disabilities.

Lack of Preparation of Teachers

Phelps and Stempel (1989) believe that many teachers in the early grades pay little attention to handwriting because they themselves have been given little training in methods of teaching it. Many elementary teachers assume that handwriting is a skill that children learn informally, that handwriting will come easily and by osmosis, and that children will be bored by the repetition necessary for acquiring a reliable skill. They cannot look into the future and foresee some 8th grade teacher faced with poorly prepared students who write illegibly and slowly. Teachers often lack the understanding that handwriting is a skill that demands "a competent level of instruction" (Alston and Taylor 1987). They seem unaware that children will practice to achieve mastery when they can see positive results.

> Classroom teachers may not be aware of the long-term benefits of careful consistent teaching of handwriting.

Classroom teachers may not be aware of the long-term benefits of careful consistent teaching of handwriting. The curricula in our schools are so packed with requirements that it is often difficult to include the basics. Although the time required for teaching handwriting is not so great, it has to be incorporated regularly into a class schedule. Novice teachers, if they teach the mechanics of writing at all, are often thrown upon the resource of using publishers' copybooks. They expect children to copy, self-teach, and internalize the material. And yet, without direct

44

teaching, the attempt to learn writing often ends in disaster. Any 1st grade child can find and lock onto endless inefficient ways of scribbling around the same letter. Many cases of apparent dysgraphia are the result of inadequate teaching.

Teachers should not be blamed for their lack of preparation. The inadequate attention paid to handwriting appears to be based on a lack of emphasis at the level of state and local school system guidelines. Nolen, McCutchen, and Berninger (1990) state, "The responsibility for the nation's literacy...belongs not to the classroom teacher alone, but also to the institutions that educate teachers and the states that certify them." These authors conducted a survey of state certification requirements in teaching reading and writing. They received replies from forty-eight out of fifty states. Twenty-nine states required coursework in reading for elementary certification. The data received on writing was not definitive. Only eight states reported writing coursework requirements. There was no apparent mention of handwriting, although handwriting might have been included under the general term of Language Arts. In a brief discussion of Public Law 94-142, the authors allude to the fact that the law suggests no means by which classroom teachers could update their information about writing disorders, and that local schools often implement any reeducation in brief inadequate workshops (Nolen, McCutchen, and Berninger 1990).

American schools are not alone in their neglect of handwriting. According to Alston and Taylor (1987), there is also inconsistency in the teaching of handwriting in British schools. "In the absence of educational guidelines, freedom of what or how one will teach is left to the individual school staff or even to the individual teacher."

In the late 1960s, I taught at a private school that prided itself on its creative and gifted children. The school boasted a long-held belief that emphasis on handwriting would destroy a child's freedom of expression. The school's collective handwriting was atrocious. Spelling was worse. As a neophyte remedial specialist, I needed to identify 1st and 2nd grade children in need of extra help. I administered the Slingerland Screening tests to all our children at the beginning of the 1st and 2nd grades (Slingerland 1969). Roughly half of the 2nd graders were conspicuously identifiable as in trouble with reversals, inversions, and confusions. Standardized tests revealed levels of reading and spelling that were below expectation.

When a new principal arrived at the school, he took one horrified look at the children's work and told the remedial department to oversee the *correct* teaching of handwriting. As an initial step, the 1st, 2nd, and 3rd grade teachers compared the handwriting forms each was using. It was hard to believe that one small school could incorporate so many different patterns for the same letters. A child, moving from one grade to another, was confronted every year with an entirely new set of letter forms. Faced with that unexpected discovery, the teachers came to a consensus on how each letter should be consistently written. They agreed to teach these letter forms directly instead of turning unsupervised children loose with individual writing books.

> First and 2nd graders loved being taught how to do an accurate job.

The children were ecstatic! First and 2nd graders loved being taught how to do an accurate job. Teachers quickly learned that when they were writing on the board, they had to display extra care. If an l or a k was slightly off vertical, a chorus of happy young voices would chide, "Teacher! Remember! No leaning towers!" Youngsters at that level wanted to be shown what was *correct.* They did not mind practicing because they desired to be successful and to produce. They did not resent structure—they welcomed it.

A year later there was a dramatic change in Slingerland screening scores. The number of 2nd, 3rd, and 4th graders having difficulty with written language was significantly lower. The school was no longer turning so many borderline children into problems.

References

Alston, J., and Taylor, J. 1987. *Handwriting: Theory, Research and Practice.* London & Sydney: Croom Helm.

Berninger, V. W. 1994. *Reading and Writing Acquisition: A Developmental Neuropsychological Perspective.* Madison, WI: Brown & Benchmark.

Briggs, D. 1970. The influence of handwriting on assessment. *Educational Research* 13(1): 50-55.

Nolen, P., McCutchen, D., and Berninger, B. 1990. Ensuring tomorrow's literacy: A shared responsibility. *Journal of Teacher Education* 41: 63-72.

Peck, M., Askov, E., and Fairchild, S. 1980. Another decade of research in handwriting: Progress and prospect in the 1970s. *Journal of Educational Research* 89: 283-98.

Phelps, J., Stempel, L., and Speck, G. 1985. The children's handwriting scale: A new diagnostic tool. *Journal of Educational Research* 79: 46-50.

Phelps, J., and Stempel, L. 1987. Handwriting: Evolution and evaluation. *Annals of Dyslexia* 37: 228-39.

Phelps, J., and Stempel, L. 1989. Help for handwriting: Procedures developed at Scottish Rite Hospital. *Education* 109(4): 388-89.

Slingerland, B. H. 1969. *Slingerland Screening Tests for Identifying Children with Specific Language Disability*. Cambridge, MA: Educators Publishing Service.

Vail, P. 1986. By hand with ergs and ohms. *Newsletter of the New York Branch of the International Orton Dyslexia Society* 10(2): 1.

Zaporozhets, A., and Elkonin, D. 1971. *Psychology of Preschool Children*. Cambridge, MA: MIT Press.

Chapter 2

Handwriting and Its Relationship to Cognitive Development, Reading Acquisition, and Academic Success

By permission of Bill Whitehead and Creators Syndicate, Inc.

Introduction

In recent years, an explosion of scientific interest in the human brain, its structures, and its processes has intrigued educators. How and when is the brain shaped and developed? Will imaging technology allow us to see and understand the neural systems that underlie our students' thinking? The answers to questions like these seem to be at hand and promise to reveal new and exciting ways to help students learn.

Nowhere is the study of cognitive development more fascinating and multifaceted than in the area of language and literacy. Early results indicate that language domains are highly overlapped and interrelated in the mind. Educational psychologist Virginia Berninger and others have defined the study of language as a whole, whether it is language by ear (speech perception), by mouth (speech production), by eye (reading), or by hand (writing).

As a literacy skill, the role of handwriting is particularly interesting. Before we can run, we must learn to walk. Similarly, long before students can write sophisticated compositions by hand, they must learn to recognize and write the letters of the alphabet. Researchers are affirming that handwriting is a foundational skill with connections to many aspects of language development and academic performance. Recent studies show the far-reaching consequences for students who lack handwriting abilities, and demonstrate that handwriting is a prerequisite for advanced literacy skills. Consider these facts.

- **Handwriting is a complex skill that involves the mind and the body.** The act of writing a letterform is a series of steps that begins in the brain. With instruction and practice, these steps become more and more rapid until they are automatic.

  First, students must have a clear mental image of the letter to be written and the pattern for writing it efficiently. Next, a motor plan can be formed. Finally, these instructions are carried out by fine-motor functions of the hand. To better define this complex process, the term *orthographic-motor integration* is sometimes used in place of *handwriting*.

- **Handwriting competency lays the groundwork for academic achievement.** In the early grades, handwriting skill accounts for much of the variance in children's ability to compose sentences and stories. Automatic production of letters is one of the most important predictors of compositional skill. In the later grades, handwriting continues to play a role in students' ability to write well and succeed at school.

- **When handwriting is automatic, more working memory is available for higher-order tasks.** Studies of the brain have demonstrated that the mind can perform only one conscious cognitive activity at a time. Space in working memory is at a premium as a student undertakes a demanding task such as writing an essay. For this reason, students have a big advantage when basic skills such as handwriting and spelling are automated. Working memory is freed from attention to letter formation and legibility, and mental capacity is available to focus on the content and quality of the writing.

In this chapter, Karin Harman James presents findings, based on functional magnetic resonance imaging (fMRI), that suggest that self-generated action, in the form of handwriting, is a crucial component in setting up brain systems for reading acquisition. Kenneth Pugh and colleagues explain the relationship of neurobiology to literacy. Finally, Stephen Peverly, along with colleagues at Columbia University, reveals that handwriting skill predicts the quality of students' note-taking even at the college level. Together, these articles point to handwriting as an important contributor to cognitive development, reading acquisition, and academic success.

ZANER-BLOSER'S
15-MINUTE HANDWRITING LESSON

I. Model
Teacher models letter formation. Students form a clear mental image of the letter by observing the strokes it contains. Stroke descriptions (auditory) and writing in the air (kinesthetic) are also used. (3 minutes)

2. Practice
Students trace and write letters in isolation, in words, and in sentences. A green dot identifies the correct starting point for each letter. Clear models with directional arrows guide student practice. (10 minutes)

3. Evaluate
Students pause to look at their writing and decide if it is easy to read. Four *Keys to Legibility*—Shape, Size, Slant, and Spacing—form a rubric for self-evaluation. (2 minutes)

Excerpts from

Sensori-Motor Experience Leads to Changes in Visual Processing in the Developing Brain

Karin Harman James

Developmental Science, Pages 279–288, Vol. 13, Issue 2 (March 2010).

A fundamental question in developmental cognitive neuroscience concerns how changes in neural activation during development can inform theories of cognitive development. If we can understand how the child's brain changes with specific experiences, we will come closer to uncovering how learning happens – a crucial component in understanding human behaviour. Demonstrating neural changes during learning and development can inform and constrain cognitive theory, leading to further experimentation using purely behavioural measures as well as methods such as functional magnetic resonance imaging (fMRI). Although research into the relationship between human behaviour and brain function continues to lead to important discoveries, very little research is devoted to documenting the *emergence* of a given neural response pattern during development. The study of emergence provides insights into the potential cause of particular neural responses. To study the emergence of a neural response, however, one must be able to document the absence of the response followed by its presence; that is, to document a change. One method of investigating the emergence of neural responses is through the study of the developing brain using fMRI. Many typical neural responses that are present in the adult brain are absent or different in a child's brain (Casey, Tottenham Liston & Durston, 2005). Documenting the stages that lead to adult-like neural signatures can help us to understand why the brain responds to certain stimuli the way it does, which in turn can inform theories of cognitive development.

One type of neural response that is well documented in the adult brain is functional specialization – the tendency for brain areas or networks to respond more to one category of stimulus than to others. Functional specialization is considered to be integral to efficient processing. In many cases, functional specialization is thought to emerge from extensive experience (Gauthier, Skudlarski, Gore & Anderson, 2000a), but the type of experience seems to be important. That is, mere exposure to a particular stimulus category will not lead to functional specialization in the adult (Gauthier & Tarr, 2002). Although we assume that functional specialization for letters reflects our extensive experience with reading text, the specific type of experience that is necessary for the development of this pattern of neural response is not known. The requirements for specialization to emerge for individual letters may be different from those for words. For example, letters are learned before words during development, and children learn to write individual letters before they learn to read words (sometimes 3 or 4 years before). However, *how* children process letters in isolation is rarely studied. We believe that the question of how children learn to recognize letters is an important one, and one that can help us to understand how functional specialization develops. Can this specialization develop as a result of familiarity? By mere exposure? Or is a certain *type* of learning experience needed? Here, we make use of a learning paradigm that keeps familiarity and exposure constant while manipulating *how* letters are learned in order to try to gain an understanding of the experiences that may lead to the emergence of neural responses that reflect functional specialization in the developing brain.

Although functional specialization has often been characterized as a neural response pattern that is stimulus-specific, it may, in fact, reflect the recruitment of a specialized type of *processing* that is required for efficient recognition of a particular stimulus category (Gauthier, 2000). We suggest that the specialized processing that occurs during letter perception may be the result of our sensori-motor experience with letters. Physical interaction with the environment through sensori-motor interactions informs visual processing, and could potentially be crucial for normal object recognition to develop. Previous research suggests that recognition performance is particularly enhanced when learning requires integration across sensory and motor systems (Wexler & van Boxtel, 2005; Harman, Humphrey & Goodale, 1999; James, Humphrey & Goodale, 2001), suggesting that sensorimotor experience may be a crucial force in the emergence of functional specialization.

> We suggest that the specialized processing that occurs during letter perception may be the result of our sensori-motor experience with letters.

Neural activation patterns change after motor experience with objects. For example, when we visually perceive objects that we have had motor experience with, the motor system is active (Chao & Martin, 2000; Grezes & Decety, 2002; James & Atwood, 2009). This has recently been found to occur when we view letters as well (James & Gauthier, 2006), suggesting that our history of interacting with letters through writing is stored and perhaps re-activated upon visual presentation. We have proposed that the motor system is active during the visual presentation of letters because letters are learned using a combination of sensory and motor behaviours, including seeing, hearing, speaking, and writing. In addition, and crucial to this hypothesis, we propose that these sensori-motor experiences are stored and may lead to functional specialization for letters. Recently we have shown that adults who learn to write pseudo-letters develop functional specialization for these stimuli (greater activation to studied pseudo-letters than to unstudied pseudo-letters) in the left fusiform gyrus – the same region that is specialized for letters (James & Atwood, 2009). In contrast, adults who learned these stimuli with only visual experience did not develop the same specialized response. We interpret this as evidence supporting our claim that sensori-motor experience with letters through writing may be a crucial component for the development of functional specialization. To truly test this hypothesis however, we needed to use real letters of the alphabet in a system that is not already efficient at letter processing – the brain of the pre-school child.

> Sensori-motor experience with letters through writing may be a crucial component for the development of functional specialization.

Materials and Methods
Participants

Twelve healthy children (4 years 3 months to 5 years 4 months) with no known neurological diseases or psychological disorders participated in the present study. Seven of the children were female and five were male. All were native English speakers, and parents reported normal visual acuity. All children preferred to draw with their right hands spontaneously, and parents reported a right-hand preference for all children. Upon arriving at the first imaging appointment, the participants were randomly assigned to either the experimental or the control group. All research was approved by the Indiana University Protection of Human Participants Board. Informed written consent was obtained from the parents and they were compensated with gift certificates; the participants were compensated with a small toy or book.

Stimuli and Procedure

Imaging Sessions. Prior to the initial imaging session, children were acclimated to an MRI environment by allowing them to watch a short cartoon in our MR simulator, an artificial MRI environment. This environment also allows simulated sound to ensure that the participants are not afraid of loud noises. We are also able to monitor head movement, and stop the cartoon when excessive head movement occurs. This technique allows the children to learn how much they can move in the environment. If they felt comfortable lying still in this simulated environment they were then acclimated to the actual MRI machine.

After initial familiarization with the MRI environment, children passively viewed blocked presentations of isolated letters, isolated false fonts (stimuli that have the same features as letters, but are not actual letters), and simple shapes (see Figure 1). Sixteen-second blocks of stimuli were interspersed with 10-s fixation blocks; a block of each stimulus type was repeated three times within a given run, resulting in approximately 4-minute runs (Figure 1). Stimuli were in 3" x 2" squares (see Figure 1) presented centrally, for 2 seconds each. Between each stimulus, a 500-ms fixation cross was presented. Three runs were administered per experimental session, allowing data to be collected from nine blocks of a given stimulus type. Participants were required simply to view the stimuli passively. Neural activation, measured by the blood oxygen-level-dependent (BOLD) signal in the entire brain, was then recorded during exposure to the stimuli. Imaging sessions took approximately 20 minutes in total. Beginning one week after the first scanning session, participants returned once a week for four weeks to complete training sessions.

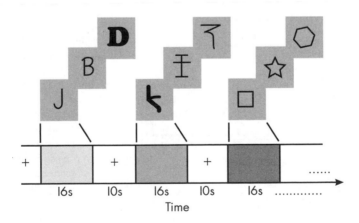

FIGURE I. *Graphic depiction of fMRI design and stimuli used in the present study (see text for design details.)*

Training Sessions. Training sessions were modeled after those used in a recent study on the effects of writing practise on letter recognition in children (Longcamp, Zerbato-Poudou & Velay, 2005). Each training session involved three types of task. First, all participants performed a four-alternative forced-choice letter identification task to assess their letter recognition ability (Figure 2a). Next, an experimenter read a short story to all participants, sitting next to the child so that s/he could view the text. The letters and words that the child was to practice were highlighted within the text and pointed to by the experimenter (Figure 2b). The children in the experimental (sensori-motor training) group then copied the letters and words that were highlighted in the story from a piece of paper (Figure 2c), and were given feedback on writing accuracy. In the control (visual training only) group, the participants simply identified the words and letters from the story instead of writing them (Figure 2c); they too were given feedback on their verbal response. The number of stimuli and time of exposure were the same in both groups. In both groups children were shown, and practiced, both upper- and lower-case letters. Finally, in the first training session, all children were asked several questions from the Bader reading inventory (Bader, 2005) to assess their phonological and visual processing of letters and words. These included: an assessment of print concepts; phoneme awareness; letter knowledge phonological awareness and language comprehension. This last task was administered to ensure that all participants were at a similar level in terms of letter and word knowledge at the beginning of the study. Each training session took approximately 30 minutes. One week after the last training session, the participants returned for the posttraining scanning session.

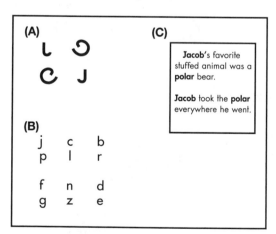

Figure 2. (A) An example of the four-alternative forced-choice task: participants were asked to 'point to the "j"'. (B) Words that contained the letters to be studied were highlighted in the story text. Participants were given examples in both upper and lower case. (C) The letters were presented in this format on a piece of paper: participants then either named or wrote the letters with feedback.

Imaging-Data Analyses Data analysis procedures reflected the question of primary interest: whether or not BOLD activation in the fusiform gyrus changes after sensori-motor training with letter stimuli.

Results

The imaging data suggest that prior to any training, the left fusiform gyrus was engaged more during letter perception than during the perception of other stimuli, but that after sensori-motor training the amplitude of the percentage signal change significantly increased during letter perception (see Figures 4 and 5). This is not as a result of familiarity with the stimuli, as the increase occurred only after sensori-motor training and not after visual training. The increase in neural response to

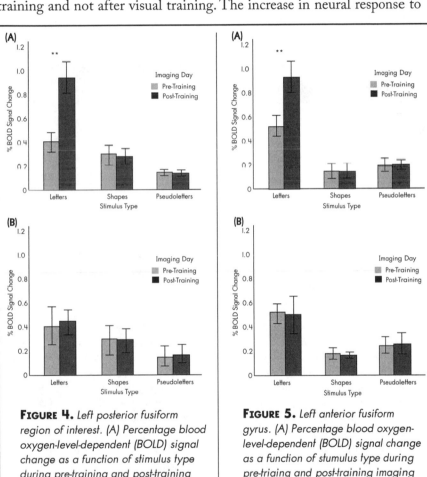

FIGURE 4. Left posterior fusiform region of interest. (A) Percentage blood oxygen-level-dependent (BOLD) signal change as a function of stimulus type during pre-training and post-training imaging sessions for the sensori-motor training group. (B) Percentage BOLD signal change as a function of stimulus type during pre-training and post-training imaging sessions for the visual-only training group. On this and all other graphs error bars represent standard error of the mean; ** depict significant differences at p < .01; and * depict differences at p < .05.

FIGURE 5. Left anterior fusiform gyrus. (A) Percentage blood oxygen-level-dependent (BOLD) signal change as a function of stumulus type during pre-triaing and post-training imaging sessions for the sensori-motor training group. (B) Percentage BOLD signal change as a function of stimulus type during pre-training and post-training imaging sessions for the visual-only training group.

letters after sensori-motor training also occurred in the right anterior fusiform gyrus, but no changes were observed in the right posterior fusiform (see Figures 6 and 7).

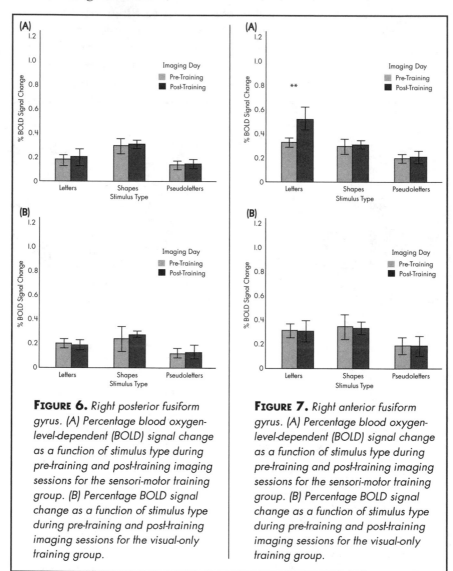

FIGURE 6. *Right posterior fusiform gyrus. (A) Percentage blood oxygen-level-dependent (BOLD) signal change as a function of stimulus type during pre-training and post-training imaging sessions for the sensori-motor training group. (B) Percentage BOLD signal change as a function of stimulus type during pre-training and post-training imaging sessions for the visual-only training group.*

FIGURE 7. *Right anterior fusiform gyrus. (A) Percentage blood oxygen-level-dependent (BOLD) signal change as a function of stimulus type during pre-training and post-training imaging sessions for the sensori-motor training group. (B) Percentage BOLD signal change as a function of stimulus type during pre-training and post-training imaging sessions for the visual-only training group.*

Discussion

The current study is the first to investigate the effects of sensori-motor experience on the neural activation patterns of young children. It is also the first study to document neural responses in pre-school children to letters, shapes and unfamiliar 2D objects (pseudoletters).

As a result, we can report several novel and interesting findings. First, we have found that, even for pre-literate children, there appear to be some hemispheric differences in how the brain responds during letter and shape perception. The left fusiform gyrus, especially in the anterior portion, responded more to letters than to shapes and pseudo-letters, even prior to our training manipulation (Figures 4 and 5). In contrast, however, the right fusiform responded similarly to letters, shapes and pseudo-letters (Figures 6 and 7). This finding suggests that early on, before children learn to read, the brain is organizing to achieve a left-hemisphere dominance for perceiving print. It seems that this hemispheric dominance does not simply result from the complexity of the letter stimuli, because the pseudoletters contained exactly the same features as the letters, only in a different organization – arguably, these stimuli are just as complex as letters. We cannot say, of course, when this hemispheric dominance for letters begins to develop; however, it should be noted that these children did have significant experience with letters despite not being able to read. That is, all children could sing the alphabet song, and all could name a minimum of 80% of the alphabet. In addition, all children could print their name. This suggests that perhaps familiarity with these stimuli has led to some hemispheric specialization. However, the children were also very familiar with the simple shapes, and could draw them as well. Even at this early age, letters are being processed differently from other, similar objects. This may be as a result of the emphasis that parents and other caregivers assign to these stimuli even at this age. It may also be as a result of perceiving letters in groups (words), even though the groups are 'meaningless' to a certain extent. We contend that part of the difference among letters and other shapes may lie in the manual construction that is happening when children learn to write letters.

Moreover, our second result of interest was the dramatic increase in activation that occurred in a putative *visual* area only after sensori-motor, that is, printing, experience. This increase supports the idea that printing practice, resulting in interactions among sensori-motor systems, may lead to the functional specialization that develops in three of our ROIs (Figures 4, 5, and 7). The increase in percentage signal change after printing training cannot be caused by familiarity, because both groups were familiar with the stimuli and had very similar exposures. The only difference

> **We contend that part of the difference among letters and other shapes may lie in the manual construction that is happening when children learn to write letters.**

in the experiences of the two groups was in the type of interactions that the participants had with the stimuli – one visual motor and one visual only. It is acknowledged, however, that the visual-motor association may not be the only type of association that changes the response properties in this area. We did not exhaustively test all possible associations, but were interested primarily in sensory-motor associations. That being said, the 'visual-only' practice involved saying the letters aloud (as did the printing practice), which is also a motor response. Thus, another way of stating our results is that the manual motor associations resulted in a different response in visual association areas than did an oral motor association.

The results of our study support behavioural work that has shown learning benefits from sensori-motor experiences. Educators have implemented sensori-motor learning strategies when teaching children to recognize shapes, including letters (Montessori, 1912). Indeed, some dyslexic individuals are delayed in motor tasks, implying that the motor difficulties they experience may have affected their letter-learning ability (Stoodley, Harrison & Stein, 2005). Similarly, children exhibiting developmental dyspraxia, a disorder manifesting in reduced motor skills, often have difficulty with letter identification and with learning to read (e.g. Portwood, 2000). Recent empirical work has shown that children recognize letters more efficiently after printing practice than when printing is not involved in learning (Longcamp et al., 2005). Thus, the accumulated *applied* evidence also converges with our results, which suggest that printing, which involves the coupling of visual and motor systems, is an important contributor to letter recognition.

> Recent empirical work has shown that children recognize letters more efficiently after printing practice than when printing is not involved in learning (Longcamp et al., 2005).

The demonstration of *changes* in brain activation as a result of controlled experience is important for understanding why neural activation patterns emerge in given situations. The results shown here suggest that one *cause* of neural specialization in the left fusiform gyrus may be our sensori-motor experience with letters. In general, these results have significant implications for our understanding of how the child's brain changes with experience, and they also suggest that the *type* of experience may be important in causing neural changes associated with learning.

References

Bader, L.A. (2005). *Bader Reading and Language inventory*. New York: Merrill Prentice Hall.

Casey, B.J., Tottenham, N., Liston, C., & Durston, S. (2005). Imaging the developing brain: what have we learned about cognitive development? *Trends in Cognitive Science, 9* (3), 104–110.

Chao, L.L., & Martin, A. (2000). Representation of man-made objects in the dorsal stream. *Neuroimage, 12,* 478–484.

Gauthier, I., & Tarr, M.J. (2002). Unraveling mechanisms for expert object recognition: bridging brain activity and behavior. *Journal of Experimental Psychology: Human Perception and Performance, 28* (2), 431–446.

Gauthier, I., Skudlarski, P., Gore, J.C., & Anderson, A.W. (2000a). Expertise for cars and birds recruits brain areas involved in face recognition. *Nature Neuroscience, 3,* 191–197.

Grezes, J., & Decety, J. (2002). Does visual perception of object afford action? Evidence from a neuroimaging study *Neuropsychologia, 40,* 212–222.

Harman, K.L., Humphrey, G.K., & Goodale, M.A. (1999). Active manual control of object views facilitates recognition. *Current Biology, 9,* 1315–1318.

James, K.H., & Atwood, T.P. (2009). Active motor experience changes neural activation patterns to letter-like symbols. *Cognitive Neuropsychology, 26,* 91–110.

James, K.H., & Gauthier, I. (2006). Letter processing automatically recruits a sensori-motor network. *Neuropsychologia, 44,* 2937–2949.

James, K.H., Humphrey, G.K., & Goodale, M.A. (2001). Manipulating and recognizing visual objects: where the action is. *Canadian Journal of Experimental Psychology, 55* (2), 111–120.

Longcamp, M., Zerbato-Poudou, M., & Velay, J.L. (2005). The influence of writing practice on letter recognition in preschool children: a comparison between handwriting and typing. *Acta Psychologica, 119* (1), 67–79.

Montessori, M. (1912). *The Montessori Method*. New York: Frederick Stokes Company.

Portwood,M. (2000). *Developmental dyspraxia*. London: David Fulton Publishing.

Stoodley, C.J., Harrison, E.P.D., & Stein, J.F. (2005). Implicit motor learning deficits in dyslexic adults. *Neuropsychologia, 44* (5), 795–798.

Wexler, M., & van Boxtel, J.J.A. (2005). Depth perception by the active observer. *Trends in Cognitive Science, 9,* 431–438.

Excerpts from

What Does Reading Have to Tell Us About Writing?

Kenneth R. Pugh, Stephen J. Frost, Rebecca Sandak, Margie Gillis, Dina Moore, Annette R. Jenner, and W. Einar Mencl

Handbook of Writing Research, Pages 433–448, ©2006 Guilford Publications, Inc.

Neuroimaging techniques have been employed with increasing frequency in recent years to examine both typical and atypical development in cognitive domains such as language, reading, memory, mathematical reasoning, attention, and executive function (Papanicolaou, Pugh, Simos, & Mencl, 2004). Research aimed at identifying the neural systems (neurocircuitry) that underlie these complex cognitive functions has benefited in recent years from rapid advances in neuroimaging technologies (e.g., positron emission tomography [PET]; functional magnetic resonance imaging [MRI]; magnetoencephalography [MEG].

In essence, functional neuroimaging allows us to identify sets of interreleted brain regions that are engaged (activated) when the participant performs a specific cognitive task (see Papanicolaou et al., 2004, for detailed methodological discussion and contrast of different technologies). While we can assume that different cognitive functions will engage many overlapping brain regions, we also might expect domain-specific circuits, and the extant data seem to bear out this expectation. Thus, for instance, some—but not all—brain regions activated during language-processing tasks will be nonoverlapping with regions associated with visual perception, mathematical reasoning, or memory tasks (Frackowiak, Friston, Frith, Dolan, & Mazziotta, 1997).

In this chapter we consider the kinds of methodological and design challenges that must be met if functional neuroimaging is to be applied fruitfully to the study of composition in writing and its disorders. To date, relatively little neuroimaging research has been conducted in this complex language production domain. However, it can be reasonably assumed from the outset that writing will share with other language functions many overlapping neurobiological systems. Therefore, we begin by considering previous findings on the functional brain organization for spoken and written language perception and production. Berninger, Abbott, Abbott, Graham, and Richards (2002) have conducted extensive behavioral research on the interrelations among all of these language domains, stressing the need to determine how composition in writing and its difficulties relate to general competencies for language by ear (speech perception), mouth (speech production), eye (reading), and hand (writing). Moreover, each of these language domains is complex and hierarchically organized (Indefrey & Levelt, 2004); we have previously noted the need to develop methods and experimental designs that will allow us to isolate and examine component subprocesses in each domain (Pugh et al., 1997, 2000). For example, for any modality, we can draw meaningful distinctions between hierarchically organized sublexical, lexical, syntactic, and comprehension-related component processes. To varying degrees, each of these component processes is likely to be shared among the written and spoken language domains.

Behavioral research suggests that disorders of reading and writing are highly comorbid and may therefore share a common etiological basis (Berninger et al., 2002). Because more is known at present regarding the neurobiology of reading development and disability with respect to component process organization, as well as the neurobiological signatures of successful remediation on these processes, this literature is reviewed in some depth to provide a set of preliminary hypotheses about what might be anticipated as we begin to explore writing difficulties and their remediation.

A few neuroimaging studies have been conducted to date examining the neural correlates of handwriting. These studies may be thought of as beginning to reveal the neurocircuitry relevant to phonological-to-graphemic and/or graphemic-to-motor planning stages of processing during writing. In one study (Katanoda, Yoshikawa, & Sugishita, 2001), a group of Japanese particapants was instructed to write the names of pictured objects, and in a second study (Menon & Desmond, 2001), a group of English speaking participants wrote sentences from dictation. Both studies converge to suggest a role for the regions previously implicated in lesion studies: the LH superior parietal lobule and LH middle to inferior frontal gyri. While the frontal regions would appear to be partially overlapping with areas implicated in speech production (Indefrey & Levelt, 2004), the involvement of the LH superior parietal lobule appears to be more specific to writing (Katanoda et al., 2001). While the tasks employed in these initial studies do not make significant demands on higher order aspects of writing behavior, such as conceptual or grammatical processing, they do suggest neural subsystems that might be crucial to the process of generating written word forms. One might speculate that if handwriting is more compromised than more general phonological and language processes in some clinical cohorts, anomalous activation patterns in these regions might be found. In any event, these studies examining handwriting now set the stage for more elaborate studies, wherein we begin to vary demands made on each of the higher order aspects of writing behavior in order to map out more fully the hierarchically organized neurocircuitry of writing.

Again, given the likelihood of many shared neurobiological components with reading, listening, and speaking, studies that examine writing within a broader language context will be very important.

Much remains to be investigated in the functional brain mapping of language by eye, ear, hand, and mouth (especially for those hierarchically arranged processes that constitute composition). Nevertheless, based on our reading of the current literature, we would cautiously suggest that despite differences in input and output mechanisms associated with each of these "end organs," the brain regions associated with phonological, semantic, syntactic, and pragmatic operations should be highly overlapping and highly interrelated.

With respect to writing deficits, the literature discussed here might be taken to suggest that if an individual has core deficits in any one of these overlapping dimensions, behavioral deficits are likely to manifest similarly in both perception and production (and within production for both speaking and writing).

> A deficit in one process should result in a processing bottleneck, and all language-based operations that rely on this process (and the network that underlies it) will suffer accordingly.

Moreover, given these functionally and anatomically integrated networks, we would also expect complex interactions across hierarchically arranged processing functions: A deficit in one process should result in a processing bottleneck, and all language-based operations that rely on this process (and the network that underlies it) will suffer accordingly. For example, the "bottleneck hypothesis" (Perfetti, 1985), in the domain of reading, has received some support: Slow and labor-prone word identification places severe constraints on subsequent sentence processing and comprehension. We might expect to see an analog of this for writing as well (Berninger et al., 2002); if lexical, phonological, spelling, or handwriting-related networks are compromised, expressing ideas in text composition will be impeded.

References

Berninger, V.W., Abbott, R.D., Abbott, S. P., Graham, S., & Richards, T. (2002). Writing and reading: Connections between language by hand language and by eye. *Journal of Learning Disabilites, 35,* 39–56.

Frackowiak, R. J., Friston, K., Frith, C. D., Dolan, R. J., & Mazziotta, J.C. (1997). *Human brain function.* New York: Academic Press.

Indefrey, P., & Levelt, W.J.M. (2004). The spatial and temporal signatures of word production components. *Cognition, 92,* 101–144.

Katanoda, K., Yoshikawa, K., & Sugishita, M. (2001). A functional MRI study on the neural substrates for writing. *Human Brain Mapping, 13,* 34–42.

Menon, V., & Desmond, J.E. (2001). Left superior parietal cortex involvement in writing: Integrating fMRI with lesion evidence. *Cognitive Brain Research, 12,* 337–340.

Papanicolaou, A.C., Pugh, K.R., Simos, P.G., & Mencl, W.E. (2004). Functional brain imaging: An introduction to concepts and applications. In P. McCardle & V. Chhabra (Eds.) *The voice of evidence in reading research* (385–416). Baltimore: Brooks.

Perfetti, C.A. (1985). *Reading ability.* New York: Oxford University Press.

Pugh, K.R., Mencl, W.E., Jenner, A.R., Katz, I., Frost, S.J., Lee, J.R., et al. (2000). Functional neuroimaging studies of reading and reading disability (developmental dyslexia). *Mental Retardation and Developmental Disabilities Research Reviews, 6,* 207–213.

Pugh, K.R., Shaywitz, B.A., Swaywitz, S.A., Shankweiler, D.P., Katz, I., Fletcher, J.M., et al. (1997). Predicting reading performance from neuroimaging profiles: The cerebral basis of phonological effects in printed word identification. *Journal of Experimental Psychology: Human Perceptions and Performance, 2,* 1–20.

Excerpts from

What Predicts Skill in Lecture Note Taking?

Stephen T. Peverly, Vivek Ramaswamy, Cindy Brown,
James Sumowski, Moona Alidoost, and Joanna Garner

Journal of Educational Psychology, Pages 167–180, Vol. 99, No. 1 (2007),
©American Psychological Association.

Despite the importance of good lecture notes to test performance, very little is known about the cognitive processes that underlie effective lecture note taking. The primary purpose of the 2 studies reported (a pilot study and Study 1) was to investigate 3 processes hypothesized to be significantly related to quality of notes: transcription fluency, verbal working memory, and the ability to identify main ideas. A 2nd purpose was to replicate the findings from previous research that notes and verbal working memory were significantly related to test performance. Results indicated that transcription fluency was the only predictor of quality of notes

> **Results indicated that transcription fluency was the only predictor of quality of notes.**

and that quality of notes was the only significant predictor of test performance. The findings on transcription fluency extend those of the children's writing literature to indicate that transcription fluency is related to a variety of writing outcomes and suggest that interventions directed at transcription fluency may enhance lecture note taking.

Contemporary views of expertise and cognitive processing suggest that performing a skill well usually depends on the parallel execution of two or more skill-specific processes within a limited-capacity working memory system. First, domain- or skill-specific basic skills (e.g., the processes that underlie word recognition) must be executed with an acceptable degree of fluency or automaticity, so that most, if not all, of the available space in working memory can be used for the application of the higher level cognitive skills (e.g., language ability) needed

> **Working memory is defined by most as storage and processing.**

to produce successful outcomes (e.g., good comprehension). If basic skills are not automatized, the application of higher level cognitive skills can be attenuated and prevent students from achieving their educational goal (e.g., Anderson, 1990; Baddeley, 1998, 2000; Ericsson & Kintsch, 1995; Kintsch, 1998; Perfetti, 1986; Schneider & Shiffrin, 1977; Shiffrin & Schneider, 1977). Second, individual differences in the capacity of working memory can lead to differences in the efficient execution of processes in working memory, which also can lead to differences in skill outcomes (Baddeley, 2001; Just & Carpenter, 1992; Swanson & Siegel, 2001). In other words, greater capacity in working memory enables greater efficiency in the processing and monitoring of higher order information (e.g., application of the knowledge of the language to interpret words). Finally, individual differences in higher level cognitive resources also can account for individual differences in task outcomes. In reading, for example, if word recognition (a basic skill) is automatized, individual differences in reading comprehension are highly correlated with language ability (Rayner, Foorman, Perfetti, Pesetsky, & Seidenberg, 2001; Vellutino, Fletcher, Snowling, & Scanlon, 2004).

> **Greater capacity in working memory enables greater efficiency in the processing and monitoring of higher order information.**

Although we know a great deal about the development of expertise in a number of domains (Anderson, 1982; Chi, Glaser, & Farr, 1988), we do not know much about the cognitive skills that underlie expertise in lecture note taking. Past elementary school, most teachers communicate information through lecture (Putnam, Deshler, & Schumaker, 1993), and lecture notes, a cryptic written record of important information presented in class (Piolat, Olive, & Kellogg, 2005), are an important part of academic studying for adolescents and young adults (Thomas, Iventosch, & Rohwer, 1987). Most college students, for example, rate lecture note taking as an important educational activity (Dunkel & Davy, 1989), and most take notes in classes (approximately 98%; Brobst, 1996; Palmatier & Bennett, 1974). In addition, research has shown that recording (encoding) and reviewing notes from classes is related to good test performance (Bretzing & Kulhavy, 1981; Fisher & Harris, 1973; Kiewra, 1985; Kiewra et al., 1991; Kiewra & Fletcher, 1984; Peverly, Brobst, Graham, & Shaw, 2003; Rickards & Friedman, 1978; Titsworth & Kiewra, 2004).

Our and others' analyses of note taking (Kiewra & Benton, 1988; Kiewra, Benton, & Lewis, 1987; Kobayashi, 2005; Peverly, 2006; Piolat et al., 2005) suggest that it is a difficult and cognitively demanding skill—students must hold lecture information in verbal working memory (VWM); select, construct, and/or transform important thematic units before the information in working memory is forgotten; quickly transcribe (via writing or typing) the information held in working memory, again before the information is forgotten; and maintain the continuity of the lecture (which also consumes working memory resources). Thus, expertise in note taking may be related to three variables: transcription fluency, working memory, and the higher level processes needed to identify important information in lecture. Hypothetically, inadequate lecture notes could result from a breakdown in any one of these variables. For example, because of the substantial cognitive load typically present during lecture (Piolat et al., 2005), slow transcription speed could strain the capacity limitations of working memory and cause students to forget some of the information in working memory (through decay or interference) and lose continuity of the lecture.

Conclusions and Implications

Contemporary views of cognitive processing and expertise (e.g., Anderson, 1990; Baddeley, 2000; Ericsson & Kintsch, 1995; Kintsch, 1998; Schneider & Shiffrin, 1977; Shiffrin & Schneider, 1977) argue that learning skills, including any school-based tasks, such as reading and writing, depend on performing a hierarchy of skills simultaneously (in parallel). In the execution of these skills, at least three conditions must hold. First, domain-specific basic skills must be executed with an acceptable degree of fluency or automaticity, so that most, if not all, of the space in working memory can be used for the application of the higher level cognitive skills needed to produce successful outcomes. If basic skills are not automatized, the application of higher level cognitive skills can be attenuated and prevent students from achieving their goal, even if their cognitive and metacognitive resources are substantial. Second, as implied in the previous sentence, individuals must have the cognitive resources (knowledge, strategies, executive monitoring) necessary to enable them to attend, interpret, and process the information in VWM once basic skills become automatized. Finally, individuals must have the VWM capacity necessary to process information adequately.

Data from these studies suggest that the basic skill of transcription fluency is related to quality of notes. Faster transcription fluency enables students to record more and higher quality information from a lecture. These data also suggest that VWM is not independently related to skill in note taking. However, this should be verified in future research with different complex span tasks, given the lack of consensus among researchers about what such tasks actually measure (Daneman & Hannon, 2001). Also, future research should measure note takers' selective attention, as Engle (2002) argued that capacity is related to the "ability to control attention [and avoid distraction] to maintain information in an active, quickly retrievable state" (p. 20). It may be the ability to attend, not the capacity of VWM, that partially accounts for skill in taking notes. Finally, the main idea task (pilot study) did not contribute to the skill of note taking. Logically, some variable must be related to the ability to identify and construct important information during a lecture. Future researchers may want to use a listening rather than a reading comprehension task. Although both measure the same higher level cognitive processes (Kintsch, 1998), the former is not confounded by differences in word recognition speed.

> Systematic instruction in handwriting in elementary school might have a positive effect on the quality of notes taken by high school and college students.

The findings from the pilot study and Study 1 on the relationship of transcription fluency to notes' quality may have important educational implications. First, systematic instruction in handwriting in elementary school might have a positive effect not only on the quantity and quality of essays written by children in elementary and middle school (Berninger et al., 1997; Graham et al., 2000; Jones & Christensen, 1999) but on the quality of notes taken by high school and college students. Longitudinal research is needed to evaluate this conjecture. Second, a transcription fluency component (among other components) should be included in instruction on lecture note taking to evaluate whether it can improve older (high school and college) students' handwriting fluency and whether improvements in fluency result in higher quality notes.

References

Anderson, J.R. (1982). Acquisition of cognitive skill. *Psychological Review, 89,* 369–406.

Anderson, J. R. (1990). *The adaptive character of thought.* Hillsdale, NJ: Erlbaum.

Baddeley, A. D. (1998). *Human memory: Theory and practice.* Boston: Allyn & Bacon.

Baddeley, A. D. (2000). The episodic buffer: A new component of working memory? *Trends in Cognitive Sciences, 4,* 417–423.

Baddeley, A. D. (2001). Is working memory still working? *American Psychologist, 56,* 849–864.

Berninger, V. W., Vaughan, K. B., Abbott, R. D., Abbott, S. P., Rogan, L. W., Brooks, A., et al. (1997). Treatment of handwriting problems in beginning writers: Transfer from handwriting to composition. *Journal of Educational Psychology, 89,* 652–666.

Bretzing, B. H., Kulhavy, R. W. (1981). Notetaking and passage style. *Journal of Educational Psychology, 73,* 242–250.

Brobst, K. E. (1996). The process of integrating information from two sources, lecture and text. (Doctoral dissertation, Teachers College, Columbia University, 1996). *Dissertation Abstracts International, 57,* 217.

Chi, M.T.H., Glaser, R., & Farr, M. (Eds.). (1988). *The nature of expertise.* Hillsdale, NJ: Erlbaum.

Daneman, M., & Hannon, B. (2001). Using working memory theory to investigate the construct validity of multiple-choice reading comprehension tests such as the SAT. *Journal of Experimental Psychology: General, 130,* 208–223.

Dunkel, P., & Davy, S. (1989). The heuristic of lecture notetaking: Perceptions of American and international students regarding the value and practice of notetaking. *English for Specific Purposes,* 33–50.

Engle, R. W. (2002). Working memory capacity as executive attention. *Current Directions in Psychological Science, 11,* 19–23.

Ericsson, K. A., & Kintsch, W. (1995). Long-term working memory. *Psychological Review, 102,* 211–245.

Fisher, J. L., & Harris, M. B. (1973). Effect of note-taking and review on recall. *Journal of Educational Psychology, 65,* 321–325.

Graham, S., Harris, K. R., & Fink, B. (2000). Is handwriting causally related to learning to write? Treatment of handwriting problems in beginning writers. *Journal of Educational Psychology, 92,* 620–633.

Jones, D., & Christensen, C. A. (1999). Relationship between automaticity in handwriting and students' ability to generate text. *Journal of Educational Psychology, 91,* 44–49.

Just, M. A., & Carpenter, P. A. (1992). A capacity theory of comprehension: Individual differences in working memory. *Psychological Review, 99,* 122–149.

Kiewra, K. A. (1985). Investigating notetaking and review: A depth of processing alternative. *Educational Psychologist, 20,* 23–32.

Kiewra, K. A., & Benton, S. L. (1988). The relationship between information processing ability and notetaking. *Contemporary Educational Psychology, 13,* 33–44.

Kiewra, K. A., Benton, S. L., & Lewis, L. B. (1987). Qualitative aspects of notetaking and their relationship with information-processing ability and academic achievement. *Journal of Instructional Psychology, 14,* 110–117.

Kiewra, K. A., DuBois, N. F., Christian, D., McShane, A., Meyerhoffer, M., & Roskelley, D. (1991). Note-taking functions and techniques. *Journal of Educational Psychology, 83,* 240–245.

Kiewra, K. A., & Fletcher, H. J. (1984). The relationship between levels of notetaking and achievement. *Human Learning: Journal of Practical Research & Applications, 3,* 273–280.

Kintsch, W. (1998). *Comprehension: A paradigm for cognition.* Cambridge, England: Cambridge University Press.

Kobayashi, K. (2005). What limits the encoding effect of note-taking? A meta-analytic examination. *Contemporary Educational Psychology, 30,* 242–262.

Palmatier, R. A., & Bennett, J. M. (1974). Notetaking habits of college students. *Journal of Reading, 18,* 215–218.

Peper, R. J., & Mayer, R. E. (1986). Generative effects of note-taking during science lectures. *Journal of Educational Psychology, 78,* 34–38.

Perfetti, C. A. (1986). Cognitive and linguistic components of reading ability. In B. Foorman & A. W. Siegel (Eds.), *Acquisition of reading skills: Cultural constraints and cognitive universals* (pp. 11– 40). Hillsdale, NJ: Erlbaum.

Peverly, S. T. (2006). The importance of handwriting speed in adult writing. *Developmental Neuropsychology, 29,* 197–216.

Peverly, S. T., Brobst, K., Graham, M., & Shaw, R. (2003). College adults are not good at self-regulation: A study on the relationship of self-regulation, note-taking, and test-taking. *Journal of Educational Psychology, 95,* 335–346.

Piolat, A., Olive, T., & Kellogg, R. T. (2005). Cognitive effort during note taking. *Applied Cognitive Psychology, 19,* 291–312.

Putnam, M.L., Deshler, D.D., & Schumaker, J.B. (1993). The investigation of setting demands: A missing link in learning strategy instruction. In L.S. Meltzer (Ed.), *Strategy assessment and instruction for students with learning disabilities* (pp. 325–354). Austin, TX: PRO-ED.

Rayner, K., Foorman, B. R., Perfetti, C. A., Pesetsky, D., & Seidenberg, M. S. (2001). How psychological science informs the teaching of reading. *Psychological Science in the Public Interest, 2,* 31–74.

Rickards, J. P., & Friedman, F. (1978). The encoding versus the external storage hypothesis in note taking. *Contemporary Educational Psychology, 3,* 136 –143.

Schneider, W., & Shiffrin, R. M. (1977). Controlled and automatic human information processing: I. Detection, search, and attention. *Psychological Review, 84,* 1–66.

Shiffrin, R. M., & Schneider, W. (1977). Controlled and automatic human information processing: II. Perceptual learning, automatic attending, and a general theory. *Psychological Review, 84,* 127–190.

Swanson, H. L., & Siegel, L. (2001). Learning disabilities as a working memory deficit. *Issues in Education, 7,* 1–48.

Thomas, J. W., Iventosch, L., & Rohwer, W. D. (1987). Relationships among student characteristics, study activities, and achievement as a function of course characteristics. *Contemporary Educational Psychology, 12,* 344–364.

Titsworth, B. S., & Kiewra, K., A. (2004). Spoken organizational lecture cues and student notetaking as facilitators of student learning. *Contemporary Educational Psychology, 29,* 447–461.

Vellutino, F.R., Fletcher, J.M., Snowling, M.J. & Scanlon, D.M. (2004). Specific reading disability (dyslexia): What have we learned in the past four decades? *Journal of Child Psychology and Psychiatry, 45,* 2–40.

PEANUTS

PEANUTS reprinted by permission of United Feature Syndicate, Inc.

Chapter 3

Handwriting Is a Perceptual-Motor Skill

Saul Steinberg, *Untitled*, 1948
Ink on paper
Originally published in *The New Yorker*, February 28, 1948
© The Saul Steinberg Foundation/Artists Rights Society (ARS), New York

Introduction

Unlike many academic skills, handwriting involves the mind and the body. Teaching a child how to hold a pencil or form a letter calls to mind a coach explaining how to bat a ball. However, handwriting is more than a physical skill. It is called a *perceptual-motor skill* because mental images and patterns govern the fine-motor functions of the hands and wrists. Understanding what letter **a** looks like, what it means, and what pattern is required to form it are important perceptual precursors to the physical act of writing **a**.

In recent years, occupational therapists and others have called attention to the deficit of fine-motor skills among many children today. Fine-motor skills involve the small muscles of the body that are used for tasks such as grasping, stacking, fastening clothing, and writing. The deficit in these skills may be the result of children choosing television and video games over more old-fashioned toys that build hand skill, such as lacing cards, play dough, blocks, and puzzles. Children who need extra help with fine-motor development may benefit from exercises specially designed to build strength in the hands and wrists.

Fine-motor development is important, but it doesn't tell the whole story. The articles in this chapter illustrate that although handwriting instruction can be broken down into many component areas, it really is more than the sum of its parts. High-quality, multi-modal handwriting instruction helps students develop and integrate a variety of cognitive and motor skills. Ultimately, students learn to make their thoughts visible in letters and words that communicate with others. Consider these points.

- **Successful handwriting depends on a range of mental and physical sub-skills, not just fine-motor abilities.** Sensory, perceptual, cognitive, psychosocial, and motor functions all play a part. Children develop in each area at different rates. A good handwriting curriculum promotes growth in all these domains while providing the direct instruction and practice vital to developing this as a reliable literacy skill.

- **Diverse play activities help young children build readiness skills for handwriting.** Play, both gross-motor (running, jumping) and fine-motor (building, stacking, cutting and pasting), helps children acquire important readiness skills for handwriting. These include hand dominance, hand-eye coordination, and spatial awareness.

- **Traditional handwriting instruction is the best cure for students who struggle with handwriting.** Recent studies indicate that many children who are referred to therapists for handwriting problems lack the benefit of high-quality classroom instruction. Often, too little class time is devoted to handwriting, and teachers feel ill-prepared to teach it. Findings suggest that traditional instruction produces better results than focusing on individual components such as fine-motor skills.

The articles in this chapter provide insight into the many component skills that underlie handwriting. First, Lynne Pape and Kelly Ryba enumerate these areas and discuss the importance of readiness. Then, author Nory Marsh shows what an efficient pencil grasp looks like. Finally, Peggy Denton and colleagues share research results demonstrating that handwriting instruction outperforms sensorimotor-based intervention when it comes to improving students' handwriting skills.

ZANER-BLOSER
MULTIMODAL INSTRUCTION

Eyes
- Look at letter models with directional arrows in student books and on wall strips.
- Look at letters to form a mental image. Identify basic strokes that make up letters.
- Look and self-evaluate with four Keys to Legibility: Shape, Size, Slant, Spacing.

Ears
- Listen to a complete stroke description for each letter.
- Listen to stories, songs, and rhymes about letters and handwriting skills (grades preK, K, l).

Hands
- Touch letterforms with ZB's *Touch and Trace Cards*.
- Touch and build fine-motor skills with teacher edition suggestions and ZB's *Fine Motor Skills Development Kit*.
- Touch and learn how to grasp a pencil comfortably and efficiently.
- Touch and practice with hundreds of teacher edition suggestions for using Wikki Stix®, sandpaper, shaving cream, sponges, and other common materials.

Movement
- Move and "skywrite" letters in the air, following correct stroke descriptions.
- Move with fingerplays, songs, and games (grades preK, K, l).
- Move and practice with hundreds of teacher edition suggestions for learning letters through painting, modeling, jumping, and more.

Performance Components Needed for Handwriting

Lynne Pape and Kelly Ryba

Practical Considerations for School-Based Occupational Therapists, ©2004 American Occupational Therapy Association.

Students use handwriting to communicate facts, ideas, thoughts, and feelings. At the same time, it provides the teacher with a mechanism to evaluate what a student has learned.

Students with specific disabilities may have difficulty mastering—or be unable to master—all of the components needed to use handwriting to communicate. It is important that occupational therapists understand all of these components. Because letter formation requires use of the hands, many people assume that handwriting is primarily a fine motor task. Parents or teachers frequently believe that a child's fine motor difficulties are the source of his or her handwriting problems. However, the fine motor component is just one small part of what is needed for students to be able to use writing to express their ideas.

Prewriting Skills

Before a child is exposed to handwriting, specific prewriting skills should be present. Vreeland (1998) has indicated that most children have developed the prewriting skills needed for letter formation by the second half of the kindergarten year. Starting handwriting instruction before a child has mastered these prewriting skills may cause poor writing habits, a dysfunctional pencil grip, and over-all discouragement (Alston & Taylor, 1987).

> The fine motor component is just one small part of what is needed for students to be able to use writing to express their ideas.

The Developmental test of Visual Motor Integration (VMI) is one assessment used to predict readiness for writing. A student's score is based on the ability to copy the first nine figures as stated by Beery (1982): vertical, horizontal, circle, plus sign, right and left diagonal lines, square, X, and triangle. In 1989, Beery revised that statement saying instead that handwriting should not be addressed until the child can copy the oblique cross (X) that typically occurs at 4 years, 11 months, as it requires that the child draw the diagonal lines required to form many letters.

Studies have found significant relationships with VMI scores as predictors of handwriting performance accuracy (Maeland, 1992; Sovik, 1975). Weil and Admundson (1994) found a significant difference between performance on the test and the ability to copy letters. This verified that kindergarten students should be ready for handwriting instruction during the latter part of the year.

In 1994, Tseng and Murray determined that the VMI was the best predictor of handwriting legibility. Tseng and Cermak (1993) reviewed ergonomics and perceptual-motor components and agreed that the nine basic prewriting shapes should be mastered before handwriting is introduced. Cornhill and Case-Smith (1996) also reviewed studies and conducted their own testing that indicate that visual-motor integration abilities were related signifi-

---

Prewriting skills are handwriting's foundations.

---

cantly to handwriting success. Students identified as having good handwriting scored higher on tests that measured motor accuracy, visual-motor integration, and in-hand manipulation (Maeland, 1992; Sovik, 1975; Tseng & Murray, 1994).

As indicated, prewriting skills are handwriting's foundations. By the latter half of kindergarten, most students have developed these necessary skills (Weil & Admundson, 1994). For those students with disabilities, however, this may not be the case. It is imperative that the occupational therapist educates the team as to the components needed as precursors before beginning handwriting. In this way, the educational team can determine how to approach the teaching of these skills. Students classified as mentally retarded or with multiple disabilities might never achieve all of the prewriting components; however, expectations are that they will be exposed to handwriting as a part of the curriculum.

Vreeland (1998) compiled a list that includes the following handwriting prerequisites.

Hand Dominance. Hand dominance develops as a result of the ability to coordinate the two sides of the body. Between ages 4 and 6 years, a child typically shows a hand preference when using tools and when performing fine motor tasks. This preference encourages consistent hand use so that skills can be developed for those tasks that require precision.

Crossing Midline and Bilateral Integration. Students need to be able to cross the midline of their bodies when forming specific letters and when writing across a page. They also need to be able to stabilize the paper while writing with the other hand. Students who have difficulty with bilateral integration may continue to switch hands during activities because of their inability to cross their midlines.

Functional Pencil Grip. A student needs an efficient, functional grasp that allows the controlled movements needed for letter formation. Schneck and Henderson (1990) identified the dynamic tripod and the lateral tripod as common functional pencil grips. The tripod grasp is formed by three fingers functioning together; the dynamic quadropod is formed by four fingers functioning together. Schneck (1991), however, also looked at the grips of students who had good handwriting and those who had poor handwriting. She found that proprioceptive and kinesthetic feedback affected handwriting legibility more than did pencil grip alone.

> A student needs an efficient, functional grasp that allows the controlled movements needed for letter formation.

Expanding on Schneck's findings, Tseng (1998) developed a comprehensive pencil grip classification. Her findings supported those studies that found the lateral tripod and dynamic quadropod equal to the dynamic tripod in legibility, speed, or both. Dennis and Swinth (2001) examined the influence of pencil grasp on the handwriting legibility of fourth-grade students during both short and long writing tasks. They found that the type of grasp used did not affect legibility as much as the length of the writing task. They also found the lateral quadropod to be a functional pencil grip.

Koziatek and Powell (2003) looked at how the type of pencil grip affected the handwriting speed and legibility of fourth-grade students. The Evaluation Tool of Children's Handwriting, discussed later in this chapter, was used to determine legibility. Photgraphs were taken of students' pencil grips as they wrote. The researchers found that four main pencil grips were used among the 99 students observed: 38 students used the dynamic tripod, 18 students used the dynamic quadropod, 22 students used the lateral tripod, and 21 sutdents used the lateral quadropod. Use of any particular grip did not affect legibility.

The literature now supports the use of these four types of mature pencil grips. As shown studies also have indicated that use of any of these did not affect handwriting legibility or speed. School-based occupational therapists must be aware of this research as they evaluate students with handwriting difficulties. Achieving the perfect dynamic tripod grasp may not be necessary for those students able to functionally use one of the three other types of recognized grasps.

Handwriting Is a Perceptual-Motor Skill

Understanding of Directional and Spatial Terms

Students must be able to recognize right from left and apply this information to external objects. They must be able to discriminate the letters and numbers needed to read and write. Finally, they must be able to translate verbal directions, such as "Start at the top and make a straight line down," into motor responses.

Ability to Copy Lines and Shapes. As discussed, there is a correlation between the ability to copy the first nine shapes on the VMI and the ability to form letters. The ability to copy the shapes is a prerequisite for learning letter formation.

Ability to Use Eyes and Hands Together. A child must be able to attend to tasks visually. Visual feedback and guidance to the hands is essential for motor output in terms of letter formation, placement, and alignment. The eyes drive the hands when writing, because early letter formation is not automatic.

Ability to Maintain an Upright Posture. The student must be able to maintain the adequate sitting posture needed for writing. There needs to be head and trunk stability to allow arm and hand mobility.

Orientation to Print. As indicated, students must be able to discriminate between letters and numbers. They also need to be able to identify letters. This is critical for the development of visual memory so that there is meaning to what is being copied or written.

Additional Performance Components

Learning to write requires motor, sensory, perceptual, and cognitive skills. These skills must be integrated into the writing process. To understand the complexity of the skills required for handwriting, it is important to discuss the following additional performance components and their contribution to the handwriting process. Vreeland (1998) grouped these components into sensory-motor, cognitive, and psychosocial areas.

> Learning to write requires motor, sensory, perceptual, and cognitive skills.

Postural Control and Stability. Upper extremity control depends on the external stability of the head and trunk. Proximal control of the upper extremity also is necessary to provide a stable support base for the control of the distal joints (Benbow, 1995). Students who have difficulty with postural control and stability may stabilize, lean, or prop their heads on their arms.

Body and Spatial Awareness. Internal body awareness allows the perception of movements and the position of body parts (proprioception) without relying on visual feedback. It assists in the development of laterality, or a child's internal awareness of the left side and right side. It also aids in directionality, the child's external awareness of left and right on himself or herself and on others and the realization that there is a right and left side to objects. It allows the child to monitor the position, movement, speed, and force of his or her writing. It provides a foundation for bilateral integration in the ability to across midline. Motor planning also relies on body awareness and proprioceptive feedback.

Students with poor body awareness may need to visually monitor their hands when performing a fine motor task, especially handwriting. Difficulty with motor planning requires a child to think about the specific movements needed for letter formation. He or she has difficulty forming and retrieving the motor memory of the letters. As a result, he or she may make the same letter three or four different ways. He or she may write slowly because of the need for the visual feedback. His or her handwriting has not reached the level of being automatic (Cermak, 1991).

Levine (1985) has indicated that some students who have poor handwriting have inadequate somatosensory perception (poor feedback about the position of the hand and fingers). A student may have problems in finger identification or in knowing the precise position of his or her arm and hand. He or she may position his or her head close to the paper to visually monitor what the hand is doing because of inadequate processing of somatosensory information. In addition, he or she frequently may attempt to adjust the pencil within his or her hand or grasp the utensil tightly to provide more feedback.

> Students with poor body awareness may need to visually monitor their hands when performing a fine motor task.

Visual-Motor, Visual-Perception, and Attention. Visual-motor ability enables the student to copy shapes, symbols, letters, and numbers. Ocular motor control allows the eyes to move and work separately from the head. This permits the child to efficiently look up at the board or at a paper on his or her desk when writing or copying. It allows the eyes to guide the hand movements needed for writing.

When beginning to print, the hand's output depends on the input and ongoing guidance of the visual system (Benbow, 1995). The student needs to visually monitor the point of his or her pencil to control stroke length and angle and to know where to intersect the lines. When writing in cursive, visual control becomes secondary to proprioceptive feedback. Various visual-perceptual components are needed for both printing and cursive to provide feedback about where to place words on the paper or on the writing line and to space words and letters properly. Visual discrimination is needed to perceive the differences between letters and numbers.

Fine Motor Components. In addition to the pencil grasp discussed previously, there are other fine motor components that affect a student's ability to manage a pencil. Benbow (1995) discussed the importance of wrist and hand function as it relates to handwriting. Wrist stability is necessary, as is the ability to oppose the thumb to the index finger to maintain a stable and open web space, stable palmar arches, and the ability to separate the two sides of the hand.

The student needs to be able to perform the in-hand manipulation needed to manage the pencil. Translation is required to position and adjust the pencil within the hand. Complex and simple rotation are necessary to pick up the pencil from the support surface and position it within the hand and to be able to rotate it to be able to erase.

Exner (1992) has identified three aspects of fine motor control that affect handwriting. The first is isolation of finger movements, which is needed to support the pencil grasp and to monitor discrete movements. The second is the grading of movements. This also is needed to support the pencil grasp and to provide fluid movements. Finally, proper timing of movements is needed to control the rhythm and flow of writing.

Cognitive Components. The effect of cognition on skill development has been discussed throughout this text. Lidz (1987) defined *cognition* as the capacity by which a person acquires, organizes, and uses knowledge. Cognition also includes multiple classes of mental capacities, such as attention, perception, memory, reasoning, problem solving, and language (Glass & Holyoak, 1986). Amundson (1992) indicated that cognitive information contributes to a student's overall handwriting dysfunction. Occupational therapists need to consider the student's attention span, memory (visual, verbal, and motor), and sequencing of events and items during assessments of conceptual skills.

Evaluating a student's level of cognition through an ability or IQ test often is required when determining if a student has a disability. Specific disabilities identified in the Individuals with Disabilities Education Act (IDEA) that may include cognitive deficits are mental retardation, autism, traumatic brain injury, or multiple disabilities. To assist in identifying realistic expectations, occupational therapists need to be aware of a student's ability level.

Psychosocial Components. Students who have difficulty writing may have self-concept or self-esteem issues as a result. They may lack the interest and motivation to write and resist tasks that require handwriting. They also may provide short answers or phrases when writing and rush through their work, not taking the time to go back and review it. This can affect overall legibility. If asked to go back and redo an assignment, a student may become very frustrated and act out.

> The acquisition of handwriting skills requires the integration of the sensory, motor, perceptual, and cognitive abilities.

A child's occupational performance includes self-care, work, and play activities. For the school-age child, work includes educational activities such as reading, writing, and calculation. Functional written communication is used both at school and at home, so the child must be able to convey information to others in a legible manner (Admundson, 2001). The acquisition of handwriting skills requires the integration of the sensory, motor, perceptual, and cognitive abilities that have been discussed. The occupational therapist needs to consider these performance components when evaluating a student's writing ability and when presenting information to the team regarding possible intervention strategies.

References

Alston, J., & Taylor, J. (Eds.). (1987). *Handwriting: Theory, research, and practice.* London: Croom Helm.

Amundson, S. J. (1992). Handwriting: Evaluation and intervention in school settings. In J. Case-Smith & C. Pehoski (Eds.), *Development of hand skills in the child* (pp. 63–78). Rockville, MD: American Occupational Therapy Association.

Amundson, S. (2001). Prewriting and handwriting skills. In J. Case-Smith, (Ed.), *Occupational therapy for children* (pp. 524–541). St. Louis, MO: Mosby.

Beery, K.E. (1989). *The Developmental Test of Visual-Motor Integration.* Cleveland, OH: Modern Curriculum Press.

Beery, K E. (1982). *The Developmental Test of Visual-Motor Integration.* Cleveland, OH: Modern Curriculum Press.

Benbow, M. (1995). Principles and practices of teaching handwriting. In A. Henderson & C. Pehoski (Eds.), *Hand function in the child: Foundations for remediation* (pp. 255–281). St. Louis, MO: Mosby.

Cermak, S. (1991). Somatosensory dyspraxia. In A. Fisher, E. A. Murray, & A. C. Bundy (Eds.), *Sensory integration: Theory and practice* (pp. 138–170), Philadelphia: F. A. Davis.

Cornhill, H., & Case-Smith, J. (1996). Factors that relate to good and poor handwriting. *American Journal of Occupational Therapy, 50,* 732–739.

Dennis, J., & Swinth, Y. (2001). Pencil grasp and children's handwriting legibility during different-length writing tasks. *American Journal of Occupational Therapy, 55,* 175–183.

Exner, C. E. (1992). In-hand manipulation skills. In J. Case-Smith & C. Pehoski (Eds.), *Development of hand skills in the child* (pp. 35–45). Rockville, MD: American Occupational Therapy Association.

Glass, A. L., & Holyoak, K J. (1986). *Cognition* (2nd ed.). Reading, MA: Addison-Wesley.

Koziatek, S., & Powell, N. (2003). Pencil grip, legibility, and speed of fourth-graders' writing in cursive. *American Journal of Occupational Therapy, 57,* 284–288.

Levine, M. (1985). *Pediatric Examination of Educational Readings at Middle Childhood (Peeramid).* Cambridge, MA: Educators Publishing Service.

Lidz, C. S. (1987). *Dynamic assessment.* New York: Guilford Press.

Maeland, A. (1992). Handwriting and perceptual-motor skills in clumsy, dys-graphic, and "normal" children. *Perceptual and Motor Skills, 75,* 1207–1217.

Schneck, C. M. (1991). Comparison of pencil-grip patterns in first graders with good and poor writing skills. *American Journal of Occupational Therapy, 45,* 701–706.

Schneck, C. M., & Henderson, A. (1990). Descriptive analysis of the developmental progression of grip position for pencil and crayon control in non-dysfunctional children. *American Journal of Occupational Therapy, 44,* 893–900.

Sovik, N. (1975). *Developmental cybernetics of handwriting and graphic behavior.* Oslo: Universitetsforlaget.

Tseng, M.H. (1998). Development of pencil grip position in preschool children. *Occupational Therapy Journal of Research, 18,* 207–224.

Tseng, M. H., & Murray, E. (1994). Differences in perceptual-motor measures in children with good and poor handwriting. *Occupational Therapy Journal of Research, 14,* 19–36.

Vreeland, E. (1998). *Handwriting: Not just in the hands.* Springfield, NH: Maxanna Learning Systems.

Weil, M., & Amundson, S. J. (1994). Relationship between visual motor and handwriting skills of children in kindergarten. *American Journal of Occupational Therapy, 48,* 982–988.

Development of a Mature Pencil Grasp

Nory Marsh

Start to Finish: Developmentally Sequenced Fine Motor Activities for Preschool Children,
©1998 Imaginart International, Inc.

An efficient grip on writing implements is an important component of handwriting "because it allows the fine movements necessary for writing" (Schneck, 1991, p. 701). Benbow, Hanft, and Marsh (1992, p. 23) identified the essential feature of an efficient grip as being that "the thumb and index finger form a circular web space allowing for skillful manipulation." Children follow a developmental progression through three general stages of pencil grasp: (a) palmar grasp, (b) static tripod grasp, and (c) dynamic tripod grasp (Schneck and Henderson, 1990).

> An efficient grip on writing implements is an important component of handwriting.

A palmar grasp—in which the writing instrument is positioned across the palm with the hand fisted and wrist either supinated or pronated—is the most immature stage. In the second stage, *static tripod grasp,* the writing instrument is usually resting in the open web space opposed between the index pad and the thumb pad. In the *dynamic tripod grasp,* the writing instrument is held and controlled between the pads of the thumb and index finger and rests on the radial side of the middle finger (Rosenbloom and Horton, 1971). An important difference between the static and dynamic tripod pencil grasps is that in the static grasp the hand, fingers, wrist, and pencil move as a single unit to control the writing instrument, whereas in the dynamic grasp, the fingers, hand, and wrist are adjusted individually, giving more refined control of the writing instrument.

Lateral tripod grasp—pencil stabilized against radial side of third digit with index pulp on top of shaft of pencil, thumb adducted and braced over or under anywhere along the lateral border of index finger, wrist slightly extended, fourth and fifth digits flexed to stabilize metacarpophalangeal arch and third digit, localized movement of digits of tripod and wrist movements on tall and horizontal strokes, forearm resting on table (Schneck, 1987).

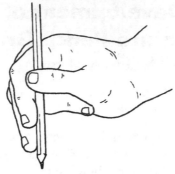

Dynamic tripod grasp—pencil stabilized against radial side of third digit by thumb pulp with index pulp on top of shaft of pencil, thumb stabilized in full opposition, wrist slightly extended, fourth and fifth digits flexed to stabilize the metacarpophalangeal arch and third digit, localized movement of digits of tripod and wrist movements on tall and horizontal strokes, forearm resting on table (Rosenbloom and Horton, 1971).

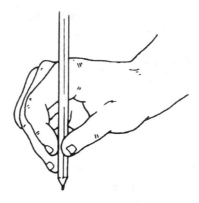

The dynamic and lateral tripod grasps are considered mature grips (Benbow, Hanft, and Marsh, 1992; Schneck, 1991; Tseng and Cermak, 1993). Children generally achieve a mature pencil grasp between the ages of four and six years (Schneck, 1991; Schneck and Henderson, 1990; Tseng and Cermak, 1993). By second grade, a child's pencil grip is usually established, and it is very difficult to modify after that time (Benbow, Hanft, and Marsh, 1992). Remember that pencil grasp is used here to refer generically to grasping any writing implement.

> By second grade, a child's pencil grip is usually established, and it is very difficult to modify after that time.

Handwriting Is a Perceptual-Motor Skill

Failure to develop a mature pencil grip may be caused by poor motor planning skills or impaired kinesthetic feedback (Tseng and Cermak, 1993). Motor planning difficulties cause inefficient pencil grips due to lack of accurate tactile and proprioceptive processing (Benbow, Hanft, and Marsh, 1992). Figure 1 illustrates pencil grips that Benbow, Hanft, and Marsh (1992) have identified as related to poor motor planning. Impaired kinesthetic, proprioceptive, and tactile feedback may lead to an awkward grip, gripping the pencil with excessive pressure and intense visual monitoring of the precise movements of the pencil (Tseng and Cermak, 1993; Benbow, Hanft, and Marsh, 1992). An extra tight grip leads to fatigue, shaking, wringing hands, and stopping and starting frequently (Benbow, Hanft, and Marsh, 1992).

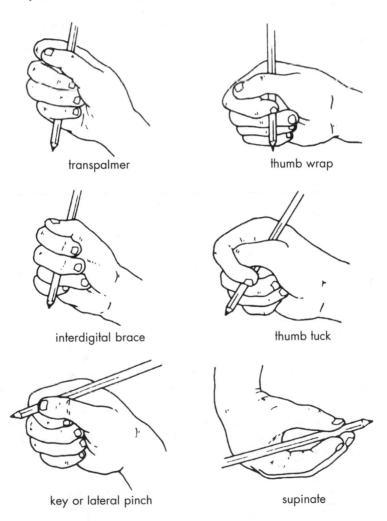

transpalmer

thumb wrap

interdigital brace

thumb tuck

key or lateral pinch

supinate

Development of a mature, functional pencil grasp is important because "inefficient grips limit the speed, range, and fluidity of distal movements needed for writing" (Benbow, Hanft, and Marsh, 1992, p. 24). In a study by Schneck (1991), first graders with mature pencil grasps demonstrated better writing skills than students with immature pencil grasps. While some variation in pencil grip may be functional for handwriting, efficient grips make handwriting easier (Tseng and Cermak, 1993). The important areas to assess in order to determine whether a pencil grip is functional are stress points, fatigue, comfort, and control (Benbow, Hanft, and Marsh, 1992).

Visual, verbal, and tactile cues may be helpful in assisting children to achieve an efficient pencil grip (Levine, 1991). For example, Levine (1991, p. 319) suggested using tactile cues such as a rubber band or string wrapped around the writing implement, triangular pencil grippers, and hexagonal-shaped crayons to assist a child in feeling and maintaining appropriate finger placement. A Stetro gripper adaptive device also works nicely to cue mature pencil grip. Writing on a vertical surface facilitates wrist extension, which also facilitates an efficient pencil grasp.

References

Benbow, M., Hanft, B., and Marsh, D. Handwriting in the classroom: Improving written communication. In Royeen, C.B. (Ed.), AOTA *Self-Study Series: Classroom Applications for School-Based Practice*, pp. 1–59. Bethesda, MD: American Occupational Therapy Association, 1992.

Levine, K.J. *Fine Motor Dysfunction: Therapeutic Strategies in the Classroom.* San Antonio, TX: Therapy Skill Builders, 1991.

Rosenbloom, L., and Horton, M.E. The maturation of fine prehension in young children. *Developmental Medicine and Child Neurology,* vol. 13: 3–8 (1971).

Schneck, C.M. Comparison of pencil grip patterns in first graders with good and poor writing skills. *American Journal of Occupational Therapy,* vol. 45, no. 8: 701–706 (1991).

Schneck, C.M., and Henderson, A. Descriptive analysis of the developmental progression of grip position for pencil and crayon control in nondysfunctional children. *American Journal of Occupational Therapy,* vol. 45, no. 10: 893–900 (1990).

Tseng, M.H., and Cermak, S.A. The influence of ergonomic factors and perceptual-motor abilities on handwriting performance. *American Journal of Occupational Therapy,* vol. 47, no. 10: 919–926 (1993).

The Effects of Sensorimotor-Based Intervention Versus Therapeutic Practice on Improving Handwriting Performance in 6- to 11-Year-Old Children

Peggy L. Denton, Steven Cope, Christine Moser

Objective. The aim of this study was to investigate the effects of two interventions (sensorimotor and therapeutic practice) on handwriting and selected sensorimotor components in elementary-age children.

Method. Thirty-eight children 6 to 11 years of age with handwriting dysfunction but no identified educational need were randomly assigned to one of the two intervention groups or a control group. Intervention groups met four times per week over 5 weeks. Handwriting was measured pre- and postintervention using the Test of Handwriting Skills. Visual perception (motor-reduced), visual-motor integration, proprioception, and in-hand manipulation were also measured.

Results. Children receiving therapeutic practice moderately improved handwriting whereas children receiving sensorimotor intervention declined in handwriting performance. The control group did not change significantly. Sensorimotor impairment was noted at pretest in three or four components and selected sensorimotor component function improved with intervention.

Conclusion. Therapeutic practice was more effective than sensorimotor-based intervention at improving handwriting performance. Children who received sensorimotor intervention improved in some sensorimotor components but also experienced a clinically meaningful decline in handwriting performance.

> Therapeutic practice was more effective than sensorimotor-based intervention at improving handwriting performance.

Introduction

Occupational therapists frequently receive referrals to treat impaired handwriting performance in elementary school-age children (Benbow, 1995: Reisman, 1991). Although keyboarding may serve as a compensatory approach for illegible handwriting in some children (Preminger, Weiss, & Weintraub, 2004), handwriting is necessary for assignments, homework, and many tests including standardized tests (high school achievement and college preparatory) for the majority of children. Elementary school-age children have been found to engage in paper and pencil tasks more frequently than manipulative tasks during a significant portion of the school day (McHale & Cermak, 1992). Thus, legible handwriting continues to be an important skill for children to develop in elementary school, and difficulty with this area can affect any child's proficiency at schoolwork.

Elementary school-age children have been found to engage in paper and pencil tasks more frequently than manipulative tasks during a significant portion of the school day.

Most occupational therapy interventions for handwriting dysfunction are based on the assumption that the relationship between sensorimotor impairment and dysfunctional handwriting is causal: that is, sensorimotor impairment results in handwriting dysfunction. It is further assumed that remediation of these underlying impaired sensorimotor components will result in improved handwriting performance (Tseng & Cermak, 1993). Feder, Majnemer, and Synnes (2000) found that 90% of the Canadian occupational therapists surveyed used sensorimotor approaches to remediate sensorimotor impairment for children with handwriting dysfunction. Similarly, Woodward and Swinth (2002) found that 92% of American school-based therapists surveyed used a multisensory approach to treat sensorimotor impairments in children with dysfunctional handwriting. Although some therapists may exclusively use a sensorimotor approach with little or no handwriting practice, others may select a skill-based approach using practice and specific motor-learning strategies. Commercially available handwriting intervention programs combine some form of sensorimotor intervention with letter formation practice (Amundson, 1998; Benbow, 1990; Laufer, 1993; Olsen, 1998). In fact, using an eclectic approach is noted as common practice in surveys of pediatric therapists (Feder et al., 2000).

The assumption that handwriting dysfunction is caused by sensorimotor impairment is evident in assessment practices as well. Feder et al. (2000) found that therapists regularly (>90%) assessed gross or fine motor skills, perceptual skills, quality of movement, and motor planning in children with handwriting and/or fine motor difficulties. Handwriting performance was assessed much less frequently (<15%).

Handwriting Is a Perceptual-Motor Skill

Occupational therapy practitioners are more likely to use sensorimotor-based interventions or an eclectic approach according to previous experimental and survey research. This tendency to combine treatment approaches in experimental studies makes it difficult to draw clear conclusions about the effectiveness of any particular intervention on a specific outcome. Systematic comparisons of the effectiveness of specifically designed occupational therapy handwriting interventions are needed to test the relative effectiveness of these approaches. Moreover, more research is needed to test the assumption that remediation of sensorimotor components leads to improved handwriting performance.

> **More research is needed to test the assumption that remediation of sensorimotor components leads to improved handwriting performance.**

Therefore, the purpose of this study was to investigate the effectiveness of two different handwriting intervention approaches on both handwriting and sensorimotor components. The following research questions guided this study:

- Did children's handwriting performance change due to the type of intervention received?

- Did children's sensorimotor component function change due to the type of intervention received?

Method

Design

This study used a three-group, pre- and posttest experimental design with random assignment to the sensorimotor (SM) ($n = 14$), therapeutic practice (TP) ($n = 15$), or control ($n = 9$) group. The raters were blinded to the children's group assignment and the children were unaware of the study's research questions.

Participants

To identify a sample of children with handwriting difficulty but no identified exceptional educational need, Gardner's Test of Handwriting Skills (THS) (1998) was administered to 200 typically developing children, 6 through 11 years of age. Approximately 25% of these children scored at least 1.5 standard deviations below the norm for their age.

Children were recruited from six private schools in two cities in the Midwest. Ultimately, 38 children, 6.0 to 11.2 years of age ($M = 9.0$, $SD = 1.1$), participated in this study. No attempt was made to balance the design by gender; 12 girls and 26 boys were included. One child broke her arm and did not participate in posttesting. Inclusion criteria for the study were: (1) between 6.0 and 12.0 years of age; (2) no known physical problems that affected their handwriting; (3) normal or corrected vision; (4) no identified exceptional educational need; and (5) poor handwriting (1.5 SD or more below the mean for their age group on THS).

Discussion

Effect of Intervention on Handwriting

For this sample of typically developing children with handwriting difficulties, therapeutic practice had a positive, albeit modest impact on children's handwriting after a relatively short period of intervention. Handwriting practice reported in the literature takes different forms, such as work sheets as part of academic instruction (Rutberg, 1998) or work sheets with feedback (Sudsawad et al., 2002). The therapeutic practice sessions in this study were conducted in small groups of 2 to 3 children with direct therapist involvement. That is, although work sheets were used as part of the intervention, children were never asked to work on them unattended. Therapists provided appropriate feedback that was systematically timed to give the children summary knowledge of their performance. Practice schedules were designed to be random rather than blocked. The task constraints were deliberately varied, and the students' metacognitive self-evaluation was consciously promoted. These results support those of Ste-Marie, Clark, Findlay, and Latimer (2004) that demonstrated therapeutic practice, based on principles of motor-learning, had a beneficial effect on handwriting performance.

> Students improved the most on those forms of handwriting that received the most practice.

The finding that handwriting performance declined in the SM group was unexpected. Unfortunately, this study took place at the end of the school year, and the children went home for the summer making further testing impossible. At the conclusion of the study, the activities used in both intervention groups were reviewed by the focus group of consulting occupational therapists. No activities were used that could explain the decrement in performance of the SM group. It is possible that instrumentation error may explain this finding. The THS has established internal reliability but no test-retest reliability. On the other hand, if these results were due to measurement error, a wide fluctuation in scores across all children with no discernable difference between the groups would be expected.

The means of the individual handwriting scales by group (Table 4) show that the largest improvements in handwriting performance in the TP group were in the dictated (M = 5.97) and copied scales (M = 6.7). Improvement on the memory scale was smaller (M = 3.6). Close analysis of the treating therapist's records reveal that dictated and copied handwriting practice dominated the interventions sessions, with less time spent on practicing handwriting from memory. It appears that the students improved the most on those forms of handwriting that received the most practice.

TABLE 4. Mean (*SD*) Pretest, Posttest, and Difference Scores for Handwriting Performance by Group and Handwriting Scale

Group Scale	Pretest		Posttest		Difference Score
Sensory Motor					
Memory	74.00	(13.48)	65.36	(11.57)	-8.60
Dictated	73.45	(7.64)	65.47	(7.13)	-7.98
Copied	85.43	(14.16)	76.07	(13.63)	-9.40
Therapeutic Practice					
Memory	71.37	(13.07)	74.93	(16.68)	3.60
Dictated	73.67	(13.14)	79.64	(16.52)	5.97
Copied	81.88	(10.78)	88.54	(10.01)	6.70
Control					
Memory	67.44	(15.19)	68.31	(12.71)	.09
Dictated	65.44	(10.41)	64.89	(9.29)	.55
Copied	72.11	(10.64)	77.92	(11.34)	5.80

Note. Difference scores were calculated as posttest–pretest.

In summary, when all of the handwriting scales were collapsed, the effect of group on handwriting change was both statistically significant and clinically strong (effect size; (f) = .72). In part these findings may reflect the large range of difference scores created when the TP group scores increased and the SM group scores declined. Yet, it also appears that therapeutic practice resulted in demonstrable improvement in handwriting performance for some, but not all children in the TP group. The decline in handwriting performance for children in the SM group was not expected and remains unexplained. Overall, the control group did not change during the course of the study. The trends noted in this study are strong enough to warrant further investigation.

Clinical Implications

Despite the limited empirical evidence that sensorimotor components are related to handwriting, they are included as key areas in handwriting evaluations (Amundson, 1992) and recommended as standard practice in occupational therapy textbooks (Amundson, 1992; Amundson & Weil, 2001; Tseng & Chow, 2003). By contrast, the findings of this current study call into question prevailing clinical assumptions about relationships between sensorimotor components and handwriting intervention. If improvement in sensorimotor function only is desired as the end goal of treatment, then sensorimotor treatment may be an appropriate intervention for handwriting dysfunction. Some of the children in this study did experience improvement in sensorimotor component function after sensorimotor treatment. However, there is no indication from this study that improvement in sensorimotor component function improved handwriting. Indeed, the reverse was found. This study found that therapeutic practice, carefully and systematically structured and implemented using motor-learning principles, was effective in improving handwriting with typically developing children with handwriting dysfunction.

> There is no indication from this study that improvement in sensorimotor component function improved handwriting.

It could be argued that the priority for occupational therapy services for typically developing children with only handwriting dysfunction is lower than for those children who have multiple needs. Yet modest but significant improvement in handwriting was noted with a relatively minimal amount of intervention time. It could also be argued that practice is an inappropriate intervention for occupational therapists to provide. If practice consists of unsupervised mass-produced work sheets, we would agree. But therapeutic practice, thoughtfully constructed and delivered, incorporating what is known about learning a motor skill, fits within occupational therapy's domain by helping children to master the important occupation of handwriting.

References

Amundson, S.J. (1992). Handwriting: Evaluation and intervention in school settings. In J. Case-Smith & C. Pehoski (Eds.), *Development of hand skills in the child* (pp. 63–78). Rockville, MD: American Occupational Therapy Association.

Amundson, S.J. (1998) *TRICS for written communication*. Homer, AK: OT KIDS.

Amundson, S.J., & Weil, M. (2001). Prewriting and handwriting skills. In J. Case-Smith (Ed.), *Occupational therapy for children* (4th ed., pp. 545–567). St. Louis, MO: Mosby.

Benbow, M. (1990). *Loops and other groups: A kinesthetic writing system*. Tuscon, AZ: Therapy Skills Builders.

Benbow, M. (1995). Principles and practices of teaching handwriting. In A. Henderson & C. Pehoski (Eds.), *Hand function in the child: Foundations for remediation* (pp. 255–281). St. Louis, MO: Mosby.

Denton, P.L., Cope, S., & Moser, C. (2006). The effects of sensorimotor-based intervention versus therapeutic practice on improving handwriting performance in 6- to 11-year-old children. *American Journal of Occupational Therapy, 60,* 16–27.

Feder, K., Majnemer, A., & Synnes, A. (2000). Handwriting: Current trends in occupational therapy practice. *Canadian Journal of Occupational Therapy, 67,* 197–204.

Gardner, M. (1998). *THS: Test of Handwriting Skills*. Hydesville, CA. Psychological and Educational Publications.

Laufer, L. (1993). *Callirobics: A multisensory approach*. Tucson, AZ: Therapy Skill Builders.

McHale, K., & Cermak, S.A. (1992). Fine motor activities in elementary school: Preliminary findings and provisional implications for children with fine motor problems. *American Journal of Occupational Therapy, 46,* 898–926.

Olsen, J.Z. (1998). *Handwriting without tears* (5th ed.). Potomac, MD: Author.

Preminger, F., Weiss, P.L., & Weintraub, N. (2004). Predicting occupational performance: Handwriting versus keyboarding. *American Journal of Occupational Therapy, 58,* 193–210.

Reisman, J.E. (1991). Poor handwriting: Who is referred? *American Journal of Occupational Therapy, 45,* 849–852.

Rutberg, J.L. (1998). *A comparison of two treatments for remediating handwriting disabilities*. Unpublished doctoral dissertation, University of Washington, Seattle.

Ste-Marie, D.M., Clark, S.E., Findlay, L.C., & Latimer, A.E. (2004). High levels of contextual interference enhance handwriting skill acquisition. *Journal of Motor Behavior, 36,* 115–126.

Sudsawad, P., Trombly, C.A., Henderson, A., & Tickle-Degnen, L. (2002). Testing the effects of kinesthetic training on handwriting performance in first grade children. *American Journal of Occupational Therapy, 56,* 26–33.

Tseng, M.H., & Cermak, S.A. (1993). The influence of ergonomic factors and perceptual-motor abilities on hand-writing performance. *American Journal of Occupational Therapy, 47,* 919–925.

Tseng, M.H., & Chow, S.M.K. (2003). Perceptual-motor function of school-age children with slow handwriting speed. In C. Royeen (Ed.), *Pediatric issues in occupational therapy.* Bethesda, MD: American Occupational Therapy Association.

Woodward, S., & Swinth, Y. (2002). Multisensory approach to handwriting remediation: Perceptions of school-based occupational therapists. *American Journal of Occupational Therapy, 56,* 305–312.

Reprinted by permission of Glenn Bernhardt.

Chapter 4

Continuous-Stroke Vertical Manuscript Supports Young Readers and Writers

Reprinted with special permission of Steve Kelley and Creators Syndicate.

Introduction

What is vertical manuscript, and why is it a good choice for young writers? Vertical manuscript is the straight-up-and-down writing style that most resembles print. Marjorie Wise and other early childhood educators introduced manuscript to American elementary schools in the 1920s. They recognized that the standard style of the time, the ornate cursive Palmer method, required a high degree of fine-motor skill and hand-eye coordination. Young children, they argued, needed a simpler, more developmentally appropriate way to write.

Today, the decision to teach the familiar upright letters of the manuscript alphabet is well-supported by custom and by a growing body of research. Recent studies point to manuscript handwriting as an important link in early literacy development that aids children as they learn about print and letter shapes. Keyboarding makes a poor substitute. Likewise, electing a more complicated italic style (such as D'Nealian) may confuse children instead of helping them make connections between what they read and what they write. Although the vertical manuscript alphabet is simple, with its straight lines and circles, it provides broad support for young writers. Consider these facts.

Vertical manuscript is familiar. Vertical manuscript is the alphabet children see in picture books and on road signs. An awareness of this environmental print leads to a natural interest in letters and their shapes. Parents and preschool teachers often introduce vertical manuscript when they teach children to write their names. Slanted or italic manuscript writing is not supported by children's everyday environment.

Vertical manuscript is easy for children to write. The basic strokes that make up the letters of Zaner-Bloser's manuscript alphabet are vertical lines, horizontal lines, circles, and slanted lines. These simple shapes occur naturally in children's drawings during the preschool years. They are also included in the nine figures children are asked to copy in the Developmental Test of Visual Motor Integration, or VMI, that is often used to measure readiness for writing: vertical, horizontal, circle, plus sign, right and left diagonals, square, X, and triangle. By contrast, the D'Nealian alphabet includes small curves and "tails" that are difficult for young children to write.

Zaner-Bloser's continuous-stroke method allows children to write manuscript letters fluidly, with fewer pencil lifts. It eliminates perceptual difficulties that can occur when visually joining a "ball and stick" to form, for example, lowercase **a**. With continuous stroke, **a** is formed with one smooth motion.

Vertical manuscript is highly legible. Just as vertical manuscript is the most legible style for traffic signs and job applications, it also helps make children's writing more readable to them and their teachers. It's a style that can be learned quickly and put to work right away in children's own writing.

Vertical manuscript supports early reading. With vertical manuscript, children learn to write the same letters they see in books, strengthening the reading-writing connection. Additionally, learning to print focuses children's attention on the distinctive shapes and features of letters in a way that simply finding a letter on a keyboard cannot. Studying the shapes of letters during handwriting instruction can lead to improved letter recognition—one of the most reliable indicators of future reading success.

Vertical manuscript is a life-long skill. Students will encounter the directions "Please print" throughout their lives. Many older students continue to prefer manuscript writing over cursive for the majority of classroom writing tasks.

The articles in this chapter explore the benefits of teaching manuscript handwriting. Marilyn Jager Adams explains how writing letters enhances early reading skills. Marieke Longcamp and colleagues share research demonstrating that handwriting outperforms keyboarding in helping children learn to identify letters. A study by kindergarten classroom researchers Debby Kuhl and Peter Dewitz finds evidence that the D'Nealian alphabet can cause confusion for young readers. Literacy expert Steve Graham concludes there is no evidence to support the use of slanted writing in the early grades. Finally, research by Jennifer Trap-Porter and others demonstrates that the D'Nealian italic alphabet provides no advantage for learning cursive writing.

ZANER-BLOSER CONTINUOUS-STROKE MANUSCRIPT

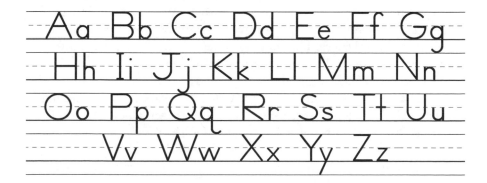

An Excerpt From

Beginning to Read: Thinking and Learning About Print

Marilyn Jager Adams

Beginning to Read: Thinking and Learning about Print, Pages 361–364, ©1990
Massachusetts Institute of Technology.

Summary: Learning Letters

Solid familiarity with the visual shapes of the individual letters is an absolute prerequisite for learning to read. To make this assertion more vivid, we may compare two "word"-learning studies, one by Peiter Reitsma (1983) and one by Lee Brooks (1977).

Reitsma's study was undertaken with twenty-nine normal, second-grade Dutch children. He presented each child with a list of ten pseudowords, four to seven letters in length, and printed on cards. Flipping through the cards, he gave each child four or eight tries, with feedback, at reading each of the pseudowords.

Three days later, Reitsma measured the speed and accuracy with which the children could read these same pseudowords, using two sets of control items for comparison. One set of control items consisted of homophonic pseudowords, spelled identically to the trained words with the exception of one single (often visually confusable) letter. The other set consisted of unrelated and previously unseen pseudowords whose pronunciations the children had repeated during training.

Those who three days earlier had been given just four practice trials read both the trained pseudowords and their homophonic contrasts significantly faster than the unrelated controls. Those who had practiced eight times read the trained pseudowords faster than either the homophonic or unrelated controls. None of the children made many errors.

Reitsma then extended this study using a set of unfamiliar real (Dutch) words, four to ten letters long, with eighteen normal first-grade children. The words were again printed on cards but this time embedded in meaningful sentences. The training sentences and, thus, the test words they contained, were read two, four, or six times by each child.

Three days later, the training words, along with sets of homophonic and unrelated control words, were presented in isolation on a computer screen, and the children were timed as they read each aloud. After only two practice trials, both the trained words and their homophones were read significantly faster than the unrelated controls. After only four practice trials, the trained words were read significantly faster than either their homophonic or their unrelated controls.

Against this remarkably spongelike word acquisition of Reitsma's young children, we may compare the performance of a group of college students trained by Brooks (1977). Brooks's adult subjects were given twelve monosyllabic, four "letter" pseudowords to learn. The spellings of six of the pseudowords reflected frequent English spelling-to-sound rules. The spellings of the other six did not and therefore had to be learned as "whole word patterns." (In fact, Brooks's purpose in conducting this experiment was to compare the speed of phonic versus whole word learning.)

The two types of words were trained in separate blocks of trials so that there should have been little confusion as to which were and which were not alphabetically decodable. With respect to differences in the learnability of the two types of pseudowords, the alphabetic items showed a slight disadvantage early in training and a slight advantage later in training. However, the point here is that, after 200 practice trials with each of the twelve items, the adults were still having trouble recognizing them. Their learning curves were still not close to asymptote.

> Solid familiarity with the visual shapes of the individual letters is an absolute prerequisite for learning to read.

Two trials for the children versus hundreds for the adults: To what can we attribute this contrast? Whereas Reitsma's items were spelled with normal familiar letters, Brooks's were spelled with an invented alphabet. Brooks's characters were exceedingly simple—∞, ∨, —, |||, ∩, ⊔; there were only six of them; and the subjects were given ten minutes of practice just on the individual letter-sound correspondences before training began. Nevertheless, Brooks's adults, in contrast with Reitsma's children, had to learn to recognize—and to recognize easily—not just the sequences of characters of which each item was comprised but also the characters themselves.

The Orthographic processor cannot begin to learn spellings until it has learned to recognize the letters from which they must be built. The Phonological processor cannot usefully learn letter sounds until the Orthographic processor has learned to discriminate the individual letters with which they must be linked. Yet the visual forms of the individual letters are abstract and highly confusable.

In view of this, I urge that instruction in letter recognition be begun long before children get to school. The goal is to ensure that the letter shapes are highly familiar and discriminable to the children before they are faced with the tasks of learning the letters' sounds or, more generally, of learning to read words. After children have become thoroughly familiar with the letters and their names, reading and writing activities follow far more easily.

Many preschoolers become familiar with letters through a common sequence of activities. First, they learn the alphabet song. Then they learn the shapes that go with each of the letter names they have learned. In both of these challenges, they may gain both motivation and guidance from "Sesame Street," especially if it is treated as a participatory program rather than passively watched. More generally, there is no substitute for the attention and praise of a real person in any enrichment activity.

For children who enter school with such background, there would seem to be little argument for avoiding careful use of letter names in the classroom. For children who enter school without it, however, this issue is more difficult. For these children, there is good reason for concern that distinctions between the names and sounds of letters will be confused if they are taught at the same time.

Both theory and data suggest that instruction on neither the sounds of letters nor the recognition of whole words should be earnestly undertaken until the child has become confident and quick at recognizing individual letters.[1] While *every* aspect of reading growth depends on the speed and accuracy of letter perception, learning to recognize and discriminate printed letters is just too big, too hard, and too fussy a task to be mastered incidentally, in tandem with some other hard and fussy task, or without an adult's focused attention to its progress and difficulties. Succinctly, what a waste to correct the pronunciation of a letter sound or word if the child's confusion was really in the visual identity of the letter.

Thus, even for poorly prepared children, I would be tempted to begin with the alphabet song. I would exploit the letter names it teaches along with any other kinds of appropriately challenging and interesting activities toward helping them learn the letters' shapes. Only after I was very sure that the children's learning of letter shapes was well under way, would I begin serious instruction in spelling-sound relations or word recognition.

It also seems like a good idea to exercise children's ability to print individual letters from the start. This is not only because of its potential for enhancing individual letter recognition but, further, because it will allow them to write words as soon as they are introduced—and, as we shall see, writing seems a solidly productive activity for the young reader.

---

[1] This is not to say that, before this, one should avoid showing printed words to children and helping them to appreciate that they symbolize spoken words, that they are comprised of individual letters, and that the letters correspond to the sounds of the corresponding words. This sort of exposure and the "print appreciation" it supports are key steps toward reading readiness.

In the initial introduction of a letter shape, and otherwise to assist development of fine motor skills, tracing may be used. Tracing exercises may be more effective if the stencils are coded to encourage a uniform sequence of motor patterns for each letter (e.g., for the letter **b,** first trace the vertical bar from top to bottom, then draw the circle). This is both because control develops through repetition and because it enhances the chances that the child will attend to the individual features of the letters and their interrelations. (Note that the basis of this recommendation is orthogonal to any puritanical notions about the hygiene of penpersonship. After the children have thoroughly learned the letters, it is okay if they want to write them in a mirror, with their toes, while standing on their heads.)

> ...it appears that neither tracing nor copying, but independent printing holds the greatest leverage for perceptual and motor learning of letter shapes.

Copying, of course, must be used; it is a necessary step toward the independent printing of a letter. But it appears that neither tracing nor copying, but independent printing holds the greatest leverage for perceptual and motor learning of letter shapes. It will be obvious when a child needs a model to produce a letter—that is, it will be obvious when reversion to copying is necessary. In such cases, copying should be encouraged and coupled with guidance about those aspects of the letter with which the child is having difficulty.

It also seems that whenever letter-sound instruction is begun, it is a good idea to present integrated letter/keyword/picture displays. These may be charts to be hung on the classroom wall or pictures in an alphabet book. In whatever showcase, such displays provide mnemonic assistance for letter shapes, letter sounds, and their couplings, at once.

Finally, given that the notion that letters spell words is so very critical, one wonders why more preschool trade books and preprimers are not produced in ways that make their print more salient. In tradebooks, at least, the possibilities of graphically or stylistically enhancing print are myriad. Again, some of Dr. Seuss's books provide good models.

Further, one wonders why so very few preschool tradebooks and preprimers are printed in uppercase type. Inasmuch as children generally learn uppercase letters first, this might provide a good early clue that letters are related to language and print.

References

Brooks, L. (1977). Visual pattern in fluent word identification. In A.S. Reber and D.L. Scarborough (eds.), *Toward a psychology of reading*, 143–181. Hillsdale, NJ: Erlbaum Associates.

Reitsma, P. (1983). Printed word learning in beginning readers. *Journal of Experimental Child Psychology, 36,* 321–339.

"If you don't learn to sign your name smaller it'll never fit on checks."

Reprinted with special permission of King Features Syndicate.

The Influence of Writing Practice on Letter Recognition in Preschool Children: A Comparison Between Handwriting and Typing

Marieke Longcamp, Marie-Thérèse Zerbato-Poudou, Jean-Luc Velay

Acta Psychologica, Pages 67–79, Vol. 119, Issue 1 (May 2005).

Abstract

A large body of data supports the view that movement plays a crucial role in letter representation and suggests that handwriting contributes to the visual recognition of letters. If so, changing the motor conditions while children are learning to write by using a method based on typing instead of handwriting should affect their subsequent letter recognition performances. In order to test this hypothesis, we trained two groups of 38 children (aged 3–5 years) to copy letters of the alphabet either by hand or by typing them. After three weeks of learning, we ran two recognition tests, one week apart, to compare the letter recognition performances of the two groups. The results showed that in the older children, the handwriting training gave rise to a better letter recognition than the typing training.

> Handwriting contributes to the visual recognition of letters.

Introduction

Nowadays, most adults probably write using a computer. Intensive use of word processing programs and the handy tools they contain (copy/paste, automatic spelling checks, etc.) is likely to modify high-level cognitive functions such as text composition (see Cochran-Smith, 1991). The present study deals with a more basic aspect of computer writing: the effects of dramatic motor changes resulting from the use of a keyboard instead of a pen. Computers are now being increasingly used at school, even at the preschool level, by very young children. If children happen to learn to write with a keyboard before they master handwriting, will this affect the way they perceive written language?

The idea that our movements organize our perceptions and contribute to setting up our spatial representations is not new and has by now become widely recognized (see Viviani, 2002). Some of the properties of objects (such as their shape, color and size) are perceived via the visual channel and others (such as their texture and temperature) by touch; all the diverse sensory inputs involved are combined together in time and space via active manipulatory movements, which also add their own information (weight, size, etc.). During childhood, we learn to associate actions with their correlated perceptions in order to build up unified, coherent representations of objects. Once the neural network underlying a given representation has been structured, any one of the inputs which was initially present suffices to reactivate the whole network (Martin, Ungerleider, & Haxby, 2000; Pulvermüller, 1999). The existence of these motor-perceptual links has been observed with neuroimaging techniques in humans; in particular, the visual presentation of pictures of objects, to which can be attributed a specific action, activated a premotor cortical area, even when no actual motor response was required (Chao & Martin, 2000). Furthermore, a growing body of lesion study data (e.g. Sirigu, Duhamel, & Poncet, 1991) suggests that sensorimotor knowledge about the functional properties of manipulatable objects is part of their representation, and can be used to recognize or name them (Martin et al., 2000). These motor-perceptual interactions involve associations of objects with potential actions: this is clearly what occurs in the case of tools.

> The fact that inability to write letters can be associated with reading deficits, due to an impaired ability to identify letters visually, is consistent with the existence of a tight coupling between the visual and sensorimotor perception of letter shapes.

Although alphabetic characters are not graspable objects, motor-perceptual links presumably contribute to their representation, since they are associated with highly specific writing movements. The fact that inability to write letters can be associated with reading deficits, due to an impaired ability to identify letters visually, is consistent with the existence of a tight coupling between the visual and sensorimotor perception of letter shapes (Anderson, Damasio, & Damasio, 1990). In addition, it has been established that writing movements can help subjects whose reading abilities are impaired: for instance, patients with pure alexia, who were no longer able to recognize letters visually, sometimes succeeded in doing so when they were asked to trace the outline of the letters with their fingers (Bartolomeo, Bachoud-Lévi, Chokron, & Degos, 2002; Seki, Yajima, & Sugishita, 1995). Handwriting movements may therefore somehow activate the visual representation of letters. The writing order of the numerous strokes composing ideograms is used as a cue to retrieve them from memory (Flores d'Arcais, 1994), which suggests that the motor scheme specific to each ideogram may be an essential component of its representation. This idea has been supported by neuroimaging studies on Japanese subjects who showed motor activation while looking at ideograms (Matsuo et al., 2001). Similarly, Longcamp, Anton, Roth, and Velay (2003) reported that, the simple visual presentation of Roman characters activated a premotor zone in the left hemisphere in right-handed subjects, even though no motor response was required. The activation of the corresponding area in the opposite hemisphere of left-handed subjects confirmed that this visually induced activation depends on the writing hand (Longcamp, Anton, Roth, & Velay, submitted for publication).

These various data converge to indicate that the cerebral representation of letters might not be strictly visual, but might be based on a complex neural network including a sensorimotor component acquired while learning concomitantly to read and write. Close functional relationships between the reading and writing processes might occur at a basic level, in addition to the interactions that have been described at a more cognitive level (Fitzgerald & Shanahan, 2000).

However, the existence of a sensorimotor component of this kind does not necessarily mean that it is involved in identifying letters. Nevertheless, there is some evidence which strongly suggests that writing movements are involved in letter memorization. For instance, repeated writing is an aid that is commonly used to help Japanese children memorize ideograms. In the same vein, Japanese adults often

Writing movements are involved in letter memorization.

report that they write with their finger in the air to identify complex characters. In fact, it has been reported that learning by writing facilitated subjects' memorization of graphic forms but not that of ideograms, words or syllables (Naka & Naoi, 1995). This effect was stronger when the forms were freely recalled in writing, but visual recognition of graphic designs was also enhanced by writing. The results of a subsequent study by Naka (1998) confirmed the positive effect of writing training on free recall of graphic designs, but no such effect was observed on visual recognition. Visual recognition was also studied by Hulme (1979), who compared children's learning of a series of abstract graphic forms, depending on whether they simply looked at the forms or looked at them as well as tracing the forms with their index finger. The tracing movements seemed to improve the children's memorization of the graphic items. Thus, it was suggested that the visual and motor information might undergo a common representation process.

There do exist some discrepancies between the results of the studies devoted to the effects of motor activity on letter memorization. Some authors have examined whether the graphic movements involved in tracing or writing may enhance the high-level cognitive processes involved in the acquisition of reading skills (see Graham & Weintraub, 1996 for a review). This was the case in the few studies in which the respective advantages of learning by handwriting versus typewriting were compared. In one study (Cunningham & Stanovich, 1990), children spelled words which were learned by writing them by hand better than those learned by typing them on a computer. However, subsequent studies did not confirm the advantage of the handwriting method (Vaughn, Schumm, & Gordon, 1992, 1993). The results obtained in these studies showed that children's word writing and recognition performances were not affected when they had used a typing method, and since the act of typing is simpler than handwriting, typewriting was thought to constitute an efficient method of teaching moderately mentally retarded students how to read and write (Calhoun, 1985).

We assume that the main process, if any, influenced by motor activity is likely to be a spatial process, in the initial step in the recognition of written characters. In other terms, writing movements may contribute to memorizing the shape and/or orientation of characters. If this is so, changing the motor conditions present during learning by using a typing method instead of a handwriting one will probably affect the subjects' representation of letters and hence their subsequent letter recognition performances. We therefore studied the early letter learning process in very young children (3–5 years) who had not yet begun to learn to read and write at school. The two modes of learning, i.e. handwriting and typing, were compared between two groups of children by testing their letter recognition performances. Since the children who participated were very young and their age range was large (2 years), and since they had obviously not all reached the same stage of cognitive and motor development, we assumed that all the children would not benefit identically from the learning. We therefore compared the learning modes as a function of the children's age. Finally, it should be pointed out that most studies dealing with the effects of writing movements on reading ability have focused on quite short retention intervals (Cunningham & Stanovich, 1990; Vaughn et al., 1992 but see Vaughn, Schumm, & Gordon, 1993). Yet as mentioned by Hulme (1979), in teaching children to read and write, one is dealing with long term memory, since the information learned is retained for periods of time. Two recognition tests were therefore carried out in the present study: the first immediately following the learning phase (T1) and the second, one week later (T2).

Methods

Participants

Seventy-six children, 41 boys and 35 girls, with a mean age of 3:10 years (46 months) and an age range of 2:9 (33 months) to 4:9 years old (57 months) participated in the experiment. They were tested in three classrooms at three different preschools.

Procedure

Learning groups

All the children were first subjected to a battery of pre-tests. An adapted version of the Bender–Gestalt test for children younger than 6 years old was used to assess their perceptual-motor development. Manual dexterity was assessed using a 9-hole pegboard in which the children had to insert nine cylindrical pieces as fast as they could. The experimenter noted the time spent and the hand used. Manual laterality was assessed using a simplified version of the Edinburgh Handedness Inventory (Oldfield, 1971). In order to evaluate their initial level of letter knowledge before learning, the children were submitted to a letter recognition pre-test. This test was exactly the same as the test used after learning. The twelve uppercase letters, which were to be learned after the pre-test, were used (B, C, D, E, F, G, J, L, N, P, R, Z). The children were seated in front of a computer screen on which four character-like patterns, including three distractors, were presented (Fig. 1). Three distractors were used with each letter: the mirror

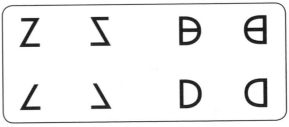

Fig 1. Two examples of visual configurations displayed on the computer screen during the letter recognition test.

image of the letter, a transformed letter (with a stroke added or missing from the letter), and the mirror image of the transformed letter. The instructions were: "Look carefully at the four letters on the screen: only one of them is the 'proper' letter, which is the letter you have learned with us. The other three are not correct. Show me this 'proper' letter with your index finger!" No speed instructions were given. The children's responses were recorded by the experimenter on the keyboard of the computer used for the test. Each of the four possible responses (upper left, upper right, lower left and lower right) was associated to a given key of the keyboard. Each letter and its distractors were presented twice in a random order (24 trials per session). The position of the four different letters and distractors on the screen varied randomly across trials.

After the letter recognition pre-test, we computed a score for each child for the number of correct responses (CR). In order to minimize the risk of getting a correct response by chance, we considered that a letter was known only when two CR were given in the two trials for this letter. This procedure reduced the number of CR but allowed us to distinguish the children who really knew the letters from those who gave random responses. The maximum score that could be scored in the test was thus 12, corresponding to 24 CR.

On the basis of all the pre-tests, we divided the child sample into two learning groups of 38 children which were matched in terms of age, sex, handedness, manual dexterity, educational level and letter recognition level. In addition, the children constituting both groups were equally distributed in each classroom in order to prevent any 'teacher effect' from occurring. In each learning group, the age range was 24 months. The 38 children of each group were sorted by age and divided into three equivalent sub-groups of 8-month ranges. Six groups were thus obtained, depending on the method used during learning, and age: Handwriting-older, Handwriting-middle, Handwriting-younger, Typing-older, Typing-middle and Typing-younger. In order to ensure that the two learning groups were not different with regard to initial letter knowledge before the beginning of learning, the CR were analyzed by means of a two (Learning mode: Handwriting vs. Typing) by three (Age: Older, Middle and Younger) ANOVA. The results of the ANOVA showed that neither the main factors (Learning mode and Age) nor their interaction reached the significance level. In particular, the slight difference between handwriting and typing in the older children was far from significant ($F(1,70) < 1$).

Learning

The aim of the experiment was for the children to implicitly learn the form of 12 uppercase letters by writing them. We used uppercase letters for several reasons: first, they are the simplest letters to write and they were the first letters that were taught at these schools, and second, the uppercase letters are what one sees on computer keyboards. Furthermore, we chose these 12 letters because they are not symmetrical, so we could use their mirror image as a distractor in the recognition tests. We did not want children to be trained with too many letters because we had just a few weeks to carry out the training and the tests. In order to make the learning more attractive, instead of teaching the 12 letters separately, they were included in four words. To form words, we added three vowels (A, O, I), which were not included in the recognition tests. The words were included in turn in a story that was told to the children by the teachers for a few weeks prior to the learning period. The four words were: LAPIN (rabbit), JOB (the rabbit's name in the story), CERF (stag) and ZADIG (the stag's name in the story). Each letter to be learned was present only once in the four words (L-P-N, J-B, CERF, Z-D-G). The learning period lasted for 3 weeks, and consisted of one half-hour session per week. The children were trained in groups of four, in presence of two experimenters, in a quiet classroom. The parents were informed about the aim of the experiment and they were asked not to have the children practice at home during the duration of the experiment.

Typing training. Each word was displayed separately on the upper left side of the computer screen, with 3 cm tall characters. The children were asked to look at the letters constituting the word, find the appropriate letters on the keyboard, and type each of them. No constraints were imposed regarding the order of the letters. When the child typed a wrong letter, the experimenter informed him/her, cancelled the wrong letter, and asked the child to find and type the correct letter. When all the letters composing the target word had been typed, the experimenter displayed the next word. The keyboard had been adapted for the purpose of the study: all the keys other than the 15 keys required to type the words (plus the backspace key and the carriage return bar for the experimenter) were removed from the keyboard. The 15 remaining keys were arranged in the central part of the keyboard. The four words were copied twice at each session, so the children typed each letter twice per session.

Handwriting training. Each word was presented on the upper left side of a piece of paper with 3 cm tall characters. The children were asked to copy the letters of the word underneath the model with a felt-tip pen. The letters could be copied anywhere on the paper and in any order. No constraints were imposed regarding the size of the letters. Since we wanted both types of training to be as similar as possible, we gave the same kind of feedback in handwriting and typing. In the typing training, the only errors that could occur were lack of a letter and confusion between two letters. In handwriting, confusion was not possible but the children could miscopy the letter. We did not correct the children when the form of the written letter was not perfect. However, if a letter was not written, the experimenter informed the child that a letter was lacking and asked him/her to find the lacking letter on the model and write it. When all the letters composing the target word had been written, the experimenter replaced the worksheet with the following one on which the next model word was presented. Each letter was copied twice at each session.

Letter recognition tests. The letter recognition tests were exactly the same as the aforementioned test performed before learning. A first test was run immediately at the end of the last learning session (T1) and repeated one week later (T2).

Discussion

The aim of this experiment was to determine whether two different types of writing training could induce different letter memorization. As a whole, the level of learning was low, since only the older children showed an increase in CR between pre-test and T1 and more precisely, only the older children who learned by handwriting. Such a low effect of learning can be explained by several causes. First, we did not explicitly teach the form of the letter because we wanted to compare two quite different writing methods and it was impossible to give comparable feedback in both types of learning. In typing, the letter is displayed with its perfect shape and no feedback has to be given about the typing movement. Thus we did not give feedback in the handwriting training to be as close as possible to the typing situation. In addition, we never directed the children's attention towards the exact form of the letter they wrote. In consequence, the learning was implicit. Furthermore, the effective time for learning was short (1.5 h within 3 weeks) with respect to the time usually required for learning to write and read. A longer time would have been more efficient but it was not possible to extend the teaching sessions. Despite this, the older children who were trained by handwriting performed more successfully in the letter recognition tests than those who were trained by typing.

> The older children who were trained by handwriting performed more successfully in the letter recognition tests than those who were trained by typing.

In this debate about the importance of motor conditions when learning to read and write, the results of the present study are in agreement with those showing that writing letters facilitates their memorization and their subsequent recognition (Hulme, 1979; Naka & Naoi, 1995). However, a negative result was obtained in a study in which learning methods differing in their motor involvement were compared in children (aged 3–6 years) (Courrieu & De Falco, 1989). In the motor situation, instead of writing, the children had to trace over a picture of the letters where the dynamics of the tracing movement were indicated graphically. After the training phase, no effects of the motor involvement which had occurred during the learning period were observed. Another negative result was obtained by Naka (1998), who observed that an advantage of handwriting showed up only when the memorization was tested by free writing recall, and not in simple visual recognition tests.

There are points that should be mentioned which may help to explain the advantage of handwriting we observed. First, the subjects were very young: they were pre-school children who had not had any previous experience of learning to read and write before the experiment. We were hence able to examine the very first step in the learning process, when the letters are still

> **Writing letters facilitates their memorization and their subsequent recognition.**

perceived as graphic forms without any particular phonological meaning. During the learning phase, the children were not required to learn the words they saw, and not even to name the letters, but only to write or type them. Likewise, in the recognition test, we did not ask the children to identify or spell words, but only to detect the letters among the distractors and to point at them without any verbalization. The whole procedure was therefore focused on a low level spatial processing of letters where sensorimotor signals might play a crucial role.

Secondly, another difference in comparison with previous studies was that learning extended over a period of three weeks, whereas in other studies on this topic, the training period generally consisted of a single session lasting anything from a few minutes to an hour. However, motor performances are known to evolve slowly, requiring many repetitions during several training sessions (Karni, 1996). The acquisition of motor skills seems to involve two main stages: an early, fast learning stage in which performances improve considerably as the result of a single training session, and a later, slow learning stage in which further gains can occur during several sessions (and even weeks) of practice (Ungerleider, Doyon, & Karni, 2002). A 3-week learning period certainly seems to provide favorable conditions for the children to set up a motor program for writing each letter and create the perceptual-motor links with its visual form. Assuming that the motor program associated with a letter is automatically reactivated when looking at it (Longcamp et al., 2003), this mechanism might help to recognize letters among close graphic forms.

Handwriting training allowed the older children to improve their performance in character recognition whereas the same training was not efficient in the children younger than fifty months. Of course, several reasons might explain this age-related difference: in particular, the lesser cognitive development of the younger children. Another reason might be that the fine motor control involved in handwriting was not mature enough in the younger children for them to produce the writing movements exactly. The fact that the graphic performances of 4-to 6-year old children have been found to correlate better with a motor score than with chronological age (van Galen, 1980) confirms that motor development is a key factor in handwriting. It has been suggested that handwriting development may be characterized by increased efficiency in inhibiting noise in the neuromotor and muscular system (van Galen, Portier, Smits-Engelsman, & Schomaker, 1993). Therefore, failure to inhibit the neuromotor noise might be the most likely cause of poor handwriting (Smits-Engelsman & van Galen, 1997). For the same maturational reasons, the peripheral kinaesthetic signals accompanying movements might be particularly noisy in younger children. The authors of studies on changes in kinaesthetic sensitivity with age have claimed that more than 30% of all 5-year-old children may be 'kinaesthetically inept' (Laszlo & Broderick, 1991). Finally, the interhemispheric relationships involved in visuo-motor coordination develop from 4 to 14 years of age, without acquiring all the characteristics present in adults (Hay & Velay, 2003). Thus, at the ages of the children who participated, a few months difference in age is undoubtedly crucial in terms of motor system maturation. In the younger children, the sensorimotor signals associated with movements might be too noisy to generate a correct sensorimotor representation of letters.

> The handwriting learning method requires the writer to perform a movement that completely defines the shape of the letter in order to build an internal model of the character.

From the sensorimotor point of view, handwriting and typing are clearly two distinct ways of writing, and these writing methods may well involve distinct central processes. The children who participated in this experiment did not type with both hands as expert typists do, nor did they even use several digits. Actually, since they had just one key to press at a time, they used their index finger, as most beginners do. During the training period, in the case of both handwriting and typing, a hand movement was therefore associated with the visual image of a given letter, but the two movements performed were quite different. On the one hand, the handwriting learning method requires the writer to perform a movement that completely defines the shape of the letter in order to build an internal model of the character. Once the learning is completed, there exists a unique correspondence between a given printed letter and the movement that is used to write this letter. On the other hand, typing is also a complex form of spatial learning in which the beginner typist has to build a cognitive map of the keyboard (see for instance Gentner, 1983; Logan, 1999). Learning typewriting consists in precisely locating a key in the keyboard and pressing it, but since the trajectory depends on the location of the finger before it goes into action, no specific relationship between the visual form of a letter and a given movement is built. Moreover, there is nothing in this pointing movement which might inform about the shape of the letters. In short, handwriting provides on-line signals from several sources, including vision, motor commands, and kinaesthetic feedback, which are closely linked and simultaneously distributed in time. No such spatio-temporal pattern occurs in typewriting. In addition to the motor differences, there exist other differences between the two writing methods. In particular, attentional differences are apparent, since learning to write a letter may require a deeper level of processing than finding a letter on a keyboard. Typing, in contrast to handwriting, inherently requires visual discrimination among letters in the process of key selection. These different aspects probably play a role in the implicit learning during both writing methods.

> Once it has been thoroughly learned and stabilized, motor memory can last for very long periods of time.

Finally, we sought to determine whether the knowledge implicitly learned by writing practice was maintained after long delays. To this aim, we observed that, in the handwriting group, the recognition performance at the end of training and after one week were identical. This is in agreement with data showing that, once it has been thoroughly learned and stabilized, motor memory can last for very long periods of time without any further practice (Shadmehr & Brashers-Krug, 1997). It is clear that much longer delays should have been tested because the learning process in question here involves memory extending over much longer periods of time.

In conclusion, the present results indicate that, provided they are not too young, handwriting learning helps children to memorize the form of a letter. Clearly, we cannot tell whether this process plays a role in reading, where whole words are perceived instead of isolated letters. Yet, as it seems to be widely accepted that letter recognition is the first stage in reading (Coltheart, Rastle, Perry, Langdon, & Ziegler, 2001), the way children perceive letters might indeed affect the way they read.

> Handwriting learning helps children to memorize the form of a letter.

Functional links have been found to exist between global motor skills performance and reading disabilities, in both children (Fawcett, Nicolson, & Dean, 1996) and adults (Nicolson et al., 1999; Velay, Daffaure, Giraud, & Habib, 2002), and further research is now required to be able to answer the question as to whether learning how to write really helps children to learn how to read.

Acknowledgments

The research was funded by the French Research Ministry (A.C.I. 'Cognitique' COG73). Marieke Longcamp was supported by a fellowship from the French Research Ministry (A.C.I. 'Cognitique'). We thank M. Besson and J.C. Gilhodes for critical comments on the manuscript and Reyna Leigh Gordon for revising the English. We are particularly grateful to the teachers of the three schools in Marseille (Chȃteau-Sec, Desautel and Valmante) who allowed us to work with their pupils during school time.

References

Anderson, S.W., Damasio, A.R., & Damasio, H. (1990). Troubled letters but not numbers: Domain specific cognitive impairments following focal damage in frontal cortex. *Brain, 113,* 749–766.

Bartolomeo, P., Bachoud-Lévi, A.-C., Chokron, S., & Degos, J.-D. (2002). Visually-and motor-based knowledge of letters: Evidence from a pure alexic patient. *Neuropsychologia, 40,* 1363–1371.

Calhoun, M.L. (1985). Typing contrasted with handwriting in language arts instruction for moderately mentally retarded students. *Education and Training of the Mentally Retarded, 20,* 48–52.

Chao, L.L., & Martin, A. (2000). Representation of manipulable man-made objects in the dorsal stream. *NeuroImage, 12,* 478–484.

Cochran-Smith, M. (1991). Word processing and writing in elementary classrooms: A critical review of related literature. *Review of Educational Research, 61,* 107–155.

Coltheart, M., Rastle, K., Perry, C., Langdon, R., & Ziegler, J. (2001). DRC: A dual route cascaded model of visual word recognition and reading aloud. *Psychological Review, 108,* 204–256.

Courrieu, P., & De Falco, S. (1989). Segmental vs. dynamic analysis of letter shape by preschool children. *Current Psychology of Cognition, 9(2),* 189–198.

Cunningham, A.E., & Stanovich, K.E. (1990). Early spelling acquisition: Writing beats the computer. *Journal of Educational Psychology, 82,* 159–162.

Fawcett, A.J., Nicolson, R.I., & Dean, P. (1996). Impaired performance of children with dyslexia on a range of cerebellar tasks. *Annals of Dyslexia, 46,* 259–283.

Fitzgerald, J., & Shanahan, T. (2000). Reading and writing relationships and their development. *Educational Psychologist, 35,* 39–50.

Flores d'Arcais, G.B. (1994). Order of strokes writing as a cue for retrieval in reading Chinese characters. *European Journal of Cognitive Psychology, 6,* 337–355.

Gentner, D.R. (1983). The acquisition of typewriting skill. *Acta Psychologica, 54,* 233–248.

Graham, S., & Weintraub, N. (1996). A review of handwriting research: Progress and prospects from 1980 to 1994. *Educational Psychology Review, 8(1),* 7–87.

Hay, L., & Velay, J.L. (2003). Interhemispheric relationships in 4-to 14-year-old children pointing to lateral targets. *Neuroreport, 14,* 1041–1044.

Hulme, C. (1979). The interaction of visual and motor memory for graphic forms following tracing. *Quarterly Journal of Experimental Psychology, 31,* 249–261.

Karni, A. (1996). The acquisition of perceptual and motor skills: A memory system in the adult human cortex. *Cognitive Brain Research, 5,* 39–48.

Laszlo, J.I., & Broderick, P. (1991). Drawing and handwriting difficulties: Reasons for and remediation of dysfunction. In J. P. Wann, A.M. Wing, & N. Søvik (Eds.), *The development of graphic skills* (pp. 259–280). London: Academic Press.

Logan, F.A. (1999). Errors in copy typewriting. *Journal of Experimental Psychology: Human Perception and Performance, 25,* 1760–1773.

Longcamp, M., Anton, J.L., Roth, M., & Velay, J.L. (2003). Visual presentation of single letters activates a premotor area involved in writing. *NeuroImage, 19,* 1492–1500.

Longcamp, M., Anton, J.L., Roth, M., & Velay, J.L. (submitted for publication). The premotor activations in response to visually presented single letters depend on the hand used to write: A study on left-handers.

Martin, A., Ungerleider, L. G., & Haxby, J. V. (2000). Category specificity and the brain: The sensory/ motor model of semantic representations of objects. In M. S. Gazzaniga (Ed.), *The cognitive neurosciences* (pp. 1023–1036). Cambridge, MA: MIT Press.

Matsuo, K., Kato, C., Tanaka, S., Sugio, T., Matsuzawa, M., Inui, T., et al. (2001). Visual language and handwriting movement: Functional magnetic resonance imaging at 3 T during generation of ideographic characters. *Brain Research Bulletin, 55,* 549–554.

Naka, M. (1998). Repeated writing facilitates children's memory for pseudocharacters and foreign letters. *Memory and Cognition, 26,* 804–809.

Naka, M., & Naoi, H. (1995). The effect of repeated writing on memory. *Memory and Cognition, 23,* 201–212.

Nicolson, R.I., Fawcett, A.J., Berry, E.L., Jenkins, I.H., Dean, P., & Brooks, D.J. (1999). Association of abnormal cerebellar activation with motor learning difficulties in dyslexic adults. *Lancet, 353(9165),* 1662–1667.

Oldfield, R.C. (1971). The assessment and analysis of handedness. *Neuropsychologia, 9,* 97–113.

Pulvermüller, F. (1999). Words in the brain language. *Behavioral and Brain Sciences, 22,* 253–336.

Seki, K., Yajima, M., & Sugishita, M. (1995). The efficacy of kinesthetic reading treatment for pure alexia. *Neuropsychologia, 33,* 595–609.

Shadmehr, R., & Brashers-Krug, T. (1997). Functional stages in the formation of human long-term motor memory. *The Journal of Neuroscience, 17,* 409–419.

Sirigu, A., Duhamel, J.R., & Poncet, M. (1991). The role of sensorimotor experience in object recognition: A case of multimodal agnosia. *Brain, 114,* 2555–2573.

Smits-Engelsman, B.C.M., & van Galen, G.P. (1997). Dysgraphia in children: Lasting psychomotor deficiency or transient developmental delay?. *Journal of Experimental Child Psychology, 67,* 164–184.

Ungerleider, L.G., Doyon, J., & Karni, A. (2002). Imaging brain plasticity during motor skill learning. *Neurobiology of Learning and Memory, 78,* 553–564.

van Galen, G.P. (1980). Handwriting and drawing: A two stage model of complex motor behavior. In G. Stelmach & J. Requin (Eds.), *Tutorials in motor behavior* (pp. 567–578). Amsterdam: North Holland.

van Galen, G.P., Portier, S.J., Smits-Engelsman, B.C.M., & Schomaker, L.R.B. (1993). Neuromotor noise and poor handwriting in children. *Acta Psychologica, 82,* 161–178.

Vaughn, S., Schumm, J.S., & Gordon, J. (1992). Early spelling acquisition: Does writing really beat the computer? *Learning Disability Quarterly, 15,* 223–228.

Vaughn, S., Schumm, J.S., & Gordon, J. (1993). Which motoric condition is most effective for teaching spelling to students with and without learning disabilities. Journal of Learning *Disabilities, 26(3),* 191–198.

Velay, J.L., Daffaure, V., Giraud, K., & Habib, M. (2002). Interhemispheric sensorimotor integration in pointing movements: A study on dyslexic adults. *Neuropsychologia, 40,* 827–834.

Viviani, P. (2002). Motor competence in the perception of dynamic events: A tutorial. In W. Prinz & B. Hommel (Eds.). *Common mechanisms in perception and action, attention and performance* (vol. XIX, pp. 406–442). Oxford: University Press.

The Effect of Handwriting Style on Alphabet Recognition

Debby Kuhl and Peter Dewitz

Paper presented at the Annual Meeting of the American Educational Research Association, April 1, 1994, New Orleans, LA.

For too long education has operated like the fashion industry. We allow ourselves to be influenced by passing fads and outside sources. This is a dangerous practice because our mistakes affect what and how children learn. Today curriculum is influenced by everyone from parents to publishers and while these influences have their place, we must be sure what happens in school is based on sound educational research. This research demonstrates how one such mistake may be affecting early readers all across the country.

Over a decade ago many school systems, including ours, adopted D'Nealian manuscript (Thurber, 1984) (also published as Modern Manuscript by other publishers) for writing instruction. Developed by Donald Thurber and published by Scott Foresman, the program was introduced into twenty-three states and is now widely used. This print form seemed perfectly logical because it made the transition from manuscript to cursive writing easier. Research on the D'Nealian form of handwriting has focused on the ease of stroke production, and there is no conclusive evidence that D'Nealian is superior to standard manuscript even though that was the goal of its creator (Connell, 1983; Duvall, 1985). The shortcoming of this well-intentioned practice was that it fails to take into consideration a critical aspect of print instruction: its potential effect on letter recognition. Only one study could be found on the relationship of letter recognition and handwriting style, and this study, with only 12 students, found that D'Nealian handwriting had no negative effects on the number of letter reversals when reading D'Nealian print, but other recognition problems were ignored (Thurber, 1984). The study did not examine the effect of D'Nealian handwriting on the letter recognition of traditional manuscript handwriting. Since letter recognition is one of the most critical skills for early readers' success, having difficulty with this skill can have a damaging impact on early reading achievement.

As my kindergarten students began to learn the alphabet and learned to write, I noticed problems they had learning to recognize letters. They consistently had difficulty identifying several letters, often making the same erroneous response to the same letter. As I recorded all responses in an attempt to analyze what they were doing, I began to notice patterns from child to child. D'Nealian manuscript appeared to be harder to learn. After collaborating with other kindergarten teachers in our district kindergarten center, I found their experiences were similar. I suspected that there was some relationship to our use of D'Nealian manuscript and the children's difficulty with letter recognition because the students appeared more successful when the letters were printed in the traditional form. I began to explore the research in an effort to understand the processes involved in learning letter names.

The D'Nealian alphabet was designed to smooth the transition from manuscript printing to cursive writing. Figure 1 presents some of the differences between D'Nealian and traditional handwriting, or the Zaner-Bloser style (Barbe,

> **Since letter recognition is one of the most critical skills for early readers' success, having difficulty with this skill can have a damaging impact on early reading achievement.**

Wasylyk, Hackney, and Braun, 1984). D'Nealian manuscript uses a continuous stroke production with a slight slant. An upswing stroke has been added to **a, d, h, i, l, m, n, t, u,** and **x.** The letters **w** and **y** are formed by joined curves rather than joined lines. The letter **k** has a closed arc added. The traditional print is perpendicular to and ends at the baseline except for descending letters.

Grapheme awareness or letter-name knowledge is an essential skill in early reading. It has been demonstrated by Chall (1967), Bond and Dykstra (1967), and others to be the best predictor of early reading achievement (Adams, 1991). While the predictive quality does not suggest that simple letter knowledge produces subsequent reading success, it does suggest that this knowledge is fundamental to the reading process.

As children learn to read, letter-name knowledge is an important aid to word recognition. When children abandon their logographic style of word recognition and move toward alphabetic reading, a stage called visual cue reading (Ehri, 1991), they use letter names as access routes for word identification (Scott and Ehri, 1990). The letter name is the cue by which the word is identified. Next, letter names provide the first cue as to the sounds of the letters. Many letter names begin with a phoneme that is also the sound most frequently represented by that letter, as in **b** and **t,** but not **w.** Later, during alphabetic reading, accurate letter recognition is essential to learning letter/sound association. Skill at alphabetic reading is necessary in order to become proficient at orthographic processing (Firth, 1985). In a sense, orthographic processing matures from letter-by-letter encoding used by kindergarten students to holistic word reading or spelling patterns by second grade (Juola, Schadler, Chabot, and McCaughey, 1977). In regard to all these processes one must conclude that letter knowledge, along with phoneme awareness, is an essential skill underlying all stages of word recognition. Even the mature reader looks at almost every word on a page and also processes most letters (McConkie and Zola, 1981). Simply stated, readers must process individual letters at some level before word recognition can become automatic. The amount of attention required to process individual letters will ultimately inhibit or facilitate word recognition. This study will discuss the perceptual processes involved in letter recognition and demonstrate how D'Nealian manuscript inhibits letter recognition both in theory and practice.

> **This study will discuss the perceptual processes involved in letter recognition and demonstrate how D'Nealian manuscript inhibits letter recognition both in theory and practice.**

Methods

Subjects

The subjects were 100 kindergarten boys and girls from two suburban schools. Fifty subjects were randomly sampled from the total kindergarten population of each school. The two schools were equal on two socio-economic indices. Each school served a middle-class population and each had a small but equal percentage of students on free and reduced lunch programs. In the D'Nealian school 5.4% of the students qualified for a free or reduced lunch, and in the traditional manuscript school 4.7% of the students qualified.

The subjects were categorized into low, average, and high ability students. In the school using D'Nealian, the classification was based on student stanine scores on the May Metropolitan Reading Readiness Test. In the school using traditional alphabet instruction, the classification was based on teacher evaluation of related classroom performance. No standardized test is given in this school to kindergarten students.

Classroom Instruction

Alphabet instruction in both schools began in the fall of the year and focused on a letter of the week. Both programs included multi-sensory experiences with the alphabet and introduced sound symbol correspondence rules. In the traditional print school, the students received the visual models of the letters on wall charts, manipulatives, big books, worksheets, and teacher-made materials. In the D'Nealian print school, the children used the D'Nealian model on alphabet charts, teacher-made materials, language experience writing, and worksheets. They were also exposed to traditional print in big books, manipulatives, and library books, as those materials are often not available in D'Nealian print. Neither school emphasized formal handwriting instruction in kindergarten, but the teachers demonstrated the correct stroke production as children used the letters in their writing.

Experimental Procedures

The children's knowledge of the alphabet was measured in late May after both schools had completed alphabet instruction. The subjects were evaluated by the same individual during the same calendar week. Each student read the alphabet from two sets of 3" x 5" cards with one set of cards printed in the D'Nealian alphabet and the other set printed in the traditional alphabet. The stimuli on the cards were photocopied lowercase letters taken from commercially prepared alphabet charts of both print styles. The cards were presented one type style at a time in random order, alternating the order of presentation for print style after each subject. The cards within each stack were also shuffled following each presentation in order to insure the letter order remained random. The response of each subject was recorded as given. If children failed to give a response or stated that they didn't know, the response was recorded as "doesn't know."

Results

Error frequencies for individual letters were calculated, and a confusion matrix was generated to determine the kinds of perceptual confusion that children experience with the two different handwriting systems. The error frequencies are presented in Table 1. When reading the traditional alphabet, the kindergarten students in the traditional classrooms made the most number of errors on letters that share the most distinctive features. Thus there were a substantial number of errors on **b, d,** and **q,** as is normally expected because they are reversal-rotational errors. The letters **b** and **d** caused the most difficulty with 9 errors and 8 errors respectively.

When children in D'Nealian classrooms read the traditional alphabet, new errors occurred. In addition to the difficulty with **b, d,** and **q,** errors were also made on the letters **f, g, j, l,** and **u.** Twenty students made errors on the letter **l,** 10 on the letter **j,** and 9 on the letter **g.** The responses to **l** and **j** reveal the influence of the D'Nealian system. The errors on the traditional **l** and **j** were made by students in the D'Nealian classrooms who read these letters as **i**. In the D'Nealian alphabet, **i** and **j** have the same distinctive features and only differ because the letters are reversals of one another. The distinctive features of **i** and **j** are carried over from the D'Nealian alphabet and cause confusion in learning the traditional alphabet.

> When children in D'Nealian classrooms read the traditional alphabet, new errors occurred.

The D'Nealian alphabet causes confusion even for those students who are taught it and must recognize it. The confusion the D'Nealian students have is presented in Figure 2, a confusion matrix. In the D'Nealian alphabet, **b** and **d** still caused considerable letter confusion, but additional problems occurred on **i, j, k, u, w, y,** and **g.** The letter **k** in D'Nealian handwriting illustrates the problem for the children. In the D'Nealian handwriting, an arc is added to the **k** making it resemble the capital **R** in the traditional system. The letter **k** is rarely confused with other letters in the traditional alphabet, but in D'Nealian it shares features with **R** and was misread by almost half of the students in the study. Additional confusion exists between **w** and **m** and **y** and **g** because the distinctive features are more similar in D'Nealian than in traditional print.

When the students in the traditional classroom read the D'Nealian alphabet, their error patterns were very similar to the D'Nealian students. They made the most number of errors on letters that were also difficult for the D'Nealian students. However, the traditional students were more successful on the D'Nealian **g, h,** and **j** than were their counterparts in the D'Nealian classroom. In the traditional alphabet, the **j** has the features of a curve and a dot, whereas in the D'Nealian alphabet, the **i** has the same features. The traditional students were never exposed to the D'Nealian **i;** therefore, they had no potential source of confusion.

Discussion

In this study I set out to demonstrate that handwriting style has a significant effect on letter recognition. The research question was generated from classroom experiences and personal observation. Some kindergarten children in my classroom appeared to struggle with learning the alphabet, and regular recording of their errors suggested that the D'Nealian alphabet might be a possible cause of their problem.

The data reveals that D'Nealian manuscript causes more confusion than does traditional manuscript and interferes with the ability of students in D'Nealian classrooms to read traditional print. It is important that the early reader be taught a handwriting style that minimizes confusion. The present study demonstrates that D'Nealian manuscript is not only harder to learn than traditional print, but D'Nealian creates substantially more letter recognition errors and causes more letter confusion than does the traditional style. One of the foundations of word recognition is the ability to recognize the printed symbols of our alphabet. It is the interplay of those individual letters that constitute words, and words communicate meaning. If the individual letters cause confusion, then word recognition is likely to be impeded, as is early reading development. The attention of early readers should not be distracted by print variation.

TABLE I. Frequency of letter recognition errors

	Traditional Alphabet		D'Nealian Alphabet	
	Traditional Students	D'Nealian Students	Traditional Students	D'Nealian Students
a	0	8	6	5
b	9	11	14	11
c	2	2	4	2
d	8	18	11	14
e	0	2	2	2
f	1	6	1	6
g	2	9	4	12
h	0	5	1	9
i	1	2	43	22
j	1	10	4	15
k	2	1	35	12
l	3	20	43	31
m	0	3	2	1
n	1	4	3	7
o	0	0	3	0
p	0	2	5	1
q	3	9	14	12
r	1	3	3	3
s	2	0	4	0
t	0	0	8	5
u	2	7	19	12
v	0	4	2	6
w	1	2	12	9
x	0	2	7	2
y	2	3	25	12
z	1	0	2	3
Total Errors	42	133	277	214

Continuous-Stroke Vertical Manuscript Supports Young Readers and Writers

FIGURE 1. A comparison of D'Nealian and Zaner-Bloser manuscript

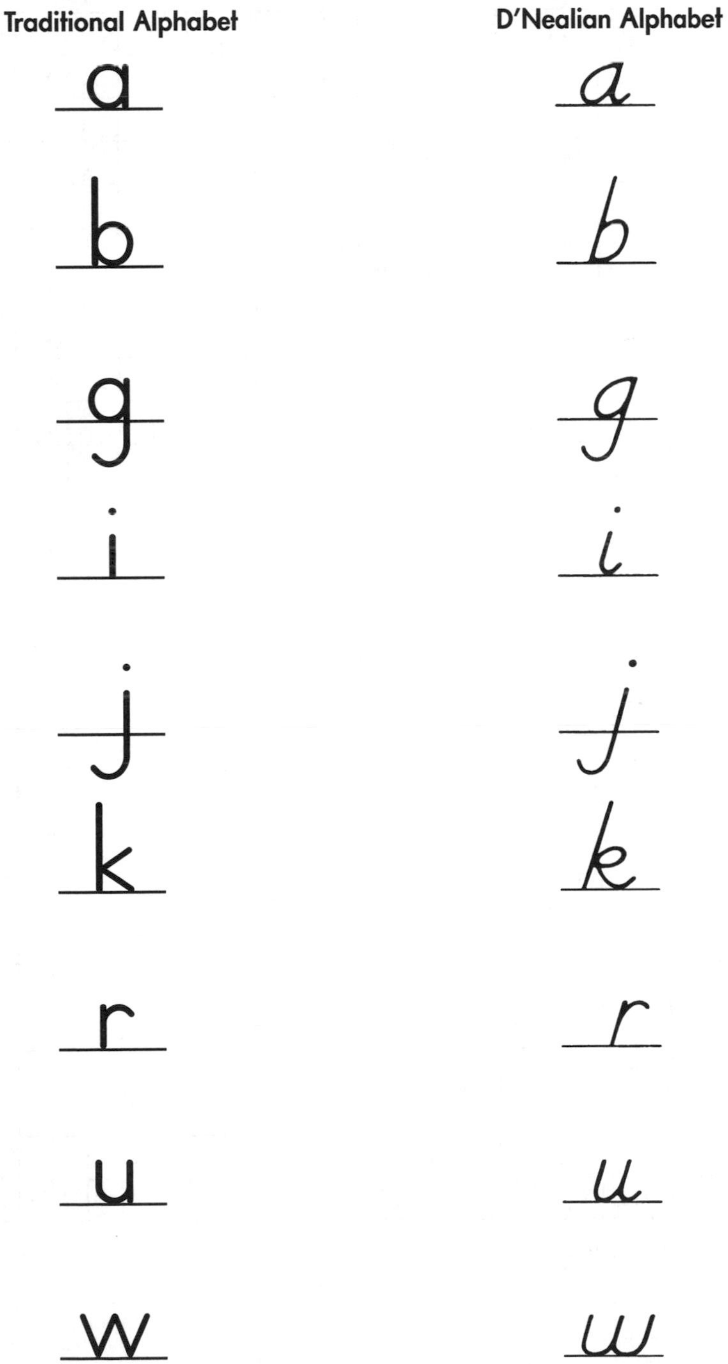

Traditional Alphabet	D'Nealian Alphabet
a	a
b	b
g	g
i	i
j	j
k	k
r	r
u	u
w	w

FIGURE 2. Error matrix for D'Nealian manuscript

	a	b	c	d	e	f	g	h	i	j	k	l	m	n	o	p	q	r	s	t	u	v	w	x	y	z
a		1		3										1			1									
b	2		6																							
c																										
d		7	1						1																	
e												1											1			
f																				1						
g				1												3									4	
h							2		1			1		3						1						
i										13	3															
j			1				3		19			22								1						
k			1																						1	
l			1						2		1					1										
m																				2		4		1		
n	1			1				8												2	1			1	1	
o																										
p	1	1		2								1					2			1						
q							2																	1		
r		2							1			9	1		1											
s																										
t				1	2									1												
u																						1			3	
v				1										1							3	1				
w					1												1					1				
x																										
y				1													2				1	1				1
z				1																					1	
*	1			2	3			1	2	2	1	1					2	3		2	4	2	3		2	1

*Student did not know

References

Adams, M.J. (1991). *Beginning to Read, Thinking and Learning about Print.* MIT Press, Cambridge, MA.

Barbe, W.B., Wasylyk, T.M., Hackney, C.S., and Braun, L.A. (1984). *Zaner-Bloser Creative Growth in Handwriting (Grades K–8).* Columbus, OH: Zaner-Bloser.

Bond, G.L. and Dykstra, R. (1967). The cooperative research program in early reading instruction. *Reading Research Quarterly, 2,* 5–142.

Chall, J.S. (1967). *Learning to Read: The Great Debate.* New York: McGraw-Hill.

Connell, D. (1983). Handwriting: Taking a look at alternatives. *Academic Therapy, 18,* 413–420.

Duvall, B. (1985). Evaluating the difficulty of four handwriting styles used for instruction. *ERS Spectrum, 3,* 13–18.

Firth, U. (1985). Beneath the surface of developmental dyslexia. In K.E. Patterson, J.C. Marshall, and M. Coltheart (Eds.) *Surface Dyslexia* (pp. 301–330. London: Erlbaum.

Juola, J.F., Schadler, M., Chabot, R.J., and McCaughey, S. (1977). The development of visual information processing skills related to reading. *Journal of Experimental Psychology, 25,* 459–476.

McConkie, G.W. and Zola, D. (1981). Language constraints and the functional stimulus in reading. In A.M. Lesgold and C.A. Perfetti (Eds.) *Interactive process in reading* (pp. 155–175). Hillsdale, NJ: Erbaum.

Scott, J.A. and Ehri, L.C. (1990). Sight word reading in prereaders: Use of logographic vs. alphabetic access routes. *Journal of Reading Behavior, 22,* 149–166.

Thurber, D.N. (1984). *D'Nealian Manuscript: A Continuous Stroke Approach to Handwriting.* Novato, CA: Academic Therapy Publications.

Are Slanted Manuscript Alphabets Superior to the Traditional Manuscript Alphabet?

Steve Graham

Childhood Education, Pages 91–95, Vol. 70 (1993),
©Association of Childhood Education International.

On "Back to School" night, a 1st-grade teacher was sharing with parents her plans for their children during the first half of the year. When one parent asked about handwriting, the teacher eagerly noted that they would be using the D'Nealian handwriting program (Thurber, 1993a).

The teacher went on to explain that the D'Nealian program did not use the traditional manuscript alphabet, which is characterized by round, upright letters that resemble type. Instead, they would use a modified script in which the manuscript letters are slanted and most of the "small" or lower-case letters resemble their cursive counterparts. She then showed the parents a chart containing the D'Nealian alphabet, emphasizing that the modified manuscript letters make the transition between manuscript and cursive writing easier and quicker for young children.

While most of the parents were unfamiliar with the D'Nealian alphabet or the concept of slanted manuscript letters, only a few voiced any comments. One parent noted that it seemed like a waste of time to learn a new script when her child could already write most of the traditional letters "quite well." Another parent, however, indicated that her older child had learned to write using D'Nealian, and that it was "simply marvelous." After hearing the first two comments, a third parent asked the teacher to "please tell us again why you think this new alphabet is better."

The teacher related many of the claims made by advocates for the newer, slanted manuscript style (Coon & Palmer, 1993; Thurber, 1993b). She reiterated that the new, slanted manuscript alphabet made the transition to cursive writing easier, saving a considerable amount of

> One parent noted that it seemed like a waste of time to learn a new script when her child could already write most of the traditional letters "quite well."

instructional time. She further indicated that the new, slanted alphabets, such as D'Nealian, used continuous strokes to form manuscript letters, resulting in better rhythm, greater speed, more writing and fewer letter reversals. She also stressed that this type of alphabet was better for children with learning disabilities and other handicaps.

As she repeated and expanded her rationale, the teacher did not refer to the research that addresses whether slanted manuscript alphabets are superior to the traditional ones. And none of the parents thought to request evidence to support the claims. This paper examines the merits of the claims made by this 1st-grade teacher and the other advocates of slanted manuscript alphabets.

Claim I: Slanted Manuscript Alphabets Make the Transition to Cursive Writing Easier

The basic claim made by developers and advocates of slanted manuscript letters is that such alphabets do a better job than traditional manuscript in facilitating the transition to cursive writing (McDougal, Littell, 1993; Thurber, 1993b). If this claim is valid, students who learn to print using a slanted manuscript alphabet should become better cursive writers than those who learn to print using traditional manuscript.

Farris (1982) examined this issue in a longitudinal study. At the beginning of the school year, she randomly assigned 86 kindergarten students to two treatment groups. From kindergarten to the first part of 2nd grade, one group was taught slanted manuscript using the D'Nealian program; the other group was taught traditional manuscript using the Zaner-Bloser program. During 2nd grade, each of the two groups made the transition to cursive writing using their respective handwriting programs.

Near the end of 2nd grade, a sample of the students' cursive writing was scored using 15 separate criteria (no information on the reliability of the scores was provided). Overall, students who had been taught traditional manuscript produced more legible cursive writing than students in the D'Nealian group. Students in the D'Nealian group were more likely to misshape cursive letters, extend strokes above and below the guidelines and vary the size of letters. Consequently, in this study the production of cursive writing was not enhanced by D'Nealian instruction.

Similarly, Trap-Porter, Cooper, Hill, Swisher and LaNunziata (1984) compared the cursive writing of 134 1st-grade students who had been taught traditional manuscript using Zaner-Bloser and 112 1st-grade students who had been taught slanted manuscript using D'Nealian. Each student copied the lower-case cursive letters from their respective programs. There were no differences between the two groups of students in the number of cursive letters omitted when copying or, more important, in the number of cursive strokes made correctly. Again, the production of cursive writing was not enhanced by the use of the D'Nealian method.

Finally, in a study by Ourada (1993), 45 3rd-grade students were divided into two groups on the basis of academic skills and behavior. None of the children had previously been taught cursive writing. One of the groups spent four weeks learning to write slanted manuscript letters using the D'Nealian alphabet, followed by eight weeks of cursive writing instruction using the same program. The other group followed the same schedule, but reviewed how to write traditional manuscript letters and learned cursive script using the Zaner-Bloser program.

A cursive writing sample collected at the end of the 12-week instructional period was scored for overall legibility as well as letter formation, slant and size (information on reliability of scores was not provided). Unfortunately, Ourada (1993) did not use statistical procedures to analyze the obtained scores. As a result, this author conducted a series of chi-square analyses to determine if the cursive writing of the two groups differed (see Graham, 1992). He found no differences between the two groups in slant (X=.94) or size of cursive letters (X^2=.38, df=1). While students in the D'Nealian group were more likely to produce papers with acceptable letter formation (X^2=4.2, df=1, $p < .05$), this proved to be a minor distinction. The overall legibility of the papers written by the two groups did not differ significantly (X^2=.91, df=1).

Analysis of the available research shows that whether slanted alphabets or more traditional manuscript letters were taught, the resulting quality of children's cursive writing was the same or exhibited only minor and unreliable distinctions. It is possible that slanted manuscript alphabets did not lead to superior cursive writing because they do not facilitate the transition to cursive to the extent claimed. Developers of the D'Nealian (Thurber, 1993a) and McDougal, Littell (1993) handwriting programs have argued that because their manuscript letters are slanted and closely resemble cursive letters, the transition to cursive writing is simple—mainly a matter of adding connecting strokes.

In an analysis of the D'Nealian and McDougal, Littell handwriting programs (Graham, 1992), the author found that almost half (46 percent) of the cursive letters in each program are substantially different from their manuscript counterparts. An additional 21 percent of the cursive letters in D'Nealian and 26 percent of those in the McDougal, Littell program involve small changes in letter formation, such as tightening a curve or shortening a line, in order to add a connecting stroke. While lower-case letters are more constant than upper-case letters, approximately 70 percent of all manuscript letters in either program require some modification for cursive writing beyond simply adding connecting strokes. Consequently, students have to learn not only all of the upper- and lower-case manuscript letters, but a modified or completely different form for most of the cursive letters. Learning cursive writing in these programs is not a simple transition.

It has also been argued that slanted manuscript alphabets facilitate the transition to cursive writing by saving instructional time. For example, Thurber (1983, 1993a) has claimed that D'Nealian cuts in half the time needed to teach cursive. The basis for claims of this nature, however, is unclear. Both the D'Nealian and the McDougal, Littell programs introduce cursive writing one-third of the way through 2nd grade. By the end of the year, all of the upper- and lower-case cursive letters are covered.

Using the more traditional alphabet, the Zaner-Bloser method provides two options for making the transition to cursive writing. One of the options mirrors the approach taken by D'Nealian and McDougal, Littell: students make the transition to cursive early in 2nd grade and cover all of the cursive letters by the end of the year. With this option, there is no difference in transition time between the two types of manuscript letters. With the second option, cursive writing is introduced in 3rd grade. Although students spend an extra year working on manuscript, the amount of time spent making the transition to cursive is again about one year.

In summary, the available evidence failed to substantiate the claim that the transition to cursive writing is enhanced by using a slanted manuscript alphabet. Programs using either slanted or more traditional manuscript letters produced no reliable differences in children's cursive writing.

> ...the available evidence failed to substantiate the claim that the transition to cursive writing is enhanced by using a slanted manuscript alphabet.

Claim 2: Slanted Manuscript Alphabets Use Continuous Strokes To Form Manuscript Letters—Resulting in Better Rhythm, Greater Speed, More Writing and Fewer Reversals Than Traditional Manuscript

Most manuscript letters can be formed by using either a single continuous stroke or two or more basic strokes (e.g., horizontal lines, vertical lines, slant lines, circles, parts of circles). The developers of the two slanted manuscript programs intentionally designed the majority of their manuscript letters so that they could be formed using a single stroke. They claim that this feature of their manuscript alphabet results in writing that is more rhythmical, faster and less directionally confusing.

It must be noted, however, that the continuous stroke method also can be used to form traditional manuscript letters. The Zaner-Bloser program, for example, provides two options for producing manuscript letters. One option involves using four basic strokes to form letters. With this option, the pencil is lifted from the paper when forming three out of every five manuscript letters (e.g., **T, t**). A second option involves using a single stroke to form manuscript letters. With this option, the pencil is lifted from the paper when forming less than half (44 percent) of the manuscript alphabet. In comparison, the pencil is lifted when forming 33 percent of the manuscript letters in the D'Nealian alphabet and 39 percent of the manuscript letters in the McDougal, Littell alphabet.

The differences between continuous stroke manuscript options are even smaller when just lower-case letters are considered. With the D'Nealian and McDougal, Littell programs, only six lower-case letters (**f, i, j, t,** and **x**) require a pencil lift. Only two additional letters (**k** and **y**) require a pencil lift with the Zaner-Bloser continuous stroke option. Neither of these letters is particularly common in English words (Zetterson, 1969).

Regardless of the similarities or differences between various handwriting programs, any claims regarding the advantages of a continuous stroke method, for either slanted or traditional manuscript letters, must be considered premature at this point. Beyond testimonials collected by publishers (cf. Coon & Palmer, 1993), no evidence exists that children write more rhythmically, faster or more as a consequence of learning a manuscript alphabet based on continuous stroke letter formation. These claims have simply not been investigated by researchers.

The only issues that have been addressed by researchers involve the effect of continuous stroke letter formation on frequency of reversals and quality of manuscript writing. In a Master's Thesis (Oglesby, 1982) cited by Thurber (1993b), 12 underachieving 2nd-graders were randomly divided into two groups that received nine weeks of manuscript instruction using either the D'Nealian or Zaner-Bloser method. Students assigned to the Zaner-Bloser group used the traditional manuscript alphabet without the continuous stroke option. Every three weeks, the quality of students' manuscript writing (e.g., legibility, letter formation, spacing) was assessed by four teachers (no information on reliability of scores was provided).

Although the overall results of the investigation favored the D'Nealian group, scores on specific handwriting measures were extremely erratic across the three testing sessions (unexplainably going up and

Continuous-Stroke Vertical Manuscript Supports Young Readers and Writers down or vice versa). Therefore, the reliability of the teachers' evaluations, and ultimately the validity of the study, must be questioned.

In the only other study located, Farris (1982) examined the manuscript handwriting performance of 1st-grade students who had used either the D'Nealian or Zaner-Bloser method since kindergarten. Again, students in the Zaner-Bloser group used the traditional manuscript alphabet without the continuous stroke option. Manuscript handwriting samples collected at two points during the year were scored using 15 separate criteria (e.g., letter formation, spacing, slant). No information on the reliability of the scores was provided. Farris found no significant differences between the two groups of students on any of the criteria, including the number of letters reversed.

Farris (1982) may have failed to find an advantage for the D'Nealian manuscript alphabet because slanted and continuous stroke letters may require a greater degree of fine-motor control than the letters in the Zaner-Bloser alphabet without the continuous stroke option. This issue was addressed by Duvall (1985), who assessed the difficulty of the lowercase manuscript letters in these two programs. She found that the letters in the D'Nealian alphabet involve more motions that occur later in children's development, require more retracing of lines and force the hand to change direction more often. In contrast, when using the Zaner-Bloser alphabet without the continuous stroke option the writer has to pay more attention to visual information, such as where strokes begin and meet.

> ...the letters in the D'Nealian alphabet involve more motions that occur later in children's development.

Last, supporters of slanted manuscript alphabets have argued that their continuous stroke letters are especially helpful for students with special needs, reducing frustration and increasing writing fluency (Coon & Palmer, 1993; Jordan, no date; Thurber, 1993b). The author found no scientific evidence, however, to support these claims. As Brown (1993) noted, "No research has been found that would support the use of one system in handwriting over the other in remedial and special education" (p. 68).

Conclusion

A slanted manuscript may not be the best choice for young children for several reasons. First, there is no credible evidence that these alphabets make a difference in children's handwriting. Making the transition to cursive writing does not appear to be enhanced by using a special alphabet like D'Nealian. Similarly, claims that slanted manuscript alphabets are superior because most of their letters are formed with a single, continuous stroke have not been validated.

Second, the use of slanted manuscript alphabets creates several practical problems for teachers. They have to respond to questions from parents who are worried because the new letters do not look "like print" (these alphabets are unusual enough that even the publishers use traditional manuscript in student workbooks). Teachers also have to learn how to write the new letters themselves in order to appropriately model their formation during instruction.

More important, many young children already know how to write to some degree before starting kindergarten or 1st grade. The letters that they learn how to write prior to starting school are, usually, the traditional manuscript. Learning a special alphabet like D'Nealian means that many children would have to relearn letters they can already write. As a result, a "hidden" transition takes place for children who are taught a slanted manuscript alphabet during kindergarten or 1st grade. This transition is also required of children who have been taught traditional print, then transfer to a school using a program such as D'Nealian. Given the lack of supportive evidence and the practical problems involved in implementation, slanted manuscript letters cannot be recommended as a replacement of the traditional manuscript alphabet.

References

Askov, E., & Peck, M. (1982). In H. Mitzel (Ed.), *Encyclopedia of educational research* (pp. 764–766). New York: Free Press.

Brown, V. (1993). D'Nealian handwriting: What it is and how to teach it. In G. Coon & G. Palmer (Eds.), *Handwriting research and information: An administrator's handbook* (pp. 62–71). Glenview, IL: Scott, Foresman.

Coon, G., & Palmer, G. (Eds.). (1993). *Handwriting research and information: An administrator's handbook.* Glenview, IL: Scott, Foresman.

Duvall, B. (1985). Evaluating the difficulty of four handwriting styles used for instruction. *ERS Spectrum, 3,* 13–20.

Farris, P. (1982). *A comparison of handwriting strategies for primary grade students.* Arlington, VA: ERIC Document Reproduction Service (CS 209 360).

Graham, S. (1992). Issues in handwriting instruction. *Focus on Exceptional Children, 25,* 1–4.

Jordan, D. (no date). Research: *Handwriting issues and special needs.* Glenview, IL: Scott, Foresman.

McDougal, Littell (1993). *Handwriting connections.* Evanston, IL: Author.

Oglesby, B. (1982). *A comparative study of the difference in the manuscript handwriting performance of six below-average second-grade students who experienced the De'Nealian method of handwriting instruction for a nine-week period when compared to six below-average second-grade students who experienced the Zaner-Bloser method of handwriting instruction for a nine-week period, as measured by four judges' scores on a teacher-made checklist.* Unpublished master's thesis, University of North Florida, Jacksonville.

Ourada, E. (1993). Legibility of third-grade handwriting: D'Nealian handwriting versus traditional Zaner-Bloser. In G. Coon & G. Palmer (Eds.), *Handwriting research and information: An Administrator's handbook* (pp. 72–87k). Glenview, IL: Scott, Foresman.

Thurber, D. (1983). *D'Nealian manuscript—An aid to reading development.* Arlington, VA: ERIC Document Reproduction Service (CS 007 057).

Thurber, D. (1993a). D'Nealian handwriting. Glenview, IL: Scott, Foresman.

Thurber, D. (1993b). How D'Nealian handwriting meets the needs of all writers. In G. Coon & G. Palmer (Eds.), *Handwriting research and information: An administrator's handbook* (pp. 50–61). Glenview, IL: Scott, Foresman.

Trap-Porter, J., Cooper, J., Hill, D., Swisher, K., & LaNunziata, L. (1984). D'Nealian and Zaner-Bloser manuscript alphabets and initial transition to cursive handwriting *Journal of Educational Research, 77,* 343–345.

Zettersten, A. (1969). *A statistical study of the graphic system of present-day American English.* Lund, Sweden: Studentlitteratur.

D'Nealian and Zaner-Bloser Manuscript Alphabets and Initial Transition to Cursive Handwriting

Jennifer Trap-Porter, John O. Cooper,
David S. Hill, and Karen Swisher: The Ohio State University
Louis J. LaNunziata: University of North Carolina, Wilmington

Journal of Educational Research, Pages 343–345, Vol. 77,
No. 6 (July/Aug, 1984), ©Taylor & Francis Informa UK LTD - Journals.

Traditionally, manuscript handwriting instruction has preceded instruction in cursive handwriting. Proponents of this approach suggest that the manuscript letter strokes are easier to perform than cursive strokes for kindergarten and first-grade students. The similarity between the manuscript letters and reading materials is considered an advantage for beginning readers and writers (Huitt, 1972).

The practice of progressing from manuscript to cursive strokes is not without opposition. Early (1976) found that exclusive use of cursive writing did not impair initial progress in reading or spelling. His results suggested that instruction in two alphabets was unwarranted. Lehaman (1980) argued that manuscript strokes are not easier to initiate than cursive forms. Further, he contended that the use of manuscript writing may lead to frustration if students are given the impression that they should stop manuscript writing and learn "real" handwriting.

Recently, a new manuscript alphabet, the D'Nealian Manuscript (Scott, Foresman & Company, 1978), was developed. D'Nealian manuscript letters are written with a slant and show more resemblance to the cursive letters than do traditional manuscript alphabets. Most D'Nealian manuscript letters are formed with one continuous stroke.

Though materials used for sales promotion of the D'Nealian manuscript alphabet state that the program will facilitate transition between manuscript and cursive writing (Scott, Foresman & Company, 1982, p. 1), data are not available to support this claim. The purpose of this study was to test the effect of training under two manuscript alphabets, D'Nealian and Zaner-Bloser, on first graders' initial attempts at producing cursive letters.

Method

Eleven classes of first graders attending six schools in central Ohio served as subjects. Classes were selected using the following criteria:

1. an expressed interest, and cooperation, of both principals and teachers;

2. formal handwriting instruction only in manuscript letters had been given to students; and

3. previous training in writing the D'Nealian Manuscript Alphabet or the Zaner-Bloser Manuscript Alphabet (1976) had occurred.

One group of subjects came from five classrooms in which students were taught manuscript handwriting using the D'Nealian Alphabet. Class size ranged from 15 to 31 students. Of the total 112 students in these classes, 60 were girls and 52 were boys. The other group of subjects consisted of students who were taught manuscript handwriting using the Zaner-Bloser Alphabet. Class size ranged from 18 to 33 students. Of the 134 students, 69 were boys and 65 were girls.

Setting

Students worked at their desks or tables in their classrooms. The work surface was clear except for the students' writing materials.

Materials

Subjects used one training sheet of the 26 lowercase cursive letters developed from the Zaner-Bloser Creative Growth Transitional Cursive Alphabet (1976). The letters, constructed with a line weight of one millimeter, were printed on paper with sets of parallel lines. The spaces between the headline and midline, midline and baseline, and descender space below the baseline were seven-sixteenths of an inch (1.11 centimeters). Since there were no major differences between the Zaner-Bloser and the D'Nealian cursive alphabets, the same model letter sheet was used with all subjects.

Copy Paper

Writing paper Number Two published by the Zaner-Bloser Handwriting Company was used. Spacing between the lines was seven-sixteenths of an inch (1.11 centimeters). The paper measured 8½ inches (21.59 centimeters) by 11 inches (27.94 centimeters) and contained red and green parallel lines.

Evaluative Overlay

Trap-Porter, Gladden, Hill, and Cooper (1983) designed a set of overlays to measure one-millimeter deviations of student letter samples from model letters. Using the overlays, individual letter strokes are evaluated based on slant, length, containment within boundaries on the overlay, contact with other strokes, and closed circular strokes. (See Trap et al. [1983] for a complete description of the evaluation criteria and scoring procedure.)

Procedures

The experimenter began the session with verbal interaction designed to help students feel at ease. Students were then given one sheet of model letters, one sheet of copy paper, and one standard number two pencil. Students were told to write their names on the paper and then put their pencils down. When all students had finished writing their names, the experimenter asked the students if they had ever seen letters like those on the model letter sheet. The experimenter briefly discussed manuscript and cursive forms of writing.

Specifically, the experimenter pointed out that each cursive letter is written without stopping or lifting the pencil except to dot the **i** or **j** or to cross the **x** and **t**. The experimenter also stressed that the cursive letters are slanted and that the copy paper should be slanted when writing cursive letters. The experimenter pointed out that all letters sit on the red line (baseline) and that most strokes begin and end on either the red line or the blue line above the red line. The experimenter then drew lines on the chalkboard. Students were asked to figure out how to write each letter. The experimenter explained the numbers and arrows on the model letter sheet and demonstrated how to write the letter **a**. After any student questions were answered, the experimenter told the students to copy the letters from the model letter sheet on their copy paper. Students were told to try to make each letter look just like it did on the model letter sheet: the same size and shape. Students were then told to pick up their pencil and begin.

Student behavior such as listening, working, putting pencils down, and watching were praised. At no time did any student receive any feedback on the quality or correctness of his or her writing sample. When students had finished copying the letters, the copy papers, model letter sheets, and pencils were collected. Students were thanked for working, and the experimenter left the room. The total session lasted between 20 and 30 minutes for each classroom.

Interscorer agreement

Two scorers were trained to assess the writing samples for letter strokes meeting criteria by using the evaluative overlays and procedures developed by Trap et al. (1983). The scorers practiced until a minimum of 85% agreement was met, then scoring of the samples began. The first scorer evaluated all 246 samples. Using a table of random numbers, 74 samples were selected for blind interobserver agreement checks. The second scorer was not involved in the study beyond the independent checking of samples. The second scorer did not know the purpose of the study or the difference in the groups. Percentage of agreement was calculated for each sample by dividing the number of agreements between observers by the number of agreements plus disagreements, and multiplying by 100.

The percentage of agreement on total strokes ranged from 81 to 100 with a mean of 93.3%. The percentage of agreement on the 39 Zaner-Bloser-trained students' samples ranged from 86 to 100% with a mean of 94.2%. The percentage of agreement on the 35 D'Nealian-trained students' samples ranged from 81 to 98% with a mean of 92.3%.

Results

The number of correct strokes made by each student was analyzed. For the group receiving training with Zaner-Bloser materials, the average percentage of correct cursive strokes was 73.49% for males and 72.86% for females. The male and female students in the D'Nealian group averaged 72.81% and 72.40% correct cursive strokes, respectively.

The data were analyzed to determine whether there were significant differences between groups in the number of letters omitted during the copying task. Fifty students (37.3%) in the Zaner-Bloser group omitted letters. The difference was not significant ($x^2 = 0.37$; $df = 1$; $p = 7.05$).

An analysis of variance was performed to determine the type of instruction (Zaner-Bloser and D'Nealian) and sex differences in number of correct cursive strokes made. The results of the ANOVA are reported in Table 1. The results indicated no significant type of instruction ($F = 0.78$; $df = 1,242$; $p = 7.05$) or gender difference ($F = 0.78$; $df = 1,242$; $p = 7.05$). The type by sex interaction was not significant ($F = 0.03$; $df = 1,242$; $p = 7.05$).

TABLE 1. ANOVA Summary

Source	SS	df	ms	F	p
Type of instruction	19.59	1	19.59	0.90	7.05
Sex	16.68	1	16.68	0.78	7.05
Type × sex	0.70	1	0.70	0.03	7.05
Error	5255.02	242	21.72		

Discussion

The results of this study suggest that first graders' production of cursive letters was not enhanced by instruction employing D'Nealian manuscript instructional materials. There was no difference in the number of cursive letter strokes at criteria by students who had received either Zaner-Bloser or D'Nealian instruction in manuscript letter writing.

Several factors should be considered in interpreting these results. First, the actual instruction by the first-grade teachers using the two sets of materials was not controlled. The equality of performance between the two groups may have been due to the teacher's varying from prescribed use of the materials. Second, students receiving D'Nealian instruction use writing paper with normal space-size. This study required the students to copy cursive letters on wide spaced transition writing paper. Space-size of writing paper may have affected the performance of the D'Nealian group. Third, the publishers of the D'Nealian materials suggest that students who receive D'Nealian instruction may learn cursive strokes more quickly when cursive writing instruction is given in later grades. This study did not address that possibility. Future research should consider instruction, space-size of writing paper, and the effect of instruction in early grades on the ease of acquisition of cursive strokes for older students in investigating the utility of the D'Nealian manuscript writing instructional materials.

> The results of this study suggest that first graders' production of cursive letters was not enhanced by instruction employing D'Nealian manuscript instructional materials.

References

Early, G. H. Handwriting, reading, and cursive spelling achievement. *Academic Therapy*, 1976, *12*, 67-74.

Huitt, R. Handwriting: the state of the craft. *Childhood Education*, 1972, *48*, 219-223.

Lehaman, C. Teaching and learning the craft of handwriting. *The Education Digest*, 1980, *45*, 50.

Scott, Foresman & Company. *Research and information: Handwriting research and D'Nealian handwriting methods—an update.* Chicago: Author, 1982.

Scott, Foresman & Company. *Teaching handwriting: A conversation with Donald N. Thurber.* Chicago: Author, not dated.

Scott, Foresman & Company. *D'Nealian manuscript alphabet.* Chicago: Author, 1978.

Trap-Porter, J., Gladden M. A., Hill, D. S., & Cooper, J. O. Space-size and accuracy of second- and third-grade students' cursive handwriting. *Journal of Educational Research*, 1983, *76*, 231-234.

Zaner-Bloser Company. *Creative growth manuscript alphabet.* Columbus, OH: Author, 1976. (a)

Zaner-Bloser Company. *Creative growth traditional cursive alphabet.* Columbus, OH: Author, 1976. (b)

"That's printing and this is cursive writing. In cursive all the letters hold hands."

Chapter 5

Good Handwriting: A Foundation for Proficient Writers

"Mommy! Billy's writing with the mustard!"

Reprinted with special permission of King Features Syndicate.

Introduction

Imagine a cartoon image of a writer hard at work. What do you see depicted in the thought bubble over the writer's head? Likely, you imagine the writer's thoughts to be full of interesting characters and plots or perhaps subtle ideas and connections. Whatever you imagine to be occupying the writer's mind, it probably has nothing to do with spelling, grammar, punctuation, keyboarding, or handwriting. Why should this be? After all, these skills are necessary for writing. Without them, the writer can communicate nothing.

We don't imagine a writer's thoughts to be concerned with spelling or handwriting because we understand that, for skilled writers, these tasks have become automatic. Once we learn to ride a bike, we rarely have to think about how to push the pedals. Similarly, proficient writers are free to concentrate on the content of their work as their pens fly across the page or their fingers glide over the keyboard, seemingly independent of conscious thought.

How do we give young writers this gift of automaticity, this mastery of underlying skills that will let their ideas flow? Automaticity has been defined as the ability to recall information from memory with speed, accuracy, and ease. In the area of handwriting, it is especially important and advantageous for students to develop automaticity at a young age. That's because handwriting, the act of transcribing thoughts into letters and words, is one of the most fundamental components of writing. The sooner young writers master handwriting, the sooner they can focus on using writing to help them learn, communicate, and succeed at school.

Automatic handwriting helps students write more quickly. Automatic handwriting is quick and competent. Students whose handwriting is slow and labored may not be able to write quickly enough to keep up with their thoughts as they compose. Good ideas may slip from memory before they can be recorded on paper. Those without automatic writing may also have trouble taking notes that keep pace with a teacher's instruction.

Automatic handwriting helps students write longer compositions. Students with automatic handwriting can write easily and fluently for a longer time, producing more text. Several recent studies have demonstrated that handwriting skill accounts for a large percentage of the variance of compositional fluency for primary-grade writers.

Automatic handwriting helps students write higher-scoring compositions. Automatic handwriting provides a significant advantage to young writers as they compose essays and stories. It lightens cognitive load and frees mental capacity to focus on higher-order compositional skills such as planning and revising. Students with automatic handwriting skills are able to generate more organized and sophisticated writing that earns high scores from teachers and test evaluators.

Automatic handwriting helps students think of themselves as good writers. Students who lack the instruction and practice needed to develop automatic handwriting can acquire a negative attitude toward writing. They may perceive writing as mentally and physically difficult, avoiding it whenever possible. By contrast, students who learn automatic handwriting at a young age win early praise for their written work and come to think of themselves as good writers.

Because automatic handwriting is so important for young writers, it is important to realize that handwriting skills must be taught. They can't be "caught" through other areas of the curriculum. Handwriting automaticity is achieved most reliably through direct, consistent instruction and practice. Recent studies provide the good news that such instruction seems to benefit all students, even older students and those who have had difficulty with writing.

The articles in this chapter explain in more detail the critical role handwriting plays in students' ability to compose high-quality written work. First, researchers Carol Christensen and Dian Jones discuss studies that link handwriting and written expression skills. Next, Steve Graham, Karen Harris, and Barbara Fink argue that handwriting is causally related to learning to write. Mark Torrance and David Galbraith explore the countless mental processes involved in the act of composing. Finally, Carol Christensen summarizes a wealth of recent research about handwriting and writing.

ZANER-BLOSER CURSIVE

Handwriting: An Underestimated Skill in the Development of Written Language

Carol A. Christensen and Dian Jones

Handwriting Today, Pages 56–69, Vol. 2 (2000), ©The National Handwriting Association.

Recent models of the composing process have generally focused on the complex array of cognitive and metacognitive processes involved in production of written language. Such processes involve lexical knowledge and retrieval, semantic coding, phonological coding, and syntactic structures (Bain, 1991; Berninger, 1994; Levine, 1987). As written expression tasks increase in length and complexity, higher order processes become more critical in producing text (Hooper, Montgomery, Swartz, Reed, Brown, Levine, & Wasileski, 1993). These skills facilitate the logical expression of ideas required for sophisticated sequential ideation and persuasive argumentation. Skills required to produce complex text include planning, organizing, self-monitoring, and revising (Hayes & Flower, 1980; Hooper et al., 1993; Levine, 1987, 1992). Self-monitoring, revising, and editing skills are necessary for students to detect errors to monitor written text for semantic and syntactic content and coherence, and to revise and edit appropriately (Beal, 1993; Butterfield, Douglas, & Plumb, 1994). Students also need to evaluate information and to analyze issues in order to selectively organize and plan their written expression (Bellanca & Fogarty, 1991; Gleason, 1995; Graham, MacArthur, Schwartz, & Page-Voth, 1992; Harris & Pressley, 1991). At the same time writers need to identify the audience and purpose of writing, generate information relating to the topic, and engage in sequential ideation relating to a topic.

> Cognitive theory can provide a theoretical basis for suggesting a relationship between facility in handwriting and competent written language skills.

Given the complexity of the cognitive processes involved in composing text, handwriting is often seen as a low-level and relatively unimportant skill. As such, teaching handwriting is portrayed as an antiquated and misguided instructional activity and a focus on handwriting seen as antithetical to development of the sophisticated written language skills.

However, in addition to promoting a focus of sophisticated thought, cognitive theory can provide a theoretical basis for suggesting a relationship between facility in handwriting and competent written language skills. Because of attentional limitations, individuals can perform only one conscious cognitive activity at a time. In order to perform complex cognitive tasks (such as producing written text) subcomponents of the task must be executed automatically. Automaticity is the performance of tasks effortlessly and accurately without consuming attentional resources. Thus, in order to produce creative, well structured and thoughtful written text, the writers must be able to translate their thoughts and ideas into written form automatically. This suggests that, rather than being antithetical to sophisticated written language skills, handwriting is an essential prerequisite.

While relatively few researchers have examined the relationship between handwriting and written language, those who have provide clear evidence that fluency in handwriting is strongly related to the ability to produce complex written text. For example, Graham, Berninger, Abbott, Abbott, and Whitaker (1997) found that handwriting accounted for 66 percent of the variance in compositional fluency at primary level, 41 percent of the variance in intermediate grades. For quality of written product, they found that handwriting accounted for 25 percent of the variance in primary grades and 42 percent of the variance in intermediate grades. Similarly, Graham, Berninger, Abbott, Abbott, and Whitaker (in press) found that handwriting was significantly related to compositional fluency and quality for both primary and intermediate elementary students, suggesting that the impact of handwriting extended beyond primary into intermediate grades.

Berninger, Yates, Cartwright, Rutberg, Remy, and Abbott (1992) administered a battery of predictor measures, including measures of neuromoter development, orthographic knowledge, visual-motor integration, syllable and phoneme segmentation, word finding, sentence syntax, reading, and verbal intelligence to 300 students in first, second, and third grades. They examined the influence of these measures on handwriting, spelling, and composition. They found that rapid, automatic production of alphabet letters, rapid coding of orthographic information, and speed of sequential finger movement were the best predictors of composition. Thus, they argued that low-level developmental skills, as well as component skills such as handwriting and spelling, may provide a critical foundation in the early stages of writing which influences the degree to which a child may subsequently develop higher-level composition skills.

De La Paz and Graham (1995) investigated the impact of removal of competing attentional demands required by the mechanics of writing through the use of dictation. They found that dictation improved writing quality for children at the primary level. However, dictation did not assist older elementary-aged students.

Thus, there is a coherent theoretical justification as well as empirical support for arguing that the ability to write letters automatically is an essential component of children's ability to express their thoughts and ideas in written form. Traditionally, the objective of instruction in handwriting was to ensure that children produced copybook quality letters and words. The focus was on neatness and rigid adherence to specific letter formations. Thus, handwriting was often seen as a routine and repetitive motor task. However, the skills required to produce written text go beyond simple motor functions. Writing requires that orthographic knowledge and motor processes are syncronised to produce letters, words and sentences. Thus, the term orthographic-motor integration is often used to portray the complex nature of the task (Berninger, 1994).

> The ability to write letters automatically is an essential component of children's ability to express their thoughts and ideas in written form.

Over the last few years, we have conducted a series of studies that has examined the relationship between orthographic-motor integration and children's written language skills. First we documented the magnitude of the relationship through a series of correlational studies. We measured orthographic-motor integration by asking students to write as many letters of the alphabet in order as they could. They were given one minute to do this. The measure was scored by counting the number of letters children wrote in correct alphabetical order excluding omissions, reversals, transpositions, and substitutions. A similar measure was used by Berninger, Mizokawa, and Bragg (1991) working with individual children. We adapted the measure so that it could be used with large groups of children. This quick and simple measure accounted for a proportion of the variance in children's written language scores that surprised us.

We measured written language by asking children to write an independently generated piece of text in 15 minutes. Topics included "Watching TV," "Holidays," "My Three Wishes," and "My Role Model." Written language samples were scored on: coherent ideas and sequencing of text in relation to topic (5 marks), accurate or understandable spelling and grammar (5 marks), syntax skills related to sentence structure (5 marks), and fluency (5 marks).

Orthographic-motor integration and written language skills were assessed on over 900 students in Grades 1, 3, 5, and 8. The number of children tested in each grade together with mean scores and correlations for each measure are given in Table 1.

TABLE 1

Number of Students, Means, Standard Deviations and Correlations for Orthographic-Motor Integration and Written Language.

Grade	Number of Students		Orthographic-Motor Integration	Written Language	Correlation
1	455	Mean	17.13	9.06	.786
		SD	(6.39)	(3.24)	
2	114	Mean	23.18	13.27	.818
		SD	(6.16)	(2.34)	
3	115	Mean	30.82	12.83	.742
		SD	(10.04)	(2.46)	
5	104	Mean	50.59	12.37	.695
		SD	(14.19)	(2.24)	
8	256	Mean	58.82	12.77	.649
		SD	(13.85)	(2.83)	

The data suggested to us that orthographic-motor integration had a powerful influence on the quality and quantity of students' written language. In grade 1, orthographic-motor integration accounted for 62 percent of the variance in written language scores. The highest correlation was in grade 2 where orthographic-motor integration accounted for 67 percent of the variance. Unfortunately, the impact of orthographic-motor integration on writing skills seems to be maintained at very high levels through to grade 8 where the amount of variance accounted for is 40 percent. Thus, it appeared that as predicted by cognitive theory the inability to write letters seriously limits students' ability to develop written language skills.

While the correlations between orthographic-motor integration and written language were consistently high across all the grade levels we tested, correlation does not necessarily demonstrate causation. In an effort to demonstrate that orthographic-motor integration had a causal impact on written language, we conducted a series of experimental studies which aimed to measure the impact of instruction in orthographic-motor integration on students' ability to produce written text.

> **As predicted by cognitive theory the inability to write letters seriously limits students' ability to develop written language skills.**

The first of these studies worked with 38 students in grade 2. Nineteen students in six classrooms were identified as having orthographic-motor integration difficulties related to handwriting. Nineteen children who attended the same classrooms were selected so that they were matched on gender, age, and reading scores. The matched group showed no evidence of handwriting problems and formed the control group.

Initially students were given the same tests as used in our previous studies. These included the one minute orthographic-motor integration test and the written language measure. They were also given the Southgate Group Reading Test (Southgate, 1962). Students who had difficulties related to orthographic-motor integration and whose reading matched peers were provided with an intervention program.

The intervention was conducted in regular class time, in small groups, or individually. Activities were planned by the class teacher in consultation with the researcher and administered by teacher aides or parent volunteers.

The control group received regular assistance to develop writing skills as would normally occur in a Year 1 classroom. However, teachers indicated that they believed that all the students in participating classes actually received more specific instruction in handwriting than would normally occur, as the teachers became more aware of the processes necessary to develop writing skills. The intervention occurred within regularly scheduled handwriting lessons over an eight week period. Each student spent approximately 10 minutes per day in intervention activities.

Students who had difficulties in orthographic-motor integration were given an intervention to enhance their orthographic-motor integration skills. The intervention was based on individual assessment of the processes each child used to form upper and lower case letters. This assessment enabled specific student profiles to be developed as the basis of remediation of orthographic codes. The intervention consisted of direct teaching of efficient letter formations, and activities for promoting speed and accuracy of writing letters. Conventional formation of lower case letters was taught through teacher modeling which was followed by guided and independent practice. Initially students were given individual assistance to correct specific errors in letter formation. When they consistently used correct formations, children moved to small group instruction to practice each letter until they became proficient. A number of activities were used to encourage appropriate letter formations. For example, green dots were used to indicate the start of a letter and red dots to "stop" (as in traffic lights) were used to mark the conclusion of letters. After conventional formations were acquired, practice was provided using a number of activities. For example, children wrote "rainbow" letters. They chose three colors for each letter then wrote in each color over letter tracks. Visual association strategies were also used to facilitate memory for letter formations, for example, "w" is like a worm. Children were also given activities without the use of pencil and paper. For example, children were asked to "draw in the air the way that 's' goes," "jump around 'g' on the floor."

Other activities include completing the missing letters in an alphabet sequence where a few letters are missing initially. The number of missing letters was increased until most letters were missing. Completing dot to dot pictures was also used to guide the correct formation sequence.

Green dots were used to indicate the start of a letter.

Finally, students were given a personal graph to record the number of letters which could be written in alphabetical order within one minute. Individual scores were recorded daily with individual improvement set as the goal. Children seemed to enjoy this activity as they were able to record personal improvements and relate practice to achievement.

The means and standard deviations for students participating in the intervention and the reading match control group are given in Table 2.

TABLE 2
Means and Standard Deviations on Pretest and Posttest Measures for Grade One Students Participating in Handwriting Intervention and Reading-Matched Control Group.

Measure		Control		Experimental	
		Pretest	Posttest	Pretest	Posttest
Handwriting	Mean*	16.7	20.1	10.1	20.2
	SD	(2.4)	(2.9)	(2.4)	(6.4)
Written Language	Mean	11.2	12.3	7.4	12.5
	SD	(1.8)	(1.5)	(2.4)	(1.9)
Southgate	Mean	19.8	25.5	19.8	25.3
	SD	(4.2)	(3.1)	(4.2)	(2.6)

*n=19

Statistical analysis indicated that there was a significant effect for the pretest. Pretest handwriting significantly impacted on story writing scores. The pretest handwriting scores accounted for approximately 34 percent of the total variance. There was a significant group by time interaction (see Figure 1). This indicated that children in the control group were significantly better at handwriting and written language before the intervention. However, the difference disappeared when children with orthographic-motor integration difficulties were provided with a systematic program which provided practice in writing letters and words.

The differences were quite substantial. Before the intervention the mean for handwriting for the control group was 16.7 compared with the experimental group of 10.1. Similarly, there was a substantial difference in written language scores for the two groups before the intervention (11.2 compared with 7.4). In other words, the children with handwriting difficulties were 60 percent behind in orthographic-motor integration before the intervention and 66 percent behind in written language. Following the intervention the differences had disappeared. The mean for the control group in orthographic-motor integration was 20.1 and the experimental, 20.2. In written language the means were 12.3 and 12.5 respectively.

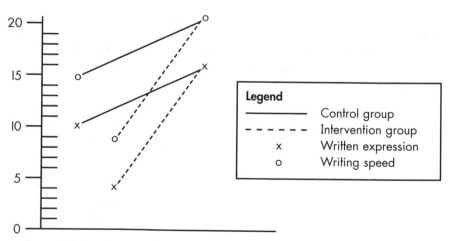

Figure I: Interaction effect on written expression scores for grade one intervention and control groups

Although the intervention was limited to practice in handwriting and did not involve any activity that directly related to written language skills, differences between the two groups in written language also disappeared. As expected, the effect of practice in handwriting was limited to written language. It did not impact on children's reading skills which remained comparable between the two groups at both pre- and posttest.

This provided convincing evidence that difficulties in orthographic-motor integration related to handwriting are causally related to competence in written language. It also indicated that a systematic program designed to ensure that children can write letters and words smoothly and efficiently can lead to significant improvement in their written language skills. However, the intervention provided a specialized program to a small number of children. The utility of instruction in handwriting in a broader context with regular classroom teachers had yet to be established.

Impact of Teacher Education

In a third set of studies, we worked with teachers rather than children to examine the impact of teaching handwriting skills at a systemic rather than clinical level. Twenty-nine Grade 1 teachers participated in two in-service training programs. Fourteen teachers participated in a traditional program covering methods to enhance children's written language. Fifteen participated in a program that encouraged them to ensure that the children in their classes practiced handwriting each day. The activities that we had used in our earlier intervention were shared with the teachers. Each program lasted for only one hour.

Before the in-service education programs were delivered, children in all classes were tested on orthographic-motor integration and written language using the same measures we had previously used. To check that differences were not due to more capable children or teachers being assigned to one of the groups, we also used a word identification measure to test reading skill. There were no statistical differences between the two groups of children before delivery of the in-service programs. We assessed children again at the end of the school year to measure the impact of encouraging teachers to provide instruction in handwriting. Students were assigned to a number of different classes in the following year. At the end of the second year, we assessed children for a third time. Table 3 provides a summary of the means and standard deviations at each assessment point.

TABLE 3

Pretest, Posttest, and Delayed Posttest Means and Standard Deviations for Experimental and Control Groups

Measures		Pretest		Posttest		Delayed Posttest	
		Ctl.	Exp.	Ctl.	Exp.	Ctl.	Exp.
Handwriting	Mean	7.06	7.31	13.87	19.85	23.84	33.43
	SD	(2.47)	(1.97)	(1.17)	(3.11)	(6.71)	(6.43)
Written Language	Mean	2.76	3.03	9.57	10.24	10.25	13.02
	SD	(0.69)	(0.66)	(1.49)	(1.34)	(1.95)	(1.7)
Word Identification	Mean	6.91	7.39	9.57	10.05	11.64	11.71
	SD	(1.59)	(1.58)	(.76)	(0.82)	(.84)	(.72)

There were no differences between children in the control or experimental groups before the in-service education programs. However, at the end of the year, children in the classes where teachers had had in-service which encouraged them to teach handwriting had significantly better orthographic-motor integration skills and higher quality written language. The differences were quite substantial. The means for both handwriting and written language for children in the experimental group was above the cut-off for the top one percent of children in the control group.

Perhaps even more remarkable was the enduring nature of the differences. In the second year after the intervention, the children in the experimental group continued to out-strip the control group. The mean scores in both handwriting and written language were better than the top 10 percent of children in the control group. Given that the intervention consisted of only one hour of in-service education, the magnitude of effects is quite substantial.

While ensuring that children have smooth and efficient handwriting promotes their ability to express their ideas in written form, it does not impact on their reading. Measures of reading were the same for the two groups throughout the study. This indicates that the differences that were detected were not due to children's general literacy skills or teachers' ability to teach literacy. It also indicated that smooth and efficient handwriting has a direct and specific influence on children's ability to express their ideas in text.

While the nature of the relationship between handwriting and written language is impressive, we do not wish to suggest that teaching handwriting is the universal panacea for all children's problems in writing text. Rather, automaticity in handwriting is a necessary prerequisite for the ability to write creative and well structured text. The ability to put letters and words on the page effortlessly, allows the scarce cognitive resource of attention to be allocated to more complex and sophisticated aspects of writing such as ideation, organization of the text and monitoring of the product. We feel that handwriting provides a critical step in children's progress towards becoming proficient writers. Once mastered, they can focus on more difficult and complex skills. However, without mastery, handwriting appears to constitute a considerable obstacle that can exert a continuing obstruction to children's development.

> **Without mastery, handwriting appears to constitute a considerable obstacle that can exert a continuing obstruction to children's development.**

References

Bain, A. (1991). Handwriting disorders. In A. Bain, L. Bailet, & L. Moats (Eds.), *Written language disorders: Theory into practice* (pp. 23–42). Austin: Pro-Ed.

Beal, C. (1993). Contributions of developmental psychology to understanding revision: Implications for consultation with classroom teachers. *School Psychology Review, 22,* 643–655.

Bellanca, J., & Fogarty, R. (1991). *Blueprints for thinking in the cooperative classroom.* Cheltenham, Victoria: Hawker Bronlow Education.

Berninger, V.W., Mizokawa, D., & Bragg, R. (1991). Theory-based diagnosis and remediation of writing disabilities. *Journal of School Psychology, 29,* 57–59.

Berninger, V.W. (1994). *Reading and writing acquisition: A developmental neuropsychological perspective.* Dubuque, Iowa: Brown & Benchmark.

Berninger, V.W., Yates, C., Cartwright, A., Rutberg, J., Remy, & Abbott, R. (1992). Lower-level developmental skills in beginning writers. *Reading and Writing, 4,* 257–280.

Butterfield, E., Douglas, J., & Plumb, C. (1994). Topic knowledge, linguistic knowledge, and revision processes as determinants of text revision. In E. Butterfield & J. Carlson (Eds.), *Children's writing: toward a process theory of the development of skilled writing* (pp. 83–142). London: JAI Press.

De La Paz, S., & Graham, S. (1995). Dictation: Applications to writing for students with learning disabilities. In T. Scruggs, & M. Mastropieri (Eds.), *Advances in learning and behavioral disorders.* (Vol. 9, pp. 227–247). Greenwich, CT: JAI Press.

Gleason, M. (1995). Using direct instruction to integrate reading and writing for students with learning disabilities. *Reading and Writing Quarterly: Overcoming Learning Difficulties, 11,* 91–108.

Graham, S., Berninger, V.W., Abbott, R.D., Abbott, S.P., & Whitaker, D. (In press). The role of mechanics in composing of elementary students: A new methodological approach. *Journal of Educational Psychology.*

Graham, S., MacArthur, C., Schwartz, S., & Page-Voth, V. (1992). Improving the compositions of students with learning disabilities using a strategy involving product and process goal setting. *Exceptional Children, 58,* 322–334.

Harris, K.R., & Pressley, M. (1991). The nature of congnitive strategy instruction: Interactive strategy construction. *Exceptional Children, 57,* 392–404.

Hayes, J., & Flower, L. (1980). Identifying the organization of writing processes. In L.W. Gregg, & E.R. Steinberg (Eds.), *Cognitive processes in writing* (pp. 3–30). Hillsdale: Erlbaum.

Hooper, S., Montgomery, J., Swartz, C., Reed, M., Brown, T., Levine, M., & Wasileski, T (1993). Prevalence of writing problems across three middle school samples. *School Psychology Review, 2,* 610–621.

Levine, M.D. (1987). *Developmental variation and learning disorders.* Cambridge: Educators Publishing Service.

Levine, M.D. (1992). Neurodevelopmental variation and dysfunction among school-aged children. In M. Levine, W. Carey, & A. Crocker (Eds.), *Developmental-behavioral pediatrics* (2nd ed.) Philadelphia: W.B. Saunders.

Excerpts From

Is Handwriting Causally Related to Learning to Write?
Treatment of Handwriting Problems in Beginning Writers

Steve Graham,Karen R. Harris, and Barbara Fink:
University of Maryland

Journal of Educational Psychology, Pages 620–633, Vol. 92,
No. 4 (Dec, 2000), ©American Psychological Association.

The contribution of handwriting on learning to write was examined in an experimental training study involving beginning writers with and without an identified disability. First grade children, experiencing handwriting and writing difficulties, participated in 27, 15-minute sessions designed to improve the accuracy and fluency of their handwriting. In comparison to their peers in a contact control condition receiving instruction in phonological awareness, students in the handwriting condition made greater gains in handwriting as well as compositional fluency immediately following instruction and six months later. The effects of instruction were similar for students with and without an identified disability. These findings indicate that handwriting is causally related to writing, and that explicit and supplemental handwriting instruction is an important element in preventing writing difficulties in the primary grades.

Horace Greeley, the founder of the *New Yorker,* often wrote notes and letters that were difficult to decipher. After writing a letter, indicating that he would be unavailable to make a solicited presentation, he received a reply, noting that it took some time to translate his response, but that his requested date, terms, and honorarium were acceptable (Hendrickson, 1994).

Unfortunately, misinterpretations are not the only consequence of handwriting difficulties. For children, there are at least three additional unwanted results. One, poor penmanship may influence perceptions about a child's competence as a writer. When teachers or other adults are asked to evaluate two or more versions of a paper differing only in handwriting quality, neatly written papers are assigned higher marks for writing quality than papers of poorer legibility (e.g., Briggs, 1980; Chase, 1986; Hughes, Keeling, & Tuck, 1983). Two, difficulties with handwriting can interfere with the execution of composing processes during the act of writing (Graham, 1990; Scardamalia, Bereiter, & Goleman, 1982). Having to consciously attend to handwriting processes while composing may tax the writer's processing memory (see Berninger, 1999), interfering with other writing processes, such as content generation and planning. For instance, having to switch attention during composing to mechanical demands, such as having to think about how to form a particular letter, may lead the writer to forget ideas or plans already held in working memory. Third, and most important to the current study, handwriting difficulties may constrain a child's development as a writer. As Berninger, Mizokawa, and Bragg (1991) noted, difficulties mastering handwriting skills may lead young children to avoid writing and develop a mind set that they cannot write, resulting in arrested writing development.

> ...difficulties mastering handwriting skills may lead young children to avoid writing and develop a mind set that they cannot write....

In addition, handwriting may require so much effort for some young writers that they develop an approach to composing (i.e., knowledge telling) that minimizes the use of other writing processes, such as planning and revising, because they exert considerable processing demands as well (McCutchen, 1996).

In the present study, we examined the impact of supplementary handwriting instruction on the handwriting and writing performance of first grade children who produced handwriting slowly and were also experiencing difficulty learning to write. In addition to the handwriting instruction provided in the classroom, all of the participating children received additional instruction from a specially trained instructor three times a week. The supplemental handwriting program was developed so that it addressed basic processes identified in several influential data-based models of handwriting performance (Ellis, 1982; Margolin, 1984; van Galen, 1991). According to these models, writing a letter requires retrieving and holding the letter in working memory, accessing the corresponding motor program, setting the parameters for the program (e.g., establish the size of letter and speed of writing), and executing it. Correspondingly, students in the handwriting condition learned to name and identify the letters of the alphabet, were taught how to form each letter, adjusted parameters for speed or fluency by rewriting text at a faster pace, and practiced executing or writing letters in isolation, words, and sentences. These procedures were designed to teach students to write letters accurately and fluently.

Like the previous study by Berninger et al. (1997), students in the contact control condition received instruction in phonological awareness. This treatment was chosen because it is known to be beneficial to first-grade children (see Bus & van Ijzendoorn, 1999), and the data from the Berninger et al. (1997) study showed that teaching phonological awareness does not influence the process of learning to write letters.

Discussion

Theoretical Implications

In this study, we examined if handwriting is a causal factor in learning to write. Previous research has shown that individual differences in handwriting skills are related to how much and how well children write (see Graham et al., 1997; Graham & Harris, 2000), and that early, supplementary handwriting instruction can boost the writing performance of poor handwriters immediately following instruction (Berninger et al., 1997; Jones & Christensen, 1999). To assess the causal role of handwriting in early writing development, we provided supplemental handwriting instruction to first grade children who were experiencing difficulty with handwriting and writing, and then assessed the immediate as well as long-term effects of such instruction.

The findings from the current study indicate that handwriting is indeed causally related to learning to write. Students who received supplementary handwriting instruction outperformed their counterparts in the contact control condition (i.e., phonological awareness instruction) on measures assessing not only handwriting, but writing skills as well. Immediately following instruction, students in the handwriting condition were more accurate in naming and writing the letters of the alphabet, and they were also able to produce the letters of the alphabet and copy connected text more fluently. With the exception of copying text more fluently, these handwriting gains were maintained six months later. Most importantly, handwriting instruction resulted in immediate as well as more long-term improvements in students' compositional fluency skills. On a story writing probe, students in the handwriting condition composed at a much faster rate than their peers in the contact control condition at posttest (this measure was not administered at maintenance). Moreover, on a norm-referenced measure of compositional fluency, the

> The findings from the current study indicate that handwriting is indeed causally related to learning to write.

Writing Fluency subtest from the WJ-R (Woodcock & Johnson, 1990), students in the handwriting condition were more skilled at constructing written sentences immediately after instruction and six months later.

> **Most importantly, handwriting instruction resulted in immediate as well as more long-term improvements in students' compositional fluency skills.**

Consequently, the mastery of handwriting skills appears to facilitate not only the initial process of learning to write, as demonstrated by this and previous studies (Berninger et al., 1997; Jones & Christensen, 1999), but may also affect the outcomes of the learning process over time, at least up to a period of six months.

Educational Implications

In recent years, there has been a tendency to downplay or even eliminate handwriting instruction as part of the writing program (Berninger, 1999; Graham & Weintraub, 1996), as approaches such as whole language and process writing have placed greater emphasis on content and process, and much less emphasis on form. The findings from the current study as well as the investigations by Berninger et al. (1997) and Jones and Christensen (1999), however, indicate that such an approach may be ill-advised with beginning writers who experience difficulty initially mastering the intricacies of handwriting. Students in these studies benefitted from explicit and supplemental instruction in how to form and fluently write the letters of the alphabet, as they evidenced improvements in both their handwriting and compositional skills. Thus, if educators want to improve the writing of these students, they need to focus not just on the content and process of writing, but on transcription skills such as handwriting as well.

It is also tempting to assume that the development of handwriting skills can be ignored because of the advent of alternative modes of composing, such as word processing and speech synthesis (Graham, 1992). As one teacher told the first author, "I don't need to worry much about handwriting, because everyone uses word processing today." Although the use of word processing and speech synthesis has clearly increased in recent years, beginning writers still, and for the foreseeable future, do most of their composing by hand. Unfortunately, the data from this study and clinical reports by others suggests that difficulties in developing adequate handwriting skills in the early grades may lead to arrested writing development, particularly in terms of compositional fluency. For

Good Handwriting: A Foundation for Proficient Writers

example, third graders participating in a summer clinic at the University of Washington told investigators that they avoided writing, because their handwriting and spelling difficulties made it hard for others to read what they wrote (as reported in Berninger et al., 1997). Thus, until alternative methods of composing, such as word processing or speech synthesis, become the primary writing tool employed by beginning writers, handwriting should not be ignored in the early grades.

The outcomes from the current study as well as the two prior investigations (Berninger et al., 1997; Jones & Christensen, 1999) further indicate that supplemental handwriting instruction is an important element in preventing writing difficulties, at least for children who struggle to master handwriting skills in the early primary grades. The finding that students with an identified disability were just as likely to benefit from additional handwriting instruction as their nondisabled peers is particularly important because handwriting and writing difficulties are quite common among these students (Graham & MacArthur, 1987). The short-term intervention applied in this study shows that it may be possible to raise writing performance relative to same grade peers on a nationally normed test of compositional fluency. If compositional fluency can be raised by four-tenths of a standard deviation at posttest and six-tenths of a standard deviation six months later by 27, 15-minute sessions, it may be possible to raise performance even more by providing a longer intervention. Such improvements in compositional fluency may be especially important for struggling writers, as research by Berninger and her colleagues (Berninger et al., 1991) indicates that compositional fluency problems in the primary grades may be the genesis for writing problems in the upper grades.

> ...students with an identified disability were just as likely to benefit from additional handwriting instruction as their non-disabled peers...

Additional research is needed to replicate the current findings and to develop other techniques for preventing writing difficulties. A recent study by Berninger et al. (1998) indicates that early, supplemental spelling instruction may also be important in the prevention of writing difficulties. Extra spelling instruction improved both the spelling and compositional fluency of second grade students who were poor spellers. We further anticipate that early, supplemental instruction in the self-regulatory aspects of writing, particularly planning and revising, will help to prevent writing difficulties. Our own research has shown that struggling writers often experience difficulties regulating these processes when writing (De La Paz, Swanson, & Graham, 1998; Graham & Harris, 2000; Graham, 1997), and that directly teaching these processes to older elementary-level students who are poor writers results in improvements in how much and how well they write (Graham & Harris, 1996). It is also likely that efforts designed to increase the quantity and quality of the regular writing program will be beneficial as well. Such instruction should reduce the number of cases of writing failure due to poor instruction and help ameliorate the severity of writing difficulties experienced by other children whose primary problems are not instructional.

In summary, explicit supplemental instruction that helps young children write letters accurately and quickly can increase the probability that they will become skilled writers. In the present study, such instruction was a better predictor of children's success than student or family variables or even the teachers' sense of efficacy or their approach to writing. This study, along with the investigations by Berninger et al. (1997) and Jones and Christensen (1999), shows that explicit handwriting instruction is an integral component of an effective writing program for beginning writers.

References

Berninger, V. (1999). Coordinating transcription and text generation in working memory during composing: Automatic and constructive processes. *Learning Disability Quarterly, 22*, 99-112.

Berninger, V., Mizokawa, D., & Bragg, R. (1991). Theory-based diagnosis and remediation of writing disabilities. *Journal of School Psychology, 29*, 57-97.

Berninger, V., Vaughn, K., Abbott, R., Abbott, S., Rogan, L., Brooks, A., Reed, E., & Graham, S. (1997). Treatment of handwriting problems in beginning writers: Transfer from handwriting to composition. *Journal of Educational Psychology, 89*, 652-666.

Berninger, V., Vaughn, K., Abbott, R., Brooks, A., Abbott, S., Rogan, L., Reed, E., & Graham, S. (1998). Early intervention for spelling problems: Teaching functional spelling units of varying size with a multiple-connections framework. *Journal of Educational Psychology, 90*, 587-605.

Briggs, D. (1980). A study of the influence of handwriting upon grades using examination scripts. *Educational Review, 32*, 185-193.

Bus, A., & van Ijzendoorn, M. (1999). Phonological awareness and early reading: A meta-analysis of experimental studies. *Journal of Educational Psychology, 91*, 403-414.

Chase, C. (1986). Essay test scoring: Interaction of relevant variables. *Journal of Educational Measurement, 23*, 33-41.

De La Paz, S., Swanson, P., & Graham, S. (1998). Contribution of executive control to the revising problems of students with writing and learning difficulties. *Journal of Educational Psychology, 90,* 448-460.

Ellis, A. (1982). Spelling and writing (and reading and speaking). In A. Ellis (Ed.), *Normality and pathology in cognitive functions* (pp. 113-146). London: Academic Press.

Graham, S. (1997). Executive control in the revising of students with learning and writing difficulties. *Journal of Educational Psychology, 89,* 223-234.

Graham, S. (1992). Issues in handwriting instruction. *Focus on Exceptional Children, 25,* 1-14.

Graham, S. (1990). The role of production factors in learning disabled students' compositions. *Journal of Educational Psychology, 82,* 781-791.

Graham, S., Berninger, V., Abbott, R., Abbott, S., & Whitaker, D. (1997). Role of mechanics in composing of elementary school students: A new methodological approach. *Journal of Educational Psychology, 89,* 170-182.

Graham, S., & Harris, K. (2000). The role of self-regulation and transcription skills in writing and writing development. *Educational Psychologist, 35,* 3-12.

Graham, S., & Harris, K.R. (1996). Self-regulation and strategy instruction for students with writing and learning difficulties. In S. Ransdell & M. Levy (Eds.), *Science of writing: Theories, methods, individual differences, and applications* (pp. 347-360). Mahwah, NJ: Erlbaum.

Graham, S., & MacArthur, C. (1987). Written language of the handicapped. In C. Reynolds & L. Mann (Eds.), *Encyclopedia of Special Education* (pp. 1678-1681). New York: Wiley & Sons.

Graham, S., & Weintraub, N. (1996). A review of handwriting research: Progress and prospects from 1980 to 1994. *Educational Psychology Review, 8,* 7-87.

Hughes, D.C., Keeling, B., & Tuck, B.F. (1983). Effects of achievement expectations and handwriting quality on scoring essays. *Journal of Educational Measurement, 20,* 65-70.

Jones, D., & Christensen, C. (1999). Relationship between automaticity in handwriting and students' ability to generate written text. *Journal of Educational Psychology, 91,* 44-49.

Margolin, D. (1984). The neuropsychology of writing and spelling: Semantic, phonological, motor, and perceptual processes. *The Quarterly Journal of Experimental Psychology, 36,* 459-489.

McCutchen, D. (1996). A capacity theory of writing: Working memory in composition. *Educational Psychology Review, 8,* 299-325.

Scardamalia, M., Bereiter, C., & Goleman, H. (1982). The role of production factors in writing ability. In M. Nystrand (Ed.), *What writers know: The language, process, and structure of written discourse* (pp. 173-210). New York: Academic Press.

van Galen, C. (1991). Handwriting: Issues for a psychomotor theory. *Human Movement Science, 10,* 165-191.

Woodcock, R., & Johnson, M. (1990). *Woodcock-Johnson Psycho-Educational Battery—Revised.* Chicago: Riverside.

The Processing Demands of Writing

Mark Torrance and David Galbraith

Handbook of Writing Research, Pages 67–82, ©2006 Guilford Publications, Inc.

To facilitate the production of the text that you are now reading, I (Torrance) am using a common word processing application running on a personal computer. As I write, the word processor is monitoring what I typed for spelling errors. If I asked it to, it would also check to see whether the text I produced is grammatical (according to its own, somewhat arcane criteria). Elsewhere on the computer, an e-mail application is running, monitoring for incoming mail, as is bibliographic software that communicates with the word processor when I require it to do so. These are just the things I know about. In the background there appear to be a further 28 processes running, at least some of which are, I assume, essential to the effective working of the computer. Each of these is constantly either manipulating information or standing ready to do so. To accomplish all of this, each process draws, to varying degrees, on both the computer's random-access memory and its central processor. My current computer has plenty of RAM and a fast processor, and will multitask quite happily across all of these processes. This would definitely not have been true of the computer that I used 10 years ago. On that machine, running just two applications at once resulted in a radical reduction in performance and any further demands would make it grind to a halt.

There is, of course, another information-processing device involved in the production of this text. While I am writing, my mind is either simultaneously engaged in or rapidly switching between processes that perform all or most of the following functions: monitoring the thematic coherence of the text; searching for and retrieving relevant content; identifying lexical items associated with this content; formulating syntactic structure; inflecting words to give them the necessary morphology; monitoring for appropriate register; ensuring that intended new text is tied into the immediately preceding text in a way that maintains cohesion; formulating and executing motor plans for the key strokes that will form the text on the screen; establishing the extent to which the just-generated clause or sentence moves the text as a whole nearer to the intended goal; and revising goals in the light of new ideas cued by the just-produced text. These processes cannot all be performed simultaneously. Attempting to do so, as with a 10-year-old computer, would result in overload and writing would stop. The fact that I am writing this at all, therefore, is testament to the writing system's ability to coordinate and schedule a number of different processes within the limited processing resources afforded it by my mind.

Overcoming Processing Constraints

Developing writing maturity involves tailoring the writing system so as to minimize concurrent demands on the writer's cognitive resources. The discussion in the previous sections points toward three broad ways in which this might be achieved:

1. Subcomponent skills, and particularly low-level skills associated with transcription (handwriting or keyboarding) and spelling, can be practiced to the extent that they rarely invoke higher level processing mechanisms.

2. Writers may develop specific skills for maximizing the efficiency with which they use transient memory resources.

3. There are several strategic steps that writers can take—preplanning, making notes, rough drafting, and so forth—that serve to reduce the number of processes that have to be juggled during composition.

We briefly discuss each of these in the sections that follow.

Developing Automaticity in Low-Level Components

For present purposes, we think of a process as automatic if it occurs without voluntary control and interferes minimally with other processes. Pashler (1994b) observes that practice can lead to automaticity by streamlining the way in which a task is performed and thus decreasing the period for which potential bottleneck mechanisms are engaged. If, for example, spelling can be achieved without the writer actively invoking mechanisms for explicit retrieval from long-term memory (LTM)—if the writer can avoid having to stop and say, "Now are there one or two c's in necessary?" or avoid consciously computing subject-verb agreement errors (Fayol, Hupet, & Largy, 1999)—then this will leave these retrieval mechanisms free for exploring possible content.

Spelling and handwriting, the two low-level processes that are most obviously required in written production but not in speech, are obvious candidates for automatization. Bourdin and Fayol, in a series of studies with varying age groups, explored differences in recall under spoken and written conditions (Bourdin, 1999; Bourdin & Fayol, 1994, 1996, 2002). These studies tend to confirm that when written production is less practiced, it interferes with conscious retrieval processes. In simple word-recall tasks, both second- and fourth-grade children recalled substantially fewer items when they were written than when they were spoken (Bourdin & Fayol, 1994). For adults, however, this effect was absent or even reversed, with slightly better recall with written responses. Predictably, adding composition demands by requiring that participants produce sentences containing the words to be recalled (a "sentence span" task) rather than recalling them in isolation also gave poorer written recall and better spoken recall in children. Again, this effect was not found in adults (Bourdin & Fayol, 1996). However, when the further demand that sentences need to be linked (a "text span" task) was added, and when the words presented were unrelated and so difficult to combine into a coherent text, adults then also performed less well in the written modality. This suggests that even when spelling and handwriting are very well practiced, they can still compete with higher level processes.

Of course Bourdin and Fayol's findings conflate spelling and handwriting effects. However, other research suggests that there is potential for interference between higher level processes and both spelling and handwriting (Fayol, 1999). Fayol and coworkers have found that spelling errors (specifically subject-verb agreement errors in French) increase in both children (Totereau, Thevenin, & Fayol, 1997) and adults (Fayol, Largy, & Lemaire, 1994) when combined with memory tasks. With more natural writing tasks, difficulty with spelling words appears to narrow the range of vocabulary that writers use. Wengelin (2005) found that her sample adult dyslexic writers were more likely to pause midword and showed substantially lower lexical diversity than nondyslexic controls. These two phenomena appeared to be related, with a high proportion of the variance in lexical diversity predicted by the extent to which writers paused midword and the extent to which they engaged in concurrent editing. This suggests, perhaps, that spelling retrieval interferes with processes involved in lexical retrieval, and/or that midword pausing in itself results in the loss of lexical items that are awaiting transcription but are less common and therefore have a lower level of activation.

There appears also to be potential for interference between the graphical processing associated and transcription and higher-level writing processes, although the evidence here is less direct. Bourdin and Fayol (2000) found that in second-grade children, repetition of even a very simple graphic pattern while orally recalling word lists resulted in a 30% reduction in recall. If, as this suggests, very low-level graphomotor processes are capable of interfering with retrieval from LTM, then training specifically focused on improving children's handwriting should benefit not only handwriting neatness but also other aspects of text generation. This appears to be the case, at least in terms of the fluency with which text is produced (Berninger et al., 1997).

The findings summarized briefly here therefore suggest both that there is potential for conflict between low-level output processes (spelling and handwriting) and processes associated with generating and structuring content, and that with increased expertise in these low-level skills this conflict becomes less likely.

References

Berninger, V.W., Vaughan, K.R., Graham, S., Abbott, R.D., Abbott, S.P., Rogan, L.W., et al. (1997). Treatment of handwriting problems in beginning writers: Transfer from handwriting to composition. *Journal of Educational Psychology. 89* (4), 652–666.

Bourdin, B. (1999). Working memory and language production: Comparison of oral and written production in adults and children. *Annee Psychologique, 99* (1). 123–148.

Bourdin, B., & Fayol, M. (1994). Is written language production more difficult than oral language production—A working-memory approach. *International Journal of Psychology. 29* (5), 591–620.

Bourdin, B., & Fayol, M. (1996). Mode effects in a sentence production span task. *Cahiers De Psychologie Cognitive, 15* (3), 245–264.

Bourdin, B. & Fayol, M. (2000). Is graphic activity cognitively costly?: A developmental approach. *Reading and Writing. 13,* 183–196.

Bourdin, B. & Fayol, M. (2002). Even in adults, written production is still more costly than oral production. *International Journal of Psychology, 37* (4), 219–227.

Fayol, M., Hupet, M., & Largy, P. (1999). The acquisition of subject-verb agreement in written French: From novices to experts' errors. *Reading and Writing, 11* (2), 153–174.

Fayol, M., Largy, P., & Lemaire, P. (1994). Cognitive overload and orthographic errors—when cognitive overload enhances subject-verb agreement errors: A study in French written language. *Quarterly Journal of Experimental Psychology A: Human Experimental Psychology, 47,* 437–464.

Pashler, H. (1994b). Graded capacity-sharing in dual-task interference? *Journal of Experimental Psychology: Human Perception and Performance, 20* (2), 330–342.

Totereau, C., Thevenin, M., & Fayol, M. (1997). The development of the understanding of number morphology in written French. In C. Perfetti, L. Rieben, & M. Fayol (Eds.), *Learning to spell* (pp. 97–114). Hillsdale, NJ: Erlbaum.

Wengelin, A. (2005). The word level focus in text production by adults with reading and writing difficulties. In D. Galbraith, M. Torrance, & L. van-Wacs (Eds.), *Writing and cognition: Research and applications.* Manuscript submitted for publication.

The Critical Role Handwriting Plays in the Ability to Produce High Quality Written Text

Carol A. Christensen

The SAGE Handbook of Writing Development,
Pages 284–299, ©2009 SAGE Publications.

Given the diversity and complexity of cognitive processes involved in the production of high quality written text, it seems counter-intuitive to suggest that handwriting is a key element in students' ability to create original and well-structured text. However, there is a sound theoretical basis and mounting empirical evidence to suggest that the relationship between handwriting and quality of written text is strong and surprisingly robust.

The focus of handwriting in the curriculum for most of the last century was on legibility, neatness and strict motor-control. Good penmanship was central to curriculum in literacy for much of the twentieth century (Schlagal, 2007). However, more recently handwriting has been seen as unimportant and irrelevant to contemporary education (Medwell and Wray, 2007).

> The relationship between handwriting and quality of written text is strong and surprisingly robust.

Schlagal argues that in recent decades two factors have pushed handwriting to the margins of curriculum. There has been a de-emphasis on basic skills with their concomitant requirement for regimes of extended practice. A focus on spelling, grammar and handwriting has been replaced by an emphasis on personal communication. Second, the contemporary focus on electronic forms of communication, particularly in regard to word-processing has led some educators to argue that there is no longer any need to teach low-level skills such as handwriting (Schlagal, 2007).

In addition, it seems that research in the 1980's on emergent writing that demonstrated that children could create meaningful texts before having access to the formal writing system, led to a curriculum focus on semantics, creativity, genre and pragmatic awareness (Hall, 1987; Teale and Sulzby, 1986; Wray and Lewis, 1997) as well as a focus on processes such as planning, monitoring and revising (Hayes and Flowers, 1980) rather than an emphasis on handwriting-related skills such as letter formation and legibility (Medwell and Wray. 2007).

It seems ironic, then, that to some extent, when handwriting is addressed in contemporary curriculum documents, the traditional emphasis found in early documents on neatness, motor control and script style remains (Medwell and Wray, 2007). Thus, current curriculum does not reflect recent research on the importance of handwriting or on the need for speed and fluency which underpins writers' ability to produce high quality written text.

Cognitive Demands of Writing. The multiplicity of cognitive processes involved in writing include: ideation related to the ability to generate original and creative ideas; syntactic awareness involved in production of grammatically accurate text; pragmatic awareness and sensitivity to audience required to produce text that communicates clearly and appropriately with the reader; technical accuracy related to spelling; and awareness of structural aspects of text such as genre. The number and complexity of these processes means that when attempting to produce text, novice writers can experience significant problems with capacity limitation of working memory or cognitive load.

Cognitive load refers to the attentional demands required to perform intellectual tasks (Sweller, 1988). Essentially the human mind has sufficient cognitive resources to attend to only one conscious intellectual activity at a time. Thus, attention is often referred to as the scarce cognitive resource (Lesgold, et al., 1988). This means that in order to perform complex intellectual tasks, an individual must be able to manage the potentially competing attentional demands that tasks may pose. This can be done in one of two ways. First, individuals can sequence tasks that have high cognitive loads. Process writing enables the writer to sequentially focus attention on one element of writing at a time. This is effective in a number of situations, however, it is not possible to sequence all the attention consuming aspects of tasks at all times.

> **Automaticity is defined as the ability to recall information from memory quickly, accurately and effortlessly.**

Automaticity provides the alternative to sequencing the cognitive processes needed to write (LaBerge and Samuels, 1974). Automaticity is defined as the ability to recall information from memory quickly, accurately and effortlessly (Schneider and Shriffrin, 1977). One characteristic of expertise is automaticity, so that experts have their knowledge available in a way that they can retrieve and use the information without consuming attention. This effortless retrieval of sub-components of complex tasks means that experts consume relatively few cognitive resources in the execution of low-level aspects of tasks and,

Good Handwriting: A Foundation for Proficient Writers

therefore, have most of their attentional resources available for sophisticated, higher-order aspects of tasks (Bransford, et al., 2000). In other words, in addition to sequencing, expert writers can manage cognitive load through automaticity.

Handwriting is one aspect of written language that cannot be sequenced in order to manage cognitive load. If novice writers focus attention on the process of getting letters and words on the page, then they do not have sufficient attentional resources to focus on higher-order and centrally important processes such as ideation, pragmatic awareness or sensitivity to genre. Thus, theoretically, automaticity in handwriting is an essential prerequisite to the production of high quality, creative and well-structured written text. Indeed, over the last 20 years in addition to theoretical analysis, there has been a steady accumulation of empirical support for the notion that handwriting plays a central role in allowing the production of high quality written text.

> **Automaticity in handwriting is an essential prerequisite to the production of high quality, creative and well-structured written text.**

Theoretical Aspects of Handwriting and Written Text. Graham, et al. (1997) argued that the necessity to switch attention from higher-order processes to the mechanical aspects of writing can interfere with planning, which in turn impacts on complexity and coherence of written work. They suggested that switching attention from the composing process to handwriting may affect the coherence and complexity of written work (Graham and Weintraub, 1996). Graham, et al. (2000) suggested that the need to switch attention from the composing process to the mechanical demands of handwriting, for example, having to think about how to form a particular letter, may result in a writer forgetting his or her ideas or plans for the text. McCutchen (1996) argued that the physical act of writing text is so demanding for young writers that they develop an approach to production of written text (knowledge telling), that minimizes the use of self-regulatory processes (e.g. planning, monitoring and revising). Thus, the cognitive load of handwriting, by exerting competing attentional demands, may make it difficult for the writer to translate his or her intentions into text.

In a review of literature, Berninger (1999) argued that there was substantial evidence to show that both transcription and working memory processes constrained the development of children's ability to compose text. This applied to children who were identified as learning disabled as well as children without learning disabilities.

In addition to problems with allocation of attention, if writers lack fluency in handwriting, they may not be able to get their ideas on the page fast enough to keep up with their thoughts. In other words, there is interference with content generation as well as with recall of ideas for text already planned. Graham and Weintraub (1996) argued that speed is an important aspect of handwriting. If handwriting is very slow, then students may not be able to record their thoughts in a way that keeps pace with their generation of ideas. Thus, they may forget their ideas before they get them on paper. Graham et al. found that speed of handwriting was significantly related to children's quality of composition.

> **If writers lack fluency in handwriting, they may not be able to get their ideas on the page fast enough to keep up with their thoughts.**

Berninger's simple view of writing (Berninger, Vaughn, Abbott, Begay, Coleman, Byrd, Curtain, Hawkins, Minch and Graham, 2002) suggested a theory of writing which consisted of three components. The first related to lower-level skill related to transcription including spelling and handwriting. The second refers to text generation processes or composing. The third related to executive functioning including planning, monitoring and revising. This model has underpinned a number of studies which have examined developmental processes contributing to children's ability to create written text.

Berninger, Mizokawa and Bragg (1991) developed a model which accounted for the relationship between lower-order skills, higher-order elements of writing such as composing and executive management, and performance on written tasks. This model was based on developmental constraints. They suggested that constraints operate at multiple levels in a dynamic relationship. Thus, Berninger, Yates, Cartwright, Rutberg, Remy and Abbott (1992) suggested that some sensory and motor capacities need to develop before the ability to integrate sensory-motor information, which underpins handwriting. This is followed by the development of higher-order cognitive skills related to writing. Berninger et al. argue that rapid coding of orthographic information, speed of finger movement and rapid production of alphabetic letters (orthographic-motor integration) may constrain the ability to transcribe ideas into text.

In addition to its impact on composition, handwriting can impact on children's attitude to writing. Berninger, Mizokawa, and Bragg (1991) suggested that if children find the acquisition of handwriting skill difficult, they tend to avoid writing tasks. This, in turn, impacts on their sense of self-efficacy in regard to writing and, consequently, they display arrested development in writing. Graham and Weintraub (1996) also argued that students' motivation may be impacted because of experiences of frustration with the writing process.

It should be kept in mind that handwriting is not just a motor act. It requires the integration of motor behaviour with knowledge of the orthography (Berninger and Graham, 1998). Memory for orthographic information, particularly letter shapes, contributes more to handwriting skill than the motor component of writing.

> If children find the acquisition of handwriting skill difficult, they tend to avoid writing tasks.

Orthographic-motor integration refers to ability to recall and produce letter shapes, groups of letters and words. Thus, handwriting requires the writer to mentally code and rehearse the visual representation of patterns of letters in words, and to integrate these patterns with motor activities (Berninger 1994).

Empirical Evidence for the Impact of Handwriting on Written Text. While there is growing evidence that handwriting plays a significant role in writers' ability to produce written text, there is variability in some research findings. In part, this is due to diversity in data collection methods based on a range of assessment methods for both handwriting and composition of written text. Assessment of handwriting has included asking students to create a piece of text, to write letters of the alphabet from memory, to copy single letters, and to copy a piece of text.

There is also diversity in participants in research on handwriting. They have been drawn from a range of backgrounds and characteristics, including normally developing young, novice writers, older students and adults. Participants have included normally achieving students, as well as students with reading and writing disabilities. In addition to a range of data collection methods and participants, a variety of analysis techniques have been used, including correlational studies, structural equation modeling, quasi experimental and experimental designs.

> Handwriting is not just a motor act.

Despite this variety in approach, there is consistency in a number of research findings. Much of the research has investigated the relationship between handwriting to two distinct aspects of written text. First, is compositional fluency which refers to the facility with which a writer can produce text. It is often measured by the amount of text produced in a specified time. Second, is the quality of written text. Measures of quality often consider issues such as: originality and creativity of thoughts and ideas contained in the text, logical sequencing and organization of the text, use of appropriate genre-specific structures, coherence of concepts expressed, detail and comprehensiveness of the coverage of the topic, sensitivity to audience, and clarity of expression which is underpinned by pragmatic awareness.

Research on handwriting and fluency of composition shows a strong and enduring relationship across a range of participant ages and methodological approaches. Research on handwriting and quality of written text is less consistent but nevertheless, points to a critically important variable.

It should be noted that the relationship between handwriting and fluency and quality of written text is due to working memory limitations and cognitive load. There is limited evidence for a relationship between appearance of handwriting and written text (Parker, Tindal and Hasbrouck, 1991).

As long ago as 1976 Rice found that for students in Grade 2, speed of handwriting predicted academic achievement as well as ability to complete written assignments. More recently, a number of studies have found significant correlations between fluency in handwriting and students' ability to produce written text. Biemiller, Regan and Gang (1993), working with children in Grades 1 to 6, reported correlations of between .34 and .76 between fluency of handwriting and fluency in composition. Similarly, Meltza, Fenton and Persky (1985) found correlations of .27 between speed of writing the alphabet and fluency in composition and .30 for quality of written text for students in Grades 4–9.

To more carefully control for influences involved in writing, Graham, Berninger, Abbott, Abbott and Whitaker (1997) used structural equation modeling to examine the relationships among handwriting, spelling and written language. They assessed 300 children in Grades 1, 2 and 3 (primary) and 300 children in Grades 4, 5 and 6 (intermediate) on two measures of handwriting: an alphabet task and a copying task. They also used a standardized spelling assessment and measured fluency and quality of composition. They found that mechanics related to spelling and handwriting accounted for 66% of the variance in compositional fluency in primary grades and 41% of the variance in intermediate grades. Mechanics accounted for a smaller proportion of the variance in quality of text; 25% in quality of composition for primary children and 42% of the variance for intermediate children. The impact of handwriting was also indicated in that Graham et al. reported that the relationship between spelling and composition was indirect and accounted for by its correlation with handwriting.

Jones and Christensen (1999), working with children in Grade 1 in Australia, found a much stronger relationship between speed and accuracy of handwriting and quality of written text than was observed in other studies. They found that when reading was controlled, handwriting accounted for 53% of the variance in written text.

Using Berninger's et al. (1991) constraints model, Berninger et al. (1992) examined the hypothesis that development of written text consists of two components. First, a process of text generation allows the writer to convert ideas into spoken language. Second, a transcription

> **When reading was controlled, handwriting accounted for 53% of the variance in written text.**

process converts spoken language into written text. They administered a number of measures to 300 children in Grades 1, 2 and 3. The data supported their hypothesis that text generation was followed by transcription. They found that lower-level developmental variables are related to early writing skill. Specifically, rapid, automatic production of alphabet letters, rapid coding of orthographic information and speed of finger movement were the best predictors of both handwriting and composition skills.

Taken as a whole, correlational studies indicate that the ability to produce letters automatically accounts for a remarkably large proportion of the variance in compositional fluency and, depending on the age of students, a large proportion of the variance in quality of written text.

References

Berninger, V. (1999), 'Coordinating transcription and text generation in working memory during composing: Automatic and constructive processes,' *Learning Disabilities Quarterly, 22(2):* 99–112.

Berninger, V., Abbott, R., Rogan, L., Reed, E., Abbott, S., Brooks, A., Vaughan, K. and Graham, S. (1998), 'Teaching spelling to children with specific learning disabilities: The mind's ear and eye beat the computer or pencil,' *Learning Disabilities Quarterly, 21(2):* 106–122.

Berninger, V., Mizokawa, D., and Bragg, R. (1991), 'Theory-based diagnosis and remediation of writing disabilities,' *Journal of Educational Psychology, 29:* 57–79.

Berninger, V., Vaughn, K., Abbott, R., Begay, K., Coleman, K., Byrd, Curtain, G., Hawkins, Minch, J., and Graham, S. (2002), 'Teaching spelling and composition alone and together: Implications for the simple view of writing,' *Journal of Educational Psychology, 94(2)* 291–304.

Berninger, V., Yates, C., Cartwright, A., Rutberg, J., Remy E., and Abbott, R. (1992) 'Lower-level developmental skills in beginning writing.' *Reading and Writing: An Interdisciplinary Journal, 4:* 257–280.

Biemiller, A., Regan, E. and Gang, B. (1993), 'Studies in the Development of Writing Speed: Age Task and Individual Differences,' University of Toronto: On, Canada. Unpublished manuscript.

Bransford, J., Brown, A. and Cocking, R. (2000), 'How people learn: Brain, mind, experience, and school.' Washington, D.C.: National Academy Press.

Graham, S., Harris, K. and Fink, B. (2000) 'Is handwriting causally related to learning to write? Treatment of handwriting problems in beginning writers.' *Journal of Educational Psychology, 92*(4): 620–633.

Graham, S., and Weintraub, N. (1996) 'A review of handwriting research: Progress and prospects from 1980 to 1994,' *Educational Psychology Review, 8:* 7–87.

Graham, S., Berninger, V., Abbott, R., Abbott, S. and Whitaker, D. (1997) 'Role of mechanics in composing of elementary school students: A new methodological approach.' *Journal of Educational Psychology, 89*(1): 170–182.

Hall, N. (1987), 'The Emergence of Literacy.' Sevenoaks: Hodder and Stoughton.

Hayes, J. and Flowers, L. (1980) 'Identifying the organization of writing processes' in L. Gregg and E. Steinberg (eds.) *Cognitive Processes in Writing.* Hillsdale, NJ: Erlbaum. pp. 3–30.

Jones, D. and Christensen, C. (1999) 'Relationship between automaticity in handwriting and students' ability to generate written text,' *Journal of Educational Psychology, 91*(1): 44–49.

LaBerge, D., and Samuels, S.J. (1974), 'Toward a theory of automatic information processing in reading,' *Cognitive Psychology, 6:* 293–323.

Lesgold, A., Rubison, H., Feltovich, P., Glaser, R., Klopfet, D., and Wang, Y. (1988), 'Expertise in a complex skill: Diagnosing x-ray pictures.' In M. T. Chi, R. Glaser, and M. Farr (Eds.), *The nature of expertise,* Hillsdale, NJ: Erlbaum, (pp. 311–342).

McCutchen, D. (1996) 'A capacity theory of writing: Working memory in composition.' *Educational psychology Review, 8:* 299–325.

Medwell, J., and Wray, D. (2007) 'Handwriting: What do we know and what do we need to know?,' *Literacy, 41:* 10-15.

Meltza, L., Fenton, T. and Persky, S. (1985), 'A developmental study of the components of written language in children with and without learning difficulties,' Paper presented at the annual meeting of the American Educational Research association, Chicago, IL.

Parker, R., Tindal, G. and Hasbrouck, J., (1991). 'Progress monitoring with objective measures of writing performance for students with learning disabilities.' *Exceptional Children, 58:* 61-73.

Rice, R., (1976), 'The use of handwriting rate for predicting academic achievement and suggesting curriculum modifications.' *Dissertations Abstracts International, 37:* 1887A.

Schlagal, B. (2007). 'Best practices in spelling and handwriting.' S. Graham, C. MacArthur, J. Fitzgerald (eds.) *Best Practices in Writing Instruction: Solving Problems in the Teaching of Literacy.* Guliford Press: NY, (pages 179–201).

Schneider, W., and Shriffrin, R. (1977). 'Controlled and automatic human information processing: Detection, search and attention.' *Psychological Review, 84:* 1–66.

Sweller, J., (1988). 'Cognitive load during problem solving: Effects on learning,' *Cognitive Science, 12:* 257–285.

Teale, W. and Sulzby, E. (eds.) (1986) *Emergent Literacy: Writing and Reading.* Norwood, NJ: Ablex.

Wray, J. and Lewis, D. (1997) 'Handwriting: what do we know and what do we need to know?,' *Literacy, 41:* 10–15.

Chapter 6

Best Practices for Handwriting Instruction

"Psssst! What font are you using?"

Reprinted with special permission of CartoonStock.

Introduction

Handwriting skills are important, but time to teach and practice them is limited in the crowded school curriculum. Using best practices can help busy teachers and administrators make the most of the short time available for handwriting instruction.

It isn't always easy to discern the best strategies for teaching handwriting. Because penmanship practice has such a long history in America, what is customary may be confused with what is effective and research-based. In many cases, the two approaches overlap, but this is not always true. For example, it is not effective for students to spend long practice sessions writing letters over and over again thoughtlessly, as they may have done in the past. For handwriting, practice makes *permanent,* not perfect. Instructional time, in which students learn to perceive a letter's shape and motor pattern, must precede short, frequent periods of practice that reinforce good letter formation and build kinesthetic memory.

The articles in this chapter describe the best practices for helping students achieve legible and automatic handwriting. Many are documented by numerous research studies and have long been part of the Zaner-Bloser method. While these practices are well-known, surveys of teachers show that they are often used inconsistently and hardly ever taught in college education courses. Following these strategies for just 15 minutes a day, 3–5 days per week, is enough to provide excellent handwriting instruction.

- **Teach letters by modeling good letter formation, providing letter models with arrows, and encouraging students to visually compare similar letters.** These techniques help students perceive letter shapes accurately and build visual and motor images that will guide their writing. *Zaner-Bloser Handwriting* teacher editions explain these strategies in each lesson, while student editions feature large clear letter models with numbered formation arrows and a green dot that shows where each letter begins.

- **Guide students as they trace, copy, and write letter forms correctly.** High-quality practice occurs when students trace, copy, and write letters with the aid of good models. Cues on students' papers, as well as watchful monitoring by the teacher, ensure that students practice correctly and form good habits. Each Zaner-Bloser student edition lesson supports students as they proceed from tracing and copying to writing letters in isolation, in words and sentences, and in their own compositions.

- **Show students how to self-evaluate by asking, "Is my writing easy to read?"** After writing a letter just 3–5 times, students should stop and examine what they wrote to further develop their knowledge about letters. In each Zaner-Bloser student edition, a "stop and check" feature gives a reminder to self-evaluate. Zaner-Bloser's four Keys to Legibility, shown below, form a rubric that helps students decide if their writing is easy to read.

- **Help students write comfortably and efficiently by teaching good positions for sitting, holding a pencil, and placing papers on their desks.** Positioning the body comfortably for writing is an important part of handwriting success. *Zaner-Bloser Handwriting* includes detailed diagrams and teaching suggestions for pencil grip, sitting position, and paper placement. These techniques should be taught early to avoid the development of awkward and inefficient habits.

Taking time to teach handwriting has been found to have positive effects on student achievement in handwriting and in writing. The authors in this chapter outline the best ways to provide instruction in handwriting. Researcher Steve Graham and others provide a snapshot of current handwriting practices in "How Do Primary Teachers Teach Handwriting? A National Survey." Graham also contributes to the helpful "Checklist for Evaluating the Quality of Handwriting Instruction." In "Handwriting Instruction in Elementary Schools," Asha V. Asher looks at handwriting instruction from the perspective of a practicing occupational therapist.

ZANER-BLOSER KEYS TO LEGIBILITY

SHAPE	**SIZE**
Legible letters have unique, recognizable shapes.	Legible lowercase and uppercase letters have consistent proportions.
SLANT	**SPACING**
Legible writing has a consistent slant.	Legible writing has consistent spacing between letters, words, and sentences.

How Do Primary Grade Teachers Teach Handwriting?

A National Survey

Steve Graham, Karen R. Harris, Linda Mason,
Barbara Fink-Chorzempa, Susan Moran, Bruce Saddler

Reading and Writing: An Interdisciplinary Journal, Pages 49–69, Vol. 21, No. 1 (Feb, 2008), ©Springer Science + Business Media.

For adults, the act of handwriting is mostly an unconscious, automatic task (Willingham, 1998). For beginning writers, however, handwriting is a more effortful activity, as the processes for producing letters still require conscious attention (Berninger, 1999; Graham, 1999). Until this skill becomes efficient and relatively automatic, it may exact a toll on the writer and ultimately writing development.

Handwriting may constrain beginning writers in at least four ways. One, these children's written text may be less accessible to others, because the legibility of their handwriting is still developing (Graham, 1999). Two, what they say in their writing may be devalued to some degree, as legibility of text can influence the evaluation of writing content. For example, when adults are asked to evaluate two or more versions of a paper differing only in handwriting legibility, lower marks for overall quality of ideas are assigned to papers that are less legible (Marshall & Powers, 1969). Three, young children's handwriting may impede their writing efforts by interfering with other writing processes (Scardamalia, Bereiter, & Goleman, 1982). For instance, having to switch attention during composing to thinking about how to form a particular letter may lead a child to forget writing ideas or plans being held in working memory. They are also likely to lose some writing ideas, as their handwriting is often not fast enough for them to record all of their ideas before they start forgetting some of them (Graham,

> **Difficulties with handwriting may constrain young children's development as writers.**

1990). Four, difficulties with handwriting may constrain young children's development as writers. McCutchen (1995) proposed that transcription skills such as handwriting are so demanding for beginning writers, that they minimize the use of other writing processes, such as planning and revising, because they exert considerable processing demands as well.

Moreover, Berninger, Mizokawa, and Bragg (1991) reported that difficulties with handwriting and spelling led children they worked with to avoid writing and develop a mind set that they could not write.

If handwriting plays an important role in shaping writing development, as the arguments above suggest, Graham and Harris (2000) argued that it is reasonable to expect that: (1) the handwriting of more skilled writers is superior to that of less skilled writers, (2) students' handwriting improves with age and schooling, (3) individual differences in handwriting predict individual differences in writing, and (4) teaching handwriting improves the writing performance of developing writers. A recent review by Graham (2006) found that the available literature provides some support for each of these assumptions.

First, the handwriting skills of children with poor handwriting are less well developed than those of their normally developing counterparts. Their handwriting is not as smooth, accurate, or legible (see Graham & Weintraub, 1996). They are also more variable in their production of letter forms (Wann & Kardirkamanathan, 1991) and produce handwriting more slowly (Weintraub & Graham, 1998). Second, there is a considerable body of research showing that handwriting improves with age and schooling (see Graham & Weintraub, 1996). Although overall legibility may peak somewhere around fourth grade (Mojet, 1991), students continue to make modifications in how they produce letter forms (for example, they may simplify script by eliminating clockwise movements (see Bolte & Hanstra-Bletz, 1991), and their fluency with handwriting increases by about 10 letters or more per minute, before it starts to level off at the start of high school (Graham, Berninger, Weintraub, & Schaefer, 1998).

Third, individual differences in handwriting predict writing achievement. As part of a study examining the relationship between text transcription skills and writing performance, Graham, Berninger, Abbott, Abbott, and Whitaker (1997) reviewed 13 studies. They reported that handwriting fluency was moderately correlated with measures of writing achievement. In the empirical study they conducted, handwriting and spelling skills together accounted for a sizable proportion of the variance in the writing skills of 600 first through sixth grade children (up to 42% of the variance in writing quality and 66% of the variance in writing

> **Difficulties with handwriting and spelling led children they worked with to avoid writing and develop a mind set that they could not write.**

output). Of these two skills, only handwriting fluency continued to make a unique contribution beyond the primary grades in accounting for variability in how much and how well students wrote.

Fourth, even though the research base is relatively thin, teaching handwriting to young writers can improve writing performance. Three studies found that handwriting instruction not only improved young students' handwriting, but one or more aspects of their writing performance as well, including sentence construction skills, writing output, and writing quality (Berninger et al., 1997; Graham, Harris, & Fink, 2000; Jones & Christensen, 1999).

> Handwriting and spelling skills together accounted for a sizable proportion of the variance in the writing skills of 600 first through sixth grade children (up to 42% of the variance in writing quality and 66% of the variance in writing output).

Despite the relative importance of handwriting, both theoretically and empirically, we know little about how it is taught to young, developing writers. In contrast to spelling (see for example Brann & Hattie, 1995; Graham, Harris, MacArthur, & Fink-Chorzempa, 2003; Traynelis-Yurek & Strong, 1999), there have been few attempts to catalogue handwriting instructional practices in today's schools. There has been some speculation (Graham & Weintaub, 1996), especially by the media, (see for example Leo, 2002) that handwriting is not emphasized or taught to young developing writers. It is difficult to verify this assumption, as the last published survey of handwriting practices was conducted in the early 1980s (Rubin & Henderson, 1982).

> Handwriting fluency continued to make a unique contribution beyond the primary grades in accounting for variability in how much and how well students wrote.

A recent study by Graham et al. (2003) provides some tentative evidence on this issue, however. They conducted a survey of the writing instructional practices of primary grade teachers randomly selected from throughout the United States. Although their study focused on the types of instructional adaptations teachers made for struggling writers, teachers were asked how often they taught handwriting skills to their students. Almost half of the teachers reported teaching handwriting daily, with one fourth indicating that they provided instruction several times a week, and another 14% indicating they taught this skill weekly. Only about 2% of the teachers indicated that they did not teach handwriting at all.

Although these findings suggest that teachers of young children do value handwriting and teach it, additional research is needed to establish replicability and to more fully determine how handwriting is taught in today's schools. The current study addressed both of these points by surveying a randomly selected sample of primary grade teachers from throughout the United States and asking them if they taught handwriting, and if this was the case, how it was taught. Teachers were also asked to describe their students in terms of their handwriting skills, including their facility with handwriting legibility and fluency, number of students with handwriting difficulties, and types of handwriting problems. Teachers were further asked about how handwriting is learned and should be taught, why children experience handwriting difficulties, and the impact of handwriting difficulties. Finally, teachers were queried about whether they liked to teach handwriting and the amount of formal preparation on teaching handwriting they received in the teacher education courses taken in college.

Students' handwriting achievement is likely influenced by the amount of handwriting instruction provided in the classroom (i.e., more instructional time should lead to improved handwriting performance), which in turn is influenced by teachers' desire to teach this skill (i.e., teachers who enjoy teaching handwriting devote more time to its mastery by students), and these attitudes are likely shaped by teachers' competence (i.e., teachers with good handwriting and greater formal preparation in how to teach handwriting will be more positively disposed to teaching it). We tested this set of assumptions by examining if the prediction of handwriting achievement (as measured by teacher judgments of students' handwriting performance) was improved by adding measures of teacher attitude to indexes of teacher competence (i.e., prior teacher education preparation in handwriting instruction and quality of teachers' handwriting), and if this prediction was further improved by adding time devoted to teaching handwriting to this set of predictors. We examined the viability of this hierarchical model for two estimates of students' handwriting skills: legibility and fluency.

> Students' handwriting achievement is likely influenced by the amount of handwriting instruction provided in the classroom.

Method

Subjects A stratified random sampling procedure was used to identify 249 first through third grade teachers from the population of primary grade teachers in the United States. The names were randomly selected from a list complied by Market Data Retrieval so that there were an equal number of teachers in grades 1, 2, and 3. This registry contained the names of over 1,600,000 elementary school teachers from over 72,000 public and private schools.

Of the 249 teachers identified, 68% (n = 169) agreed to participate in the study. Chi-square analyses revealed that there were no statistically significant differences between responders and nonresponders in terms of grade, type of school, and location of school (all ps > .09). No analysis was done for gender, as only 4 of the 249 teachers were male. Analyses of variance further indicated that there were no statistically significant differences in school size or annual expenditure for materials per pupil in the schools where the responders and nonresponders taught (both ps > .52). Consequently, responders did not differ from nonresponders on these demographic variables, providing verification that they were representative of the sample as a whole.

The 169 teachers that agreed to participate were distributed almost equally among the three grades. These teachers were overwhelmingly female, and 76% worked in a public school. Thirty-nine percent of the participants taught in a school in a suburban area, 33% in an urban area, and 27% in a rural area. Average school size was 410 students, but there was considerable variability across schools. Expenditures per pupil for instructional materials was $78.

The participating teachers averaged 15.2 years of teaching experience (Range = 1 to 40; SD = 10.2). The average class size was 19.3 (Range = 5 to 35; SD = 4.7), and approximately 70% of the children in the participating teachers' classes were White, 13% Black, 10% Hispanic, 3% Asian, and 3% Other. Teachers reported that 37% (Range = 0% to 100%; SD = 34%) of the children in their class received free or reduced cost lunch and 9% received special education services (SD = 11%). On average they reported that students spent 2 hours and 33 minutes writing during a typical week, but there was considerable variability in time spent writing (SD = 2 hours and 20 minutes). Finally, 53% of the teachers indicated that their highest degree was a Bachelor degree, 45% had a Masters degree, and 1% had a Doctoral degree.

> Handwriting is important because it influences both the reader and writer.

Discussion

Handwriting is important because it influences both the reader and writer (Graham & Harris, 2000). The reader forms impressions about the quality of ideas in a hand written paper based on the legibility of text, and illegibilities may make part or all of the text impossible to read. Handwriting can also interfere with specific aspects of writing such as content generation, especially for young children who are still mastering this skill, whereas, difficulties acquiring this skill may lead some beginning writers to avoid writing, resulting in arrested writing development (Berninger, 1999; Graham, 1999). Experimental studies further demonstrate that teaching this skill to primary grade children can have a positive impact on both their handwriting as well as their writing (Berninger et al., 1997; Graham, et al., 2000; Jones & Christensen, 1999). Despite the importance of handwriting to early writing development, there has been concern about if and how this skill is taught to young children (Graham & Weintraub, 1996; Leo, 2002).

The findings from the current study provide some welcome news for advocates of explicit and systematic handwriting instruction for young developing writers. Primary grade teachers in the current study, drawn randomly from public and private schools across the United States, indicated that they taught handwriting, with 80% of their school districts requiring the teaching of this skill and 90% of them indicating that they provided an average of 70 minutes of instruction per week. This corroborates the findings from an earlier study that most primary grade teachers in the United States teach handwriting (Graham et al., 2003). Furthermore, the average amount of time devoted to instruction was generally consistent with recommendations to devote 50 to 100 minutes of instructional time each week to handwriting (Graham & Miller, 1980).

> The average amount of time devoted to instruction was generally consistent with recommendations to devote 50 to 100 minutes of instructional time each week to handwriting.

The frequency with which a minority of the teachers taught handwriting in this and the prior Graham et al. (2003) investigation raises one reason for concern. In the previous study, 25% of teachers taught handwriting once a week or less (2% did not teach it at all), whereas in this study 10% of teachers taught handwriting just once a week and 10% did not teach it at all. Handwriting is a motor skill and like most motor skills it is best learned through spaced practice (Graham & Miller, 1980). Thus, teaching it once a week or less is not preferable to teaching it several times a week or daily.

Of course, the effectiveness of handwriting instruction is not just dependent on providing instruction, but on what happens when instruction is delivered. Another area for concern was the finding that only 12% of the participating teachers reported that they received adequate preparation to teach handwriting in their college education courses. Lack of either instructional knowledge or knowledge of handwriting development could weaken the quality of teachers' handwriting instruction. College education courses are not the sole repository of such knowledge, however, as teachers can obtain information and expertise through ongoing professional development as well as through the process of actually teaching handwriting. Unfortunately, we did not ask teachers about other sources where they may have learned about handwriting.

> Ninety percent of these teachers used one of the well known basal handwriting programs such as the Zaner-Bloser program.

Lack of formal preparation in college teacher education courses may be offset by teachers' use of commercial materials. Three out of every five teachers indicated that they used commercial materials for handwriting instruction. Ninety percent of these teachers used one of the well known basal handwriting programs such as the Zaner-Bloser program. Programs like this one provide both teaching materials and generally well designed teaching procedures (Sawyer, Graham & Harris, 1992). This provides no guarantee, though, that teachers use the materials as intended.

In any event, there were some reasons for optimism about the quality of handwriting instruction provided by teachers. First, when teaching students how to write letters, 60% or more of the teachers used the following effective practices (see Graham & Harris, 1989; 2002; Graham & Miller, 1980): modeled how to form the letter, students practiced the letter by tracing it and writing it from copy, praised students' for correct letter formation, and directed students to correct malformed letters as well as identify their best formed letters. Most teachers also taught students proper pencil grip and paper position, including how left-handers should position their paper. Slightly more than one-half of the teachers displayed examples of students' best handwriting, whereas a slightly greater percentage of teachers used specific procedures to promote handwriting fluency. Just as importantly, teachers commonly made specific

Best Practices for Handwriting Instruction

adaptations/modifications for students with poorer handwriting, including extra encouragement, one-on-one instruction, extra time to complete written assignments, and additional conferences with students about their handwriting.

These positive features of handwriting instruction are diminished somewhat by many teachers not using other proven methods and a minority of teachers using questionable procedures. For example, effective instructional practices for teaching letter formation, such as writing the letter from memory or comparing/contrasting how similar letters are formed (Graham & Miller, 1980) were applied by less than one half of the teachers. On the other hand, questionable practices, such as verbalizing the steps for forming a letter while writing it or requiring students to use a specific writing instrument (see Graham, 1992), were employed by almost a third or more of the teachers. Likewise, other than showing left-handers how to position their paper, other frequently recommended provisions (see Graham & Miller, 1980) for these students were applied by a relatively small percentage of teachers (one-third or less).

Another possible concern is that teachers' assessment of handwriting mostly involves informal techniques that rely heavily on subjective judgments. The fact that teachers' judgments about which letters are most difficult for primary grade students did not provide a good match to the letters identified as difficult via the systematic study of young children's writing (see Graham et al., 2001), which raises concerns about the accuracy of the participating teachers' evaluations.

It is interesting to note that many teachers had misconceptions about handwriting development (which also raises questions about the accuracy of their observations and knowledge about handwriting). Most of the research evidence shows that girls have better handwriting than boys and that there is no significant difference in the handwriting legibility and fluency of left handed and right handed students (Graham & Weintraub, 1996). Nevertheless, only about one-half of the participating teachers thought that girls had better handwriting, whereas slightly more than one-half of the teachers indicated that left handed children had better handwriting. Another example of teachers' misconceptions involved the development of a personal style of handwriting. Slightly more than 40% of the teachers thought that students' handwriting should not deviate from the taught style. This belief is at odds with what is currently known. It is almost a universal phenomenon for students to modify the script that they are taught, in part to increase how quickly they can write specific letters (Graham & Weintraub, 1996).

We also examined the sequential role of three factors in predicting handwriting achievement (as assessed by teachers' judgments about the legibility and fluency of their students' handwriting). We reasoned that handwriting achievement is influenced by the amount of time devoted to handwriting instruction, which in turn is influenced by teachers' desire to provide handwriting instruction, and that such attitudes are shaped by teachers' competence (as measured by the quality of teachers' handwriting and the amount of formal preparation on how to teach handwriting provided in teacher education courses). To test this line of reasoning, we examined if the prediction of handwriting achievement was improved by adding assessments of teacher attitude to our measures of teacher competence, and by considering if this prediction was further improved by adding time spent teaching handwriting to the formula. We tested this model for both teachers' judgments about students' legibility and handwriting fluency. For the most part, the data was consistent with the proposed model. For handwriting fluency, measures of teacher competence predicted student performance and prediction was enhanced by sequentially adding measures of attitudes toward teaching and instructional time to the formula. The same pattern was found for handwriting legibility, except that the addition of instructional time to the formula did not improve prediction of student performance. These findings highlight the possible importance of teachers' competence and attitudes towards the teaching of handwriting, but must be viewed cautiously, as measures of student performance, instructional time, and teachers' competence were reported and not actually measured.

> Handwriting is being taught by the overwhelming majority of primary grade teachers in the United States....recommended instructional procedures are applied unevenly.

Finally, we assumed that teachers would be aware of elements of their teaching and would be able to relate this knowledge to questions about their instructional practices. While there is evidence that professionals, including teachers, can describe what they do when questioned (e.g., Diaper, 1989), the findings from the study need to be supplemented by additional research where teachers' instructional practices in handwriting are observed and not just reported.

In summary, handwriting is being taught by the overwhelming majority of primary grade teachers in the United States. Nevertheless, only a small percentage of teachers received adequate preparation on how to teach handwriting in their college education courses, and teachers' responses to questions about their handwriting program suggests that recommended instructional procedures are applied unevenly.

References

Berninger, V. (1999). Coordinating transcription and text generation in working memory during composing: Automatic and constructive processes. *Learning Disability Quarterly, 22,* 99–112.

Berninger, V., Mizokawa, D., & Bragg, R. (1991). Theory-based diagnosis and remediation of writing disabilities. *Journal of School Psychology, 29,* 57–79.

Berninger, V., Vaughn, K., Abbott, R., Abbott, S., Rogan, L., Brooks, A., Reed, E., & Graham, S. (1997). Treatment of handwriting problems in beginning writers: Transfer from handwriting to composition. *Journal of Educational Psychology, 89,* 652–666.

Bolte, A., & Hansta-Bletz, L. (1991). A longitudinal study of the structure of handwriting. *Perceptual and Motor Skills, 72,* 983–994.

Brann, B., & Hattie, J. (1995). Spelling instruction in primary schools. *New Zealand Journal of Educational Studies, 30,* 39–49.

Diaper, D. (1989). Knowledge elicitation: Principles, techniques, and application. New York: Wiley.

Graham, S. (1990). The role of production factors in learning disabled students' compositions. *Journal of Educational Psychology, 82,* 781–791.

Graham, S. (1992). Issues in handwriting instruction. *Focus on Exceptional Children, 25,* 1–14.

Graham, S. (1999). Handwriting and spelling instruction for students with learning disabilities: A review. *Learning Disability Quarterly, 22,* 78–98.

Graham, S. (2006). Writing. In P. Alexander & P. Winne (Eds.), *Handbook of Educational Psychology* (pp. 457–478). Mahwah, NJ: Erlbaum.

Graham, S., Berninger, V., Abbott, R., Abbott, S., & Whitaker, D. (1997). The role of mechanics in composing of elementary school students: A new methodological approach. *Journal of Educational Psychology, 89,* 170–182.

Graham, S., Berninger, V., Weintraub, N., & Schafer, W. (1998). Development of handwriting speed and legibility. *Journal of Educational Research, 92,* 42–51.

Graham, S., & Harris, K. (2000). The role of self-regulation and transcription skills in writing and writing development. *Educational Psychologist, 35,* 3–12.

Graham, S., & Harris, K. R. (2002). Prevention and intervention for struggling writers. In M. Shinn, G. Stoner, & H. Walker (Eds.), *Interventions for academic and behavior problems II: Preventive and remedial approaches* (pp. 589–610). Bethesda, MD: National Association of School Psychologists.

Graham, S., Harris, K.R., & Fink, B. (2000). Is handwriting causally related to learning to write? Treatment of handwriting problems in beginning writers. *Journal of Educational Psychology, 92,* 620–633.

Graham, S., Harris, K.R., MacArthur, C., & Fink-Chorzempa, B. (2003). Primary grade teachers' instructional adaptations for weaker writers: A national survey. *Journal of Educational Psychology, 95,* 279–293.

Graham, S., & Miller, L. (1980). Handwriting research and practice: A unified approach. *Focus on Exceptional Children, 13,* 1–16.

Graham, S., & Weintruab, N. (1996). A review of handwriting research: Progress and prospects from 1980 to 1994. *Educational Psychology Review, 8,* 7–87.

Graham, S., Weintruab, N., & Berninger, V. (2001). Which manuscript letters do primary grade children write legibly. *Journal of Educational Psychology, 93,* 488–497.

Jones, D., & Christensen, C. (1999). The relationship between automaticity in handwriting and students' ability to generate written text. *Journal of Educational Psychology, 91,* 44–49.

Leo, P. (2002, April 13). Tracing the roots of illegible handwriting. *Pittsburgh Post-Gazette.*

Marshall, J., & Powers, J. (1969). Writing neatness, composition errors, and essay grades. *Journal of Educational Measurement, 6,* 97–101.

McCutchen, D. (1995). Cognitive processes in children's writing: Developmental and individual differences. *Issues in Education: Contributions from Educational Psychology, 1,* 123–160.

Mojet, J. (1991). Characteristics of the developing handwriting skill in elementary education. In J. Wann, A. Wing, N. Sovik (Eds.), *Development of graphic skills: Research, perspectives and educational implications* (pp. 53–75). London: Academic Press.

Rubin, N., & Henderson, S. (1982). Two sides of the same coin: Variation in teaching methods and failure to learn to write. *Special Education: Forward Trends, 9,* 17–24.

Scardamalia, M., Bereiter, C., & Goleman, H. (1982). The role of production factors in writing ability. In M. Nystrand (Ed.), *What writers know: The language, process, and structure of written discourse* (pp. 173–210). New York: Academic Press.

Traynelis-Yurek, E., & Strong, M. (1999). Spelling practices in school districts and regions across the United States and state spelling standards. *Reading Horizons, 39,* 279–294.

Wann, J., & Kardiramanathan, M. (1991). Variability in children's handwriting: Computer diagnosis of writing difficulties. In J. Wann, A. Wing, N. Sovik (Eds.), *Development of graphic skills: Research, perspectives and educational implications* (pp. 223–236). London: Academic Press.

Weintraub, N., & Graham, S. (1998). Writing legibly and quickly: A study of children's ability to adjust their handwriting to meet common classroom demands. *Learning Disability Quarterly, 13,* 146–152.

Willingham, D. (1998). A neuropsychological theory of motor skill learning. *Psychological Review, 105,* 558–584.

Excerpts from

Handwriting Instruction in Elementary Schools

Asha V. Asher

The American Journal of Occupational Therapy, Pages 461–471, Vol. 60 (2006),
©American Occupational Therapy Association.

Method

A survey of the process by which handwriting was taught to students from kindergarten through grade 6 was carried out by the two occupational therapists working in the district. I constructed an open-ended questionnaire, which was a format that was chosen to capture the full extent of the teachers' opinions. The suburban school district had approximately 2,900 students from kindergarten through grade 6 when the project was undertaken.

The factors incorporated in the survey evolved from the literature on handwriting, including kinds of paper used, letter formations and programs, and practice time. The survey differentiated between the ages when students were expected to write letters and when the students were taught how to form the letters using a specific directionality, because some teachers expected students to write letters before formal instruction in letter formation. Based on progression of visual-motor control (Beery, 1997), occupational therapists often recommend that letters with straight lines are taught first, followed by those with curves, and finally letters with oblique lines. However, some teachers use a different order to introduce letters; hence, a question was included about the order in which letters were introduced to the students. The questionnaire was pilot-tested with two teachers, and three different versions of the questionnaire were used on their advice. The first version pertained to teaching of manuscript letters and was distributed to teachers of kindergarten through grade 2. The second version referred to the teaching of cursive script, and it was distributed to teachers of third and fourth grades. The third version was prepared for teachers of fifth and sixth grades and queried the need to review handwriting. Each classroom teacher and the teachers providing special education and intervention services, from kindergarten through grade 6, were asked to complete the appropriate version of the survey. The number of years of teaching experience of the respondents was between 2 and 30 years. The survey was distributed during the month of October and responses were retrieved 1 week later.

Implications for Handwriting Instruction

Age When Handwriting and Correct Letter Formation Are Taught

Teachers differed in their beliefs regarding age for introducing handwriting instruction. Consider a child whose kindergarten teacher has the philosophy that writing should be taught in the first grade. If that child transitions to a first grade teacher whose philosophy dictates that handwriting should be taught in kindergarten, the child will reach second grade having received no formal instruction on how to form individual letters. The child would then use his or her resources to form recognizable letters but may pick up inefficient letter formations.

In practice, I have found that many children referred for occupational therapy use very unusual letter formations—for example, when the letter *a* is made by two or more complete clockwise circles; or when a lower-case *r*, scripted from the baseline up, cannot be differentiated from an incomplete letter *c*—which reduces speed of writing as well as legibility. Sheffield (1996) states that many cases of apparent dysgraphia are the result of inadequate teaching. She found that teaching students of grades 1, 2, and 3 the correct letter formations, and giving them adequate handwriting practice over 1 school year, resulted in a significant decrease in the number of students having difficulty with written language. Thus, it can be inferred that students need consistent instruction on how to form the individual letters, and the instruction should be coordinated with the higher grades.

> **Many cases of apparent dysgraphia are the result of inadequate teaching.**

Different Kinds of Paper Used

Of the many different kinds of paper used in the school district, the commercial program used to teach handwriting dictated some choices. Letters are formed by flexion extension strokes of the thumb, index, and middle finger, with wrist movements for the rounded and horizontal strokes. This is a learned motor skill. The excursion made by the movement components has to change when letters have to fit between differently spaced lines, or when the placement of the letter on the line changes: that is, the letter *a* is written on top of the line when writing on a single line; is touching the top and bottom lines when writing between two lines; and is between the middle and the bottom lines when using triple-lined paper. If students are provided with all three types of paper when writing is introduced, they have to adjust to three differing sets of parameters, requiring more information-processing activities. For some students, this effort may exceed the optimal challenge point (Guadagnoli & Lee, 2004) and therefore skilled behavior might potentially take longer to establish. Thus in the initial phase of handwriting instruction, teachers should consider keeping task demands consistent by minimizing the variations of paper. Once motor patterns are developed, variable practice using different kinds of paper is appropriate. It will increase the challenge level of the task, facilitating retention of performance. Although some researchers have suggested the use of different kinds of paper, Graham (1992) recommended that students should be restricted to paper with wide lines during initial handwriting instruction. Information from motor learning supports Graham's recommendation because it essentially limits the number of variables provided until the student develops some control of letter formations.

Programs Used for Writing Instruction

The different programs reported in this survey used varying formations to form some of the letters. The letter *W*, for example, was formed with continuous strokes from the left to the right in a "down, up, down, up" sequence or by repeated downward strokes changing the direction of the oblique line; the letter *d* was formed by extending the bottom of the letter *c* with a continuous vertical stroke from the bottom, up, and down again, or by starting from the top down, with a counter-clockwise loop to close the letter. A student may get differing instructions if receiving help from different teachers (e.g., special educators, intervention specialists) within the same grade level, and from parents at home, or when moving through different grades. For a child struggling with handwriting, conflicting instructions add to the motor planning challenges. Use of the different programs within one school is also frustrating to the staff, including special educators and occupational therapists who move between classes.

> Teachers should consider keeping task demands consistent by minimizing the variations of paper.

One teacher reports, "As an intervention specialist, I try to reinforce what's done in the classroom—but the classrooms teach differently, so this is difficult."

Research supporting the superiority of a particular program over another is limited. However, using one consistent program within a school district would ensure that the staff uses uniform instructions, helping students master writing more easily. Consistency of instruction together with adequate practice during acquisition of handwriting would help to establish the motor skills used for communication.

Some commercial programs use the concepts suggested by motor learning theory. Using consistent paper, the programs require several repetitions of the introduced letter, providing verbal directions to guide the directionality (i.e., the program provides blocked practice in the acquisition phase). As each new letter is introduced, and mastered, it is practiced as part of a word using the previously mastered letters. This helps to retain the previously learned letter formations. It also provides an optimal challenge by ensuring random practice conditions and including language concepts. As the students increase their repertoire of letters, the challenge point is raised by the recall of a larger number of letters for more efficient retention of learning.

Order of Introducing the Letters

The order in which each teacher introduced letters was determined by his or her particular philosophy, whether visual-motor control or language development. Students should be developmentally ready to form the basic lines (vertical, horizontal, circular, and oblique) that constitute manuscript letters by the time they enter school at age 5 (Beery, 1997). It can be deduced that if students have had adequate experiences using paper and pencil and have developed age-appropriate visual-motor integration skills, then the order of introduction of letters should not have an impact on success with handwriting. Research confirms that kindergarten students who were able to copy the first 9 forms on the Beery-Buktenica test of Visual Motor Integration (VMI) performed better on a copying task than those kindergartners who did not copy them (Daly, Kelley, & Krauss, 2003).

> Using one consistent program within a school district would ensure that the staff uses uniform instructions, helping students master writing more easily.

Practice Schedule Used

Students need to practice the motor production of letters before they have this skill available at an automatic level to convey thought. Although formal guidelines regarding the amount of practice per week have not been established, it appears that some of the teachers in this district provide less than the typical handwriting instruction of 20 to 60 min per week (Rubin & Henderson, 1982; Zaner-Bloser, 1993).

Students whose handwriting difficulties stem from poor motor memory do not retain a kinesthetic pattern for forming letters. Their writing may appear legible, but observation reveals that one particular letter may be formed in different ways; for example, the letter *a* may be formed from the top in a clockwise direction, or anti-clockwise, or from the baseline up in either direction, or in a fragmentary fashion. These students then must compare visually to determine the correctness of the letter-forms, which slows down their writing. To address the difficulties resulting from poor motor memory, Levine (1987) advocated that adequate practice with consistent repetition of efficient letter formations be provided in the classroom within a structured handwriting program. Close adult supervision is needed to ensure that students are practicing correctly, because using a consistent letter formation helps to strengthen the kinesthetic memory of that letter formation. Practice may occur under blocked and constant conditions in the introductory phase of handwriting (Baker, 1999; Poole, 1991). When a relatively stable movement representation is developed, use of random and variable practice conditions will help retention of the motor skills. Mastery of the motor skills involved in writing can then be used for effective communication.

> **Students need to practice the motor production of letters before they have this skill available at an automatic level to convey thought.**

Conclusion

The study found that educators in this school district use a variety of methods and tools to teach manuscript, with no continuity of instruction between the grade levels. Although cursive was introduced uniformly in grade 3, with some agreement in the program used, there was variation in the order of introduction of letters, paper used, and practice time provided. These instructional methods could potentially limit the effectiveness of handwriting instruction, which was confirmed by the teachers of grades 5 and 6. They reported that all students had *not* developed fluent handwriting as a tool of expression, because of which instructional time was used to review handwriting again. These consequences suggest the need for structuring handwriting instruction, which should be aligned from kindergarten through the subsequent grade levels. The students would then augment the competencies developed in the earlier grades to refine the motor skill of writing. As teachers accommodate the required increases in content areas, they need clear guidelines on effective methods to teach handwriting as a tool of written expression. School-based therapists can interpret information from the motor learning theory identified in this article, pertaining to consistency of instruction and practice, to help educators develop these guidelines.

Teachers impart initial handwriting instruction, but students with problems in handwriting are referred to occupational therapy for remediation. As school-based occupational therapists struggle to manage the myriad referrals in school (Holtzinger & Hight, 2005), they need to reflect on the initial instruction of handwriting imparted by educators, in addition to therapeutic needs identified. By contributing to the effectiveness of the initial handwriting instruction, occupational therapists can ensure that all students receive proper instruction. Then, only those students who have genuine deficits best addressed by occupational therapy would be referred for remediation, allowing therapists to better manage their caseloads. Ensuring appropriate referrals would be ethically correct and reflect professional integrity. Occupational therapists addressing handwriting instruction should align their instructional programs to those used in the student's classroom and avoid adding variables to handwriting instruction.

> Occupational therapists addressing handwriting instruction should align their instructional programs to those used in the student's classroom and avoid adding variables to handwriting instruction.

The results of the survey spurred this school district to review its handwriting instruction and to use one consistent program with specific expectations from kindergarten to the sixth grade. The instructional decision was based on philosophical beliefs and research-based evidence from the fields of both education and occupational therapy. The district team first outlined the philosophical beliefs regarding handwriting, after which they drew up a curriculum with specific objectives for each grade level as part of the language arts curriculum. Only then did they evaluate the commercial programs available to select one program that met their needs. Additional factors considered included cost of materials and availability of related programs, such as writing readiness and spelling programs. This program has been used for 5 years now. Occupational therapy referrals for students with only handwriting difficulties (i.e., students not served on Individual Education Programs) were not tracked in this district; therefore, data regarding change in the number of students served is not available. However, I have noted a shift in the quality of the referrals. Rather than the students seen previously who needed handwriting instruction, the current referrals predominantly concern students with deficits in motor or visual-perceptual function, which are appropriately remediated with occupational therapy.

In describing management of handwriting instruction, Benbow (1995) clarified that some children learn to write well regardless of the methods used to teach writing. Others are unable to learn the skill regardless of the interventions used. However, most children fall between these two extremes and readily benefit from good teaching strategies. Occupational therapists have valuable information to share that will assist educators in devising instructional strategies that help these in-between students develop an efficient mode of written communication.

References

Baker, B. (1999, June). Principles of motor learning for school-based occupational therapy practitioners. *School System Special Interest Section Quarterly, 6*, 1–4.

Beery, K.E. (1997). *The Beery Buktenica developmental test of visual-motor integration.* New Jersey: Modern Curriculum Press.

Benbow, M.D. (1999). *Loops and other groups: A kinesthetic writing system.* San Antonio, TX: Psychological Corporation.

Daly, C.J., Kelley, G.T., & Krauss, A. (2003). Relationship between visual-motor integration and handwriting skills of children in kindergarten: A modified replication study. *American Journal of Occupational Therapy, 57*, 459–462.

Graham, S. (1992). Issues in handwriting instruction. *Focus on Exceptional Children, 25*(2), 1–13.

Guadagnoli, M.A., & Lee, T.D. (2004). Challenge point: A framework for conceptualizing the effects of various practice conditions in motor learning. *Journal of Motor Behavior, 36*(2), 212–224.

Holtzinger, L.J., & Hight, V.P. (2005, Jan. 10). How satisfied are OTs in the schools? [Electronic version]. *Advance for Occupational Therapists, 21*(1), 35–41. Retrieved April 25, 2005, from http://occupational-therapy.advanceweb.com

Levine, M.D. (1987). *Developmental variation and learning disorders.* Cambridge, MA: Educators Publishing Co.

Poole, J.L. (1991). Application of motor principles in occupational therapy. *American Journal of Occupational Therapy, 45*, 531–537.

Rubin, N., & Henderson, S.E. (1982). Two sides of the same coin: Variation in teaching methods and failure to learn to write. *Special Education: Forward Trends, 9*, 17–24.

Sheffield, B. (1996). Handwriting: A neglected cornerstone of literacy. *Annals of Dyslexia, 46*, 21–35.

Zaner-Bloser Educational Publishers. (1993). *The Zaner-Bloser handwriting survey: Preliminary tabulations.* Columbus, OH: Author.

Extra Handwriting Instruction: Prevent Writing Difficulties Right from the Start

Steve Graham, Karen R. Harris, Barbara Fink

TEACHING Exceptional Children, Pages 88–91, Vol. 33, No. 2, ©2000 Council for Exceptional Children, Inc.

Place a check next to each item that describes a feature of instruction in your classroom. The completed checklist can assist you in maintaining and improving the effectiveness of your current handwriting program by summarizing what you currently do as well as pinpointing areas that may need additional attention.

CHECKLIST FOR EVALUATING THE QUALITY OF HANDWRITING INSTRUCTION

I Teach Children How to Write Each Letter by

__ Showing them how to form it.

__ Discussing how it is similar and different from other letters.

__ Using visual cues, like numbered arrows, as a guide to letter formation.

__ Providing practice tracing, copying, and writing the letter.

__ Keeping instructional sessions short, with frequent opportunities for practice and review.

__ Asking children to identify their best formed letter(s).

__ Encouraging them to rewrite or correct poorly formed letters.

__ Monitoring handwriting practice to ensure that letters are formed correctly.

__ Giving corrective feedback as needed.

I Help Children Become More Fluent Handwriters by

__ Providing plenty of opportunities to write.

__ Eliminating interfering habits that reduce handwriting fluency.

__ Having them copy short passages with the goal of writing them a little faster each time.

I Promote Handwriting Development by

__ Making sure that each child develops an appropriate and comfortable pencil grip.

__ Encouraging children to sit in an upright position, leaning slightly forward, when writing.

__ Showing them how to position their paper when writing.

__ Teaching children to name and identify the letters of the alphabet.

__ Teaching them how to write both upper- and capital letters.

___ Devoting 75 to 100 minutes per week to handwriting instruction.

___ Providing plenty of opportunities for children to use different writing instruments and paper.

___ Asking children to establish goals for improving specific aspects of their handwriting.

___ Implementing appropriate procedures for left-handers (e.g., proper placement of the paper).

___ Monitoring students' handwriting, paying special attention to their needs in letter formation, size, spacing alignment, and line quality.

___ Dramatizing progress in handwriting through charts, graphs, praise, or posting neat papers.

___ Helping children develop a positive attitude about their handwriting.

I Make Sure That I

___ Encourage students to make final drafts of papers neat and legible.

___ Maintain my belief that I can teach all children how to write fluently and legibly.

___ Set high but realistic expectations for each child's handwriting performance.

___ Keep a balanced perspective on the role of handwriting in learning to write.

I Assist Students Who Experience Difficulty by

___ Organizing my class so that I can provide additional handwriting help to those who need it.

___ Identifying and addressing problems that may impede a child's success in handwriting.

___ Talking with parents and soliciting advice on how to improve their child's handwriting.

___ Coordinating my handwriting instruction with the efforts of other professionals.

___ Placing special emphasis on teaching difficult letters (i.e., *a, j, k, n, q, u, z* and reversals).

Chapter 7

Effective Handwriting Interventions

"Sorry about the misunderstanding. Sometimes my G's look like S's."

Reprinted with special permission of CartoonStock.

Introduction

Students can experience difficulty with handwriting for many reasons. The most common reason is that too little class time has been devoted to handwriting instruction and practice. Before concluding that a student has a special need in the area of handwriting, it is important for teachers to make sure that ample time has been given to master the skill. In a response to intervention model (RTI), tier 1 should consist of regular, high-quality handwriting instruction and practice as described in the earlier chapters of this book.

Students who need more help with handwriting may exhibit the following symptoms: slow, labored writing; reversals; misshapen letters; difficulty sequencing and arranging words on paper; an inability to write for a sustained period of time. Teachers can aid progress for these students by analyzing their needs and providing targeted instruction and practice individually or in small groups.

Tier 2 interventions may focus on corrective strategies like the ones described below. Many additional strategies and suggestions are given throughout *Zaner-Bloser Handwriting* teacher editions. In planning such instruction, it is helpful to determine through observation and testing whether students learn best when information is presented in a visual, auditory, or kinesthetic/tactile mode.

Visual learners will benefit from studying letter shapes and learning how to follow models with directional arrows. Lessons for auditory learners may include the Zaner-Bloser stroke descriptions, which provide clear and consistent directions for forming letters. Kinesthetic/tactile learners will appreciate sandpaper letters to trace, writing in the air, or walking on giant letters formed with masking tape on the floor.

Sometimes, conditions such as attention deficit disorder, dyslexia, dysgraphia, and poor motor control can prevent a student's success in handwriting. Students with special needs like these may benefit from individualized (tier 3) interventions delivered by specialists outside the classroom. Even in cases like these, however, the classroom teacher can provide invaluable support through clear, consistent lessons that show an awareness of individual needs. Follow these suggestions to help all students succeed with handwriting.

Help with directionality and letter reversals. Make arrows on student papers to emphasize left to right progression. Also try coloring the entire left edge of the writing paper green as a reminder to start at the left. Teach commonly reversed letters, like **b** and **d**, on different days. Emphasize the individual strokes in each letter.

Provide supportive materials. Incorporate fine-motor skill practice into your classroom routine for younger students. For students who are having trouble with guidelines, use paper with wide rulings. Show students how to hold the pencil between the first and second fingers as an acceptable, alternate pencil grip.

Don't leave out left-handed students. Notice lefties in your classroom, and make sure they know how to position their papers and hold their pencils for comfortable, legible writing.

Emphasize legibility, not perfection. Allow older students to use manuscript writing if it is easier for them. Surround students with models of acceptable handwriting, and set a good example when you write on the board and on student papers.

The articles in this chapter provide a full spectrum of practical suggestions for helping students with handwriting. Steve Graham and Karen Harris explain that extra handwriting instruction can prevent writing difficulties. Jane Case-Smith and colleagues show how a coteaching model using occupational therapists and teachers significantly improved first-graders' handwriting legibility and speed, as well as their overall writing fluency. Lisa Kurtz provides solutions for common handwriting problems, and Kama Einhorn gives tips for classroom teachers. Finally, Clinton Hackney and William Hendricks explain how educators can help an often-overlooked population.

ZANER-BLOSER
CORRECTIVE STRATEGIES

green dot ——— U ——— red dot	⎯⎯ m ⎯ not ⎯ m ⎯
Use a green dot to show where a letter begins. A red dot can help students' aim and provide an ending point.	Alert students when they must retrace smoothly to avoid loops. Practice with finger paint, or by driving a toy car in the shape of the letter.
⎯⎯⎯ not ⎯⎯⎯	⎯ d ⎯ not ⎯ d ⎯
Messy joining strokes cause illegible cursive writing. Highlight joinings on student papers. Practice both common (**th**) and tricky (**ws**) pairs.	When circles and ovals are open, letters are hard to read. Don't let the air out of "balloon" letters! Practice smooth, closed circles in shaving cream or with pipe cleaners.

Excerpts from

Improving the Writing Performance of Young Struggling Writers

Steve Graham and Karen R. Harris

The Journal of Special Education, Pages 24–26, Vol. 39,
No. I (Spring 2005), ©SAGE Publications.

Interventions for Handwriting and Spelling

Although there is considerable research on teaching handwriting and spelling to struggling writers and children with learning problems (see Graham, 1999), little is known about the impact of such instruction on these students' overall writing development (Graham & Harris, 2000). The survey studies reviewed previously (Graham et al., 2003; Graham et al., 2004a, 2004b) revealed that primary-grade teachers believe that directly teaching these skills to developing writers is important and that, at least in terms of handwriting, failure to master basic transcription skills can have a negative impact on children's writing.

Theoretically, handwriting or spelling difficulties may hamper children's writing in several different ways (Graham, 1990; Scardamalia & Bereiter, 1986). First, having to consciously attend to transcription skills when writing may tax a child's processing memory (see Berninger, 1999), interfering with other writing processes, such as generating content or planning. For example, having to switch attention during writing to mechanical demands, such as having to think about how to spell a particular word, may lead the child to forget plans or ideas already held in working memory, influencing writing output. Simultaneously allocating attention to spelling words while planning the next unit of text during writing may also affect the coherence and complexity of content integration, influencing the overall quality of writing. It is further possible that there are fewer opportunities to make expressions more precisely fit intentions at the point of translation, if attention is occupied with spelling, affecting the process of translating ideas or words into sentences.

> We designed two experiments in which young struggling writers received extra instruction in handwriting or spelling.

To determine if difficulties with transcription skills hamper children's writing performance, we designed two experiments in which young struggling writers received extra instruction in handwriting or spelling (Graham et al., 2000; Graham, Harris, & Fink-Chorzempa, 2002). If transcription difficulties interfere with writing as theory suggests, then students who receive extra handwriting or spelling instruction should not only become better at these skills than control students (who receive instruction in phonological awareness or mathematics, respectively); there should also be corresponding improvements in their writing output, writing quality, and sentence construction skills. For the study involving extra spelling instruction (Graham, Harris, & Fink-Chorzempa, 2002), we further looked for a corresponding improvement in two important reading skills: word attack and word recognition. This was based on Ehri's (1989) proposal that spelling contributes to reading development by shaping children's phonemic awareness, strengthening their grasp of the alphabetic principle, and making sight words easier to remember.

In addition to examining the theoretical links between text transcription skills and children's writing performance (and reading in the spelling study), these two experiments addressed an important practical issue. How can we prevent writing difficulties? Although work by Englert and her colleagues (Englert et al., 1995) demonstrated that a well-designed literacy program can have a positive impact on the writing performance of primary-grade children who experience learning difficulties, there is very little data on the skills or aspects of instruction that need to be emphasized to prevent writing problems. Several previous studies have shown that instruction in handwriting (Berninger et al., 1997; Jones & Christensen, 1999) and spelling (Berninger et al., 1998) can facilitate first and second graders' writing development. The finding that there were transfer effects from handwriting and spelling to writing in these investigations suggests that supplementary instruction in either of these skills during the primary grades may be an important element in prevention efforts.

> **All children whose handwriting fluency was in the bottom quartile of their class and who were also identified by their teacher as having a handwriting problem were included in the study.**

Extra Handwriting Instruction

We screened 310 first-grade children in 12 classrooms in four urban schools to identify students at risk for handwriting problems. In each class, students copied a short sentence as many times as they could in a

90-second period. All children whose handwriting fluency (number of letters correctly written) was in the bottom quartile of their class and who were also identified by their teacher as having a handwriting problem were included in the study. These 38 children were randomly assigned to an experimental (extra handwriting instruction) or control (phonological awareness instruction) condition. The children were mostly Black (71%), and 48% of them received a free or reduced-rate lunch. These distributions were consistent with those of the student body of the participating schools. Fourteen (37%) of the students had a disability (most commonly speech and language difficulties) and an additional 18 students (47%) received reading recovery instruction. Furthermore, all of the participants, according to their teachers, were experiencing difficulties learning to write, and the results of a norm-referenced standardized writing test were consistent with the teachers' evaluation.

The handwriting treatment was designed to teach children how to write lowercase manuscript letters accurately and fluently.

Students in both conditions were individually instructed by graduate students majoring in education. Each instructor taught students from both conditions to control for possible teacher effects. The instructor met with each student three times a week (15 minutes each time) for 9 weeks.

The handwriting treatment was designed to teach children how to write lowercase manuscript letters accurately and fluently. This was accomplished through four instructional activities that were included in every lesson. Each lesson began with a warm-up activity (Activity 1) designed to teach students to name each letter of the alphabet, match letter names with their corresponding symbols, and identify where each letter in the alphabet was placed. This was followed by instruction and practice in writing individual letters (Activity 2). Every three lessons (i.e., every unit), a new set of letters was introduced. Letters that were formed using similar strokes were grouped together for instruction (e.g., *l, i, t* or *a, e, o*) and sequenced so that letter sets that were easier to learn and occurred more frequently in children's reading material were taught first. Letter instruction involved modeling how to form each of the letters in the set and discussing how they were formed, followed by practice tracing, copying, and writing each letter, with the student circling his or her best formed letters. The only major difference across the three lessons was that students practiced writing the letters in words after the first lesson.

In these same three lessons, students copied a sentence (Activity 3) that contained multiple instances of the letters being taught in that unit (e.g., "Little kids like to get letters" for the letters *l, i, t*). During the first of the three lessons, students copied the sentence, quickly and without making mistakes, for a period of 3 minutes. They then recorded their performance on a graph. During the next two lessons they were directed to do the same thing but to write a little faster. Again their performance was graphed and the teacher drew a big star on their graph whenever they met the goal for writing faster. During the fourth activity, students were taught how to write one letter from the unit in an unusual way (e.g., as long and tall) or use it as part of a picture (e.g., turning the letter *i* into a picture of a butterfly).

> **Handwriting-instructed students outperformed their counterparts in the control condition on measures assessing not only handwriting but writing skills as well.**

Handwriting-instructed students outperformed their counterparts in the control condition on measures assessing not only handwriting but writing skills as well. Immediately following instruction, handwriting-instructed students were more accurate in naming (effect size = 0.86) and writing the letters of the alphabet (effect size = 0.94), and they were also able to produce the letters of the alphabet (effect size = 1.39) and copy connected text more fluently (effect size = 1.49). With the exception of copying text more fluently, these handwriting gains were maintained 6 months later (all effect

> **These handwriting gains were maintained 6 months later.**

sizes > 0.65). Even more significantly, extra handwriting instruction resulted in immediate as well as more long-term improvements in students' writing. In comparison with control students, handwriting-instructed students were more skilled at constructing sentences immediately following instruction (effect size = 0.76) and 6 months later (effect size = 0.70). Handwriting instruction also had a positive impact on writing output (effect size = 1.21), as handwriting-instructed students produced more writing content under timed conditions than their control counterparts did when writing a story (this measure was not administered at maintenance). Consequently, the mastery of handwriting skills not only appears to facilitate the initial process of learning to write, as demonstrated by the findings from this and previous studies (Berninger et al., 1997; Jones & Christensen, 1999), but may also affect the outcomes of the learning process over time, at least up to a period of 6 months.

References

Berninger, V. (1999). Coordinating transcription and text generation in working memory during composing: Automatic and constructive processes. *Learning Disability Quarterly, 22,* 99–112.

Berninger, V., Vaughan, K., Abbott, R., Abbott, S., Rogan, L., Brooks, A., et al. (1997). Treatment of handwriting problems in beginning writers: Transfer from handwriting to composition. *Journal of Educational Psychology, 89,* 652–666.

Berninger, V., Vaughan, K., Abbott, R., Brooks, A., Abbott, S., Rogan, L., et al. (1998). Early intervention for spelling problems: Teaching functional spelling units of varying size with a multiple-connections framework. *Journal of Educational Psychology, 90,* 587–605.

Ehri, L. (1989). The development of spelling knowledge and its role in reading acquisition and reading disabilities. *Journal of Learning Disabilities, 22,* 356–365.

Englert, C., Garmon, A., Mariage, T., Rozendal, M., Tarrant, K., Urba, J. (1995). The early literacy project: Connecting across the literacy curriculum. *Learning Disability Quarterly, 18,* 253–275.

Graham, S. (1990). The role of text production factors in learning disabled students' compositions. *Journal of Educational Psychology, 82,* 781–791.

Graham, S. (1999). Handwriting and spelling instruction for students with learning disabilities: A review. *Learning Disability Quarterly, 22,* 78–98.

Graham, S., & Harris, K. R. (2000). The role of self-regulation and transcription skills in writing and writing development. *Educational Psychologist, 35,* 3–12.

Graham, S., Harris, K.R., & Fink-Chorzempa, B. (2000). Is handwriting causally related to learning to write?: Treatment of handwriting problems in beginning writers. *Journal of Educational Psychology, 92,* 620–633.

Graham, S., Harris, K.R., & Fink-Chorzempa, B. (2002). Contributions of spelling instruction to the spelling, writing, and reading of poor spellers. *Journal of Educational Psychology, 94,* 669–686.

Graham, S., Harris, K. R., Fink-Chorzempa, B., Saddler, B., Moran, S., Adkins, M., & Mason, L. (2004). *A national survey of the handwriting practices of primary grade teachers.* Unpublished raw data.

Graham, S., Harris, K. R., MacArthur, C., & Fink-Chorzempa, B. (2003). Primary grade teachers' instructional adaptations for weaker writers: A national survey. *Journal of Educational Psychology, 95,* 279–293.

Graham, S., Harris, K. R., Mason, L., Moran, S., Saddler, B., & Adkins, M. (2004). *A national survey of the spelling practices of primary grade teachers.* Unpublished raw data.

Jones, D., & Christensen. C. (1999). The relationship between automaticity in handwriting and students' ability to generate written text. *Journal of Educational Psychology, 91,* 44–49.

Scardamalia, M., & Bereiter, C. (1986). Written composition. In M. Wittrock (Ed.), *Handbook of research on teaching* (3rd ed., pp. 778–803). New York: MacMillan.

Excerpts from

Effect of a Coteaching Handwriting Program for First Graders: One-Group Pretest-Posttest Design

Jane Case-Smith, Terri Holland, Alison Lane, Susan White

The American Journal of Occupational Therapy, July 2012

Students who struggle to learn handwriting are often referred to occupational therapy for intervention. Handwriting problems are one of the most common reasons for referral to school-based occupational therapy (Feder, Majnemer, & Synnes, 2000; Woodward & Swinth, 2002). Clinicians most often provide interventions using a one-on-one model of direct services outside the classroom. As described in the literature, occupational therapy handwriting interventions frequently use sensorimotor approaches that emphasize foundational skills combined with teaching–learning approaches that emphasize cognitive strategies (Weintraub, Yinon, Hirsch, & Parush, 2009; Zwicker, & Hadwin, 2009).

Inclusive Models of Handwriting Interventions

Classroom-embedded models for delivery of occupational therapy services have been developed to meet the mandate of inclusive education in the Individuals With Disabilities Education Act (Giangreco, 1986; Rainforth & York-Barr, 1997). In these models, the occupational therapist provides assessment and intervention in the classroom, allowing the student to remain in his or her natural context (Bazyk et al., 2009). Classroom-embedded services can result in optimal accommodations for students because they are developed and evaluated in the student's natural environment. Consultation is a classroom-based service in which the occupational therapist recommends teacher-implemented adaptations and accommodations for students with disabilities and can include training the teacher in specific interventions to implement with a student (Sandler, 1997). Consultation models do not always result in ideal occupational therapist participation in services to the child; they can evolve into delegation of intervention implementation to the teacher with minimal participation of the occupational therapist. When students need ongoing assessment to plan and coordinate their program, other models of service delivery are needed (Case-Smith & Holland, 2009).

One model of inclusive intervention is coteaching. Coteaching usually consists of a general educator paired with a special education teacher or related services professional (e.g., occupational therapist or speech–language pathologist) providing instruction to a class. When an occupational therapist participates in coteaching, the teacher and therapist collaboratively plan, coordinate, implement, and evaluate the classroom instruction. As a partnership between the teacher and occupational therapist, coteaching involves jointly developing goals, making decisions about classroom management, planning instruction and interventions, and evaluating student performance (Beamish, Bryer, & Davies, 2010; Bessette, 2008; Gately & Gately, 2001). Although different models of coteaching have been proposed, most often the role of the occupational therapist is to support the traditional role of the general education teacher. In this role, the occupational therapist adapts the curriculum, modifies materials, and provides specific interventions to students. The goal of coteaching is to provide different areas of expertise that, when combined, enhance instruction for all students (Murawski & Dieker, 2004). With a well-honed partnership, co-teaching can increase learning outcomes for all students while embedding accommodations for students with disabilities (Beamish et al., 2010).

> Handwriting problems are one of the most common reasons for referral to school-based occupational therapy.

Coteaching to Support At-Risk Students

In addition to services for students who have individualized education programs (IEPs), occupational therapists provide supports and develop accommodations for learners who struggle to learn the curriculum through Response to Intervention (RTI). Partnerships in which the occupational therapist and teacher together collect data on student progress, review the data, and plan instruction with embedded interventions are needed for RTI models to effectively support at-risk learners.

We evaluated the effects of one such partnership, a handwriting and writing program called Write Start that was cotaught by teachers and an occupational therapist and addressed handwriting legibility, handwriting speed, writing fluency, and written expression in first-grade students with diverse learning needs.

Research Questions

The research questions were as follows:

1. Do students improve significantly in handwriting legibility, speed, writing fluency, and written expression immediately and at six months following the Write Start program?

2. Do groups of students categorized by baseline handwriting legibility demonstrate differences in handwriting and writing progress immediately and at six months following the Write Start program?

Method

Research Design

This prospective, one-group, pretest–posttest design compared the effects of a handwriting and writing program on three different levels of learners. Measures of handwriting and writing were administered at pretest, posttest, and six-month follow-up. Two first-grade classrooms in a Midwestern U.S. city were selected to participate. This study was approved by the Ohio State University Institutional Review Board.

Sample

Each of the two first-grade classrooms selected to participate had two or more students with IEPs. The parents were informed about the study at the start of the school year during student orientation and completed consent forms at the time of the teachers' initial assessment. Information about which students were on IEPs and about their initial academic testing was provided by the teachers. A total of 39 students (21 boys, 18 girls) received permission to enter the study. The exclusion criteria for our sample were cognitive level on academic testing <70% or severe visual or hearing loss. One child with Down syndrome was excluded from the analysis because his cognitive level did not meet our criterion; however, this child participated in the program. Six students had IEPs, a proportion similar to those among students in the district and in the metropolitan area.

Write Start Intervention

An occupational therapist, classroom teacher, and intervention specialist implemented the Write Start program in the autumn of the first-grade year. The Write Start intervention had explicit goals to prevent handwriting problems and promote fluent writing in students of all ability levels using an evidence-based approach (see Case-Smith, Holland, & White, 2011). The cotaught program involved 45-minute sessions implemented twice a week for 12 weeks (24 sessions in total). Two types of coteaching—station teaching and team teaching (Cook & Friend, 1995)—were implemented. In *station teaching*, the coteachers created and coordinated activities for small groups of students. High- and low-performing students were selected for each group (see Tanta, Deitz, White, & Billingsley, 2005). The students rotated through the different stations while the teachers and therapists managed their stations. In *team teaching*, the teacher and therapist alternated in delivering the instruction, coordinating who led instruction on the basis of their expertise and the content.

Each week, the teachers and occupational therapist met to plan that week's handwriting and writing sessions for both classrooms. They first reviewed students' progress using handwriting samples from the previous week. After discussing individual and overall class performance, they selected activities and strategies for the coming week, including adaptations and supports for individual students. Examples of individualized adaptations and supports for writing included highlighted paper, pencil grips, three-tone paper, raised-lined paper, and slant boards. Examples of accommodations for behavior included weights held in laps, sensory breaks, and additional adult cueing.

The first and second weekly sessions had a specific and consistent format. In Session 1, the occupational therapist instructed the students in writing two or three letters, and the students practiced each letter repeatedly. Using motor learning concepts, the teachers and occupational therapist modeled letter formation and provided simple, consistent verbal and visual cues and specific descriptive feedback during the students' practice. Then the students rotated in small groups to stations in which they participated in activities to promote motor planning, sensory feedback, and manipulation; visual–motor integration; and memory of correct letter formation. Most of the activities used multisensory strategies for learning letter formation. Using strategies developed by Graham et al. (2000) and Harris et al. (2006), the teacher and occupational therapist asked students to evaluate their own work and promoted peer modeling and feedback by pairing students.

In Session 2, the therapist reviewed the letters that were taught in Session 1, the students copied a sentence as a writing sample, and then the students spent 20–30 minutes writing stories or an assignment. In the final period of Session 2, called the "writing workshop," the teacher gave mini-lessons on a writing convention or concept, the students were allowed periods of independent writing, the teacher and occupational therapist conferred with students about their writing, and the students were encouraged to share their writing with each other (e.g., read each others' writing in the "share chairs"; see Harris et al., 2006). The teacher emphasized good handwriting during the writing workshop using the terms introduced to the students during the handwriting instruction. At the end of the program, the students "published" their stories, necessitating that they edit their stories to make them readable to others.

Measures

Intervention Fidelity

A fidelity measure for the Write Start program was developed using the core principles to define expected therapist and teacher behaviors and child responses (Case-Smith, Holland, & Bishop, 2011). Each instructional element was scored as performance with complete consistency, partial consistency, and inconsistency. The reliability of the fidelity instrument was established the previous year (Case-Smith et al., 2011). Graduate assistants administered the fidelity measure in 18 of the 24 Write Start sessions. In addition, Jane Case-Smith interviewed the teachers and occupational therapist at the end of the program to gather qualitative data about their coteaching experience.

Evaluation Tool of Children's Handwriting—Manuscript (ETCH–M)

Handwriting legibility and speed were assessed using the Evaluation Tool of Children's Handwriting–Manuscript (ETCH–M; Amundson, 1995). The ETCH–M sections we analyzed included lower- and upper-case alphabet legibility and lower- and uppercase alphabet speed. Percentage scores were computed for number of legible letters when writing the alphabet. Speed scores were the number of seconds the child took to write the alphabet letters. The ETCH–M demonstrated fair test–retest reliability for letter legibility ($r = .77$) and word legibility ($r = .71$) when first- and second grade students were tested 1 week apart (Diekema, Deitz, & Amundson, 1998). Feder, Majnemer, Bourbonnais, Blayney, and Morin (2007) examined the validity of the ETCH–M and found that teachers' ratings of handwriting correlated with ETCH–M scores.

Graduate research assistants administered the ETCH–M individually to students. After students completed the test's writing samples, the ETCH–M protocols were copied and blinded for scoring. Using the manual's criteria, two evaluators independently scored each ETCH–M, and the scores were then compared to determine the final legibility percentages.

Woodcock-Johnson Fluency and Writing Samples

Writing performance was measured using the Writing Fluency and Writing Samples subtests of the Woodcock–Johnson III Tests of Achievement (WJIII; Woodcock, McGrew, & Mather, 2007; McGrew, Schrank, & Woodcock, 2007). In the Writing Fluency test, students were instructed to compose sentences from three words written beside a picture. The test requires minimal idea generation, but the child must link words in a complete sentence under a time constraint. Students who did not produce three grammatical sentences within two minutes were told to stop. Those who produced three grammatical sentences were allowed to continue for seven minutes. One point was awarded for each grammatical sentence using all the written words without modification. In the Writing Samples test, the student wrote a meaningful sentence for a given purpose (a picture). The test requires retrieval of word meaning and syntactic information. The students were evaluated three times—at baseline, one week, and six months following the intervention.

Procedures

We grouped the students by initial legibility level using their pretest ETCH—M lowercase alphabet legibility score. We also checked this score using their first handwriting sample score to ensure that the ETCH—M was an accurate representation of the students' handwriting performance. The groups were defined as follows: low performing, <50% legibility; average performing, 50%–80% legibility; and high performing, >80% legibility.

Handwriting Legibility and Speed

Because the Write Start program taught the student lowercase letters, our analysis focuses on lowercase alphabet legibility. As a group, the students improved by 27 percentage points in lowercase handwriting legibility (from 62% legibility to 89% legibility), and this improvement was highly significant. They also improved significantly in handwriting speed for writing the lowercase alphabet; the mean speed decreased by 122 seconds, from 203.9 seconds to 80.9 seconds. In the uppercase alphabet, the students also made significant progress in legibility, improving by 11.2 percentage points, and in speed, improving by 97.1 seconds (see Table 1).

> As a group, the students improved by 27 percentage points in lowercase handwriting legibility (from 62% legibility to 89% legibility), and this improvement was highly significant.

Writing Fluency and Written Expression

The students also made significant gains in writing fluency and written expression (see Table 2). For all students, mean scores for Writing Fluency improved by 6.7 points, from 1.2 to 7.9, a significant gain. Writing Samples, a measure of written expression, was considered to be an indirect outcome of the Write Start program because writing ability was not the emphasis of the program. Writing Samples mean scores improved significantly from pretest (7.6) to follow-up (10.7).

TABLE 1. Handwriting Scores on the Evaluation Tool of Children's Handwriting–Manuscript, by Baseline Legibility Level

Subscale	Time	Low-Performing Group M (SD)	Average-Performing Group M (SD)	High-Performing Group M (SD)
Lowercase alphabet legibility (%)	Pretest	41.5 (4.0)	59.1(3.4)	85.9 (4.2)
	Posttest	76.5 (2.6)	88.3 (2.2)	97.3 (2.7)
	Follow-up	78.5 (2.9)	88.9 (2.5)	98.4 (3.0)
Lowercase alphabet speed (sec)	Pretest	208 (29.1)	255.1 (24.9)	148.5 (30.5)
	Posttest	111.1 (9.8)	92.5 (8.4)	61.5 (10.3)
	Follow-up	97.8 (10.2)	83.7 (8.7)	61.2 (10.7)
Uppercase alphabet legibility (%)	Pretest	51.5 (5.3)	75.3 (4.5)	88.6 (5.5)
	Posttest	65.5 (4.4)	76.4 (3.8)	90.0 (4.6)
	Follow-up	69.7 (4.1)	85.6 (3.5)	93.7 (4.3)
Uppercase alphabet speed (sec)	Pretest	210 (29.1)	203.7 (24.9)	171.5 (30.5)
	Posttest	121.9 (12.7)	113.5 (10.9)	92.8 (13.3)
	Follow-up	109.8 (9.8)	100.3 (8.4)	84.4 (10.2)

Note. Students were grouped on the basis of baseline handwriting legibility level as follows: low-performing group, <50% legibility; average-performing group, 50%–80% legibility; and high-performing group, >80% legibility.

TABLE 2. Writing Fluency and Writing Samples Scores on the Woodcock–Johnson III Tests of Achievement, by Baseline Legibility Level

Subtest	Time	Low-Performing Group M (SD)	Average-Performing Group M (SD)	High-Performing Group M (SD)
Writing Fluency raw scores	Pretest	0.2 (0.5)	0.9 (0.4)	2.5 (0.6)
	Posttest	2.1 (1.3)	5.3 (1.1)	5.9 (1.4)
	Follow-up	3.8 (1.3)	8.5 (1.1)	11.3 (1.4)
Writing Samples raw scores	Pretest	5.4 (0.6)	7.3 (0.5)	10.2 (0.6)
	Posttest	8.0 (0.5)	8.9 (0.5)	11.3 (0.6)
	Follow-up	9.9 (0.5)	10.5 (0.4)	11.7 (0.5)

Note. Students were grouped on the basis of baseline handwriting legibility level as follows: low-performing group, <50% legibility; average-performing group, 50%–80% legibility; and high-performing group, >80% legibility.

Discussion

This study examined the progress made when a diverse set of learners, including students who struggled with handwriting, participated in a cotaught handwriting and writing program. We implemented the Write Start program with the entire first-grade class, embedding additional supports and accommodations into each session. In this classroom-embedded model, we used station teaching, repeated practice, frequent and immediate adult feedback, self-evaluation, and peer modeling and support. These methods allowed the occupational therapist and teachers to meet the needs of individual students and to accommodate different learning styles.

Our model of coteaching required an hour a week to review students' progress and plan the sessions. The teachers and occupational therapist were enthusiastic about the model and revealed in the final interview that coteaching required flexibility, willingness to partner, openness to others' ideas, and time to plan. When asked about the benefits of the model, the teachers and occupational therapist noted that students received more attention and individualized instruction, interventions were easy to implement and monitor, and students learned about collaboration and cooperation from the modeling of the teachers and occupational therapist. The teachers and occupational therapist also reported that they gained skills from working together. In particular, the teachers learned strategies for teaching handwriting, and the occupational therapist learned about the first-grade curriculum and behavioral management of a classroom. Compared with traditional instruction, the teachers who participated in Write Start felt that the handwriting goals were generalized more readily into the classroom instruction and that handwriting instruction was better integrated into the writing curriculum.

> A substantial proportion of students struggle with handwriting (Cahill, 2009; Graham et al., 2008) and can benefit from additional supports but have no or limited access to occupational therapy services.

The goal of this study was to develop and evaluate a model of service delivery that would enable occupational therapists to provide services to at-risk and struggling students before they were placed on IEPs and referred for occupational therapy services. A substantial proportion of students struggle with handwriting (Cahill, 2009; Graham et al., 2008) and can benefit from additional supports but have no or limited access to occupational therapy services. To determine the effect of the

Write Start program on children who were struggling with handwriting or had illegible handwriting, we compared the progress of low-, average-, and high-performing students as determined by baseline legibility. Students with low initial handwriting legibility scores made the greatest progress, improving 34.6% in 12 weeks. The low-performing group's gains in the current study were relatively substantial and were retained at year-end testing.

The second primary variable of interest was writing fluency; our hypothesis was that once handwriting is automatic, students develop fluency and can focus on content and composition. Fluency was measured using lowercase alphabet speed and the Writing Fluency subscale. These scores improved substantially for students at all performance levels. Handwriting speed improved 87.3 seconds for the high-performing group and 110.2 seconds for the low-performing group. The average-performing group improved 171.4 seconds for writing the alphabet, which, combined with their follow-up legibility scores (89%), indicates that they had become functional handwriters. All groups improved in writing fluency, making substantial gains in the follow-up period. Their improvement after the program ended suggests that the students' handwriting had become automatic, allowing them to focus on writing and mastering writing fluency.

> Handwriting instruction for first-grade students that includes adult modeling of letter formation, use of consistent visual and verbal cues, repeated practice with immediate adult feedback, peer modeling and support, and self evaluation results in significant gains in legibility, speed, and fluency.

Students of all performance levels seemed to benefit from the Write Start program; the students who initially were struggling in handwriting improved the most in legibility, and the students who initially had good legibility made substantial gains in writing fluency. Therefore, the program was able to meet the needs of diverse learners in the natural context of the first-grade classroom. Although the model required three adults, including an occupational therapist, it is probable that the same amount of time would be needed for the teacher to provide handwriting instruction to the class and the occupational therapist to provide individualized services to children with poor handwriting.

Implications for Practice

- Handwriting instruction for first-grade students that includes adult modeling of letter formation, use of consistent visual and verbal cues, repeated practice with immediate adult feedback, peer modeling and support, and self evaluation results in significant gains in legibility, speed, and fluency.

- Integrating occupational therapy handwriting interventions into the classroom using a co-teaching model allows students with poor handwriting to receive services while remaining in their learning environment and promotes handwriting performance among all students.

- First-grade students across ability levels may benefit when coteaching teams of occupational therapists and teachers collaboratively plan and implement handwriting instruction that is linked to students' writing instruction.

Conclusion

The first-grade students who participated in the Write Start cotaught handwriting and writing program with classroom-embedded occupational therapy services made significant progress in handwriting legibility, speed, and writing fluency that was retained at the six-month follow-up. Students who demonstrated low baseline legibility made progress in handwriting and writing similar to that of students who demonstrated high baseline legibility.

As a model for inclusive, classroom-embedded occupational therapy services, Write Start appears to benefit students at risk for handwriting and writing problems and may prevent later handwriting problems. By supporting the development of writing fluency, this model enhances young children's literacy competency.

References

Amundson, S. (1995). *Evaluation of Children's Handwriting*. Homer, AK: O.T. Kids.

Bazyk, S., Michaud, P., Goodman, G., Papp, P., Hawkins, E., & Welch, M. A. (2009). Integrating occupational therapy services in a kindergarten curriculum: A look at the outcomes. *American Journal of Occupational Therapy, 63,* 160–171.

Beamish, W., Bryer, F., & Davies, M. (2010). Teacher reflections on co-teaching a unit of work. *International Journal of Whole Schooling, 2,* 3–18.

Bessette, H. J. (2008). Using students' drawings to elicit general and special educators' perceptions of co-teaching. *Teaching and Teacher Education, 24,* 1376–1396.

Cahill, S. M. (2009). Where does handwriting fit in? *Intervention in School and Clinic, 44,* 223–228.

Case-Smith, J., & Holland, T. (2009). Making decisions about service delivery in early childhood programs. *Language, Speech, and Hearing Services in Schools, 40,* 416–423.

Case-Smith, J., Holland, T., & Bishop, B. (2011). Effectiveness of an integrated handwriting program for first grade students: A pilot study. *American Journal of Occupational Therapy, 65,* 670–678.

Case-Smith, J., Holland, T., & White, S. (2011). Effectiveness of a co-taught handwriting–writing program for first grade students. *Journal of Educational Research.*

Cook, L., & Friend, M. (1995). Co-teaching: Guidelines for creating effective practices. *Focus on Exceptional Children, 28*(3), 1–12.

Diekema, S. M., Deitz, J., & Amundson, S. J. (1998). Test–retest reliability of the Evaluation Tool of Children's Handwriting–Manuscript. *American Journal of Occupational Therapy, 52,* 248–255.

Feder, K. P., Majnemer, A., Bourbonnais, D., Blayney, M., & Morin, I. (2007). Handwriting performance on the ETCH–M of students in a grade one regular education program. *Physical and Occupational Therapy in Pediatrics, 27,* 43–62.

Feder, K., Majnemer, A., & Synnes, A. (2000). Handwriting: Current trends in occupational therapy practice. *Canadian Journal of Occupational Therapy, 67,* 197–204. PubMed

Gately, S. E., & Gately, F. J. (2001). Understanding co-teaching components. *Teaching Exceptional Children, 33,* 40–47.

Giangreco, M. F. (1986). Delivery of therapeutic services in special education programs for learners with severe handicaps. *Physical and Occupational Therapy in Pediatrics, 6,* 5–15.

Graham, S., Harris, K. R., & Fink, B. (2000). Is handwriting causally related to learning to write? Treatment of handwriting problems in beginning writers. *Journal of Educational Psychology, 92,* 620–633.

Graham, S., Harris, K. R., Mason, L., Fink-Chorzempa, B., Moran, S., & Saddler, B. (2008). How do primary grade teachers teach handwriting? A national survey. *Reading and Writing, 21,* 49–69.

McGrew, K. S., Schrank, F. A, & Woodcock, R. W. (2007). *Technical manual: Woodcock–Johnson III. Normative update.* Rolling Meadows, IL: Riverside Publishing.

Murawski, W. W., & Dieker, L. A. (2004). Tips and strategies for co-teaching at the secondary level. *Teaching Exceptional Children, 36*(5), 52-58.

Rainforth, G., & York-Barr, J. (1997). *Collaborative teams for students with severe disabilities* (2nd ed.). Baltimore: Brookes.

Sandler, A. G. (1997). Physical and occupational therapy services: Use of a consultative therapy model in the schools. *Preventing School Failure, 41,* 164–167.

Tanta, K. J., Deitz, J. C., White, O., & Billingsley, F. (2005). The effects of peer-play level on initiations and responses of preschool children with delayed play skills. *American Journal of Occupational Therapy, 59,* 437–445.

Weintraub, N., Yinon, M., Hirsch, I. B., & Parush, S. (2009). Effectiveness of sensorimotor and task-oriented handwriting intervention in elementary school-aged students with handwriting difficulties. *OTJR: Occupation, Participation and Health, 29,* 125–134.

Woodcock, R. W., McGrew, K. S., & Mather, N. (2007). *Woodcock–Johnson III Test of Achievement.* Itasca, IL: Riverside Publishing.

Woodward, S., & Swinth, Y. (2002). Multisensory approach to handwriting remediation: Perceptions of school-based occupational therapists. *American Journal of Occupational Therapy, 56,* 305–312.

Zwicker, J. G., & Hadwin, A. F. (2009). Cognitive versus multisensory approaches to handwriting intervention: A randomized controlled trial. *OTJR: Occupation, Participation and Health, 29,* 40–48.

Helpful Handwriting Hints

Lisa A. Kurtz

TEACHING Exceptional Children, Pages 58–59, Vol. 27,
©1994 Council for Exceptional Children, Inc.

Classroom teachers should consider handwriting instruction to be a relevant part of the elementary-level curriculum because of the role written communication plays in a total literacy program. While the content of a student's written effort is admittedly more important than its appearance, some degree of proficiency in the mechanical aspects of writing is needed to prevent interruption in the flow of communicative intent. Teachers should consider remedial instruction not only when the student's writing is illegible, but also whenever the student writes so slowly or with such effort that it interferes with concentration on the content of the assignment. They can do much to reinforce remedial handwriting strategies for children with motor learning difficulties. This article presents practical solutions to some of the more common problems that may interfere with the mechanics of writing.

Poor Sitting Posture

Poor posture often relates to an underlying problem with low muscle tone and can significantly interfere with the ease with which a child can coordinate hand movement for visually guided work. The child should have a chair that has a flat seat and back. The chair should be at a height that allows the child's feet to rest flat with the hips, knees, and ankles all at 90-degree angles. This will help the child to achieve smooth postural adjustments as the writing arm moves across the paper. The desk height should be 2 inches above the height of the child's bent elbows (Benbow, 1988). If the desk is too high, the child will tend to elevate his or her shoulders, which can restrict freedom of movement. If the desk is too low, the child may tend to slouch over the desk or lean on the nondominant arm for support. When copying material from the chalkboard, children with writing difficulties should be seated directly in front of the material to be copied, because fine motor skill tends to be most efficient when the child is in a symmetrical body position.

Immature Pencil Grasp

Children who persist in using primitive pencil grasps may demonstrate problems with low muscle tone and may have failed to develop the ability to isolate distal movements. Their control of hand movements comes from the shoulder and elbow, as opposed to the more precise control that comes from the hand and fingers. While some degree of individual variability is acceptable, it is important to reinforce the following elements of pencil grasp (Benbow, 1988):

1. The forearm should rest on the writing surface in a neutral position, with the hand resting on the little finger. This position allows the wrist to move freely.

2. The wrist should be in a slightly extended posture (bent back), because this brings the thumb in a position where it can comfortably oppose the fingers.

3. There should be a rounded, open web space between the thumb and fingers. This position permits freedom of movement through all finger joints and also allows the finger pads to contact the pencil shaft. Tactile sensors are most efficient on the pads of the fingers, so this position optimizes sensory awareness of grip pressure and kinesthetic movements. One of the best activities for encouraging proper hand position is to practice writing, tracing, or other fine motor activities while sitting or standing at a vertical work surface, such as a blackboard or easel. When the work is presented at or slightly below eye level, the student cannot avoid holding the writing tool using the desired wrist position.

> One of the best activities for encouraging proper hand position is to practice...while sitting or standing at a vertical work surface, such as a blackboard or easel.

Children who persist in using primitive types of pencil grasps may benefit from a variety of sensorimotor activities and exercises. Games that provide deep pressure to the shoulder joints, such as wheelbarrow walking or crawling on hands and knees through an obstacle course, may be appropriate in helping such children increase control and stability at the shoulder (Oliver, 1989). Some children enjoy learning the sign language alphabet as a fun way to practice finger isolation skills. Children with weak pencil grasps may benefit from resistive pencil activities such as tracing around stencils or templates, drawing or writing in clay with a stylus, or drawing on sandpaper or pressure-sensitive carbons. The resistance causes the child to grip the writing tool more firmly, to receive increased sensory feedback and subsequently to strengthen hand muscles.

Adapted pencil holders such as triangle grips or Stetro grips may be useful for children who have difficulty remembering the proper position but have adequate control when the pencil is placed for them. Teachers can also adapt standard pencils by wrapping them with strips of tape or adhesive-backed foam padding to mark where on the shaft the pencil should be held. Old-fashioned pencil holders that keep the pencil in a vertical position are also helpful for some children, because they encourage approach and grasp with the forearm in the proper position.

Poor Stability or Positioning of Paper

Several associated characteristics may be evident in children who have trouble positioning or stabilizing the paper. These include the following:

1. There may be a tendency to switch hands frequently during manipulative play. This suggests that the child is not certain of which hand to assign a dominant role and which hand to use as an assistor.

2. Synkinesis, or motor overflow, may be observed in the less dominant hand. For example, when performing a one-handed activity, the other hand moves involuntarily.

3. There may be hesitancy or discomfort in manually or visually crossing the midline of the body. This is often a subtle problem that may be present only as a stiffness in trunk movements when writing. For example, when writing at the chalkboard the child may step sideways rather than allowing the writing arm to reach past the midline.

To help children who have difficulties with bilateral motor integration, teachers should encourage activities that require the two hands to work reciprocally. The easiest bilateral activities require using the two hands symmetrically, as in clapping games or flattening clay with a rolling pin. Slightly more difficult activities allow the nondominant hand to be in a static role while the dominant hand assumes a more dynamic role. Examples include holding a mixing bowl while stirring with the dominant hand and holding a template steady while the dominant hand traces. The most challenging bilateral activities require both hands to interact reciprocally and with different motions. Scissor activities offer this sort of experience, because one hand manipulates the scissors while the other holds and orients the angle of the paper.

Adjusting the angle of the paper may help some children with poor bilateral coordination. While good writers seem to learn best using a slight slant, increasing the slant of the paper and shifting it slightly toward the dominant hand may help a child who avoids crossing the midline, because it places the paper to the side of the midline. Once the best angle has been identified for the student, a strip of masking tape can serve as a visual reference. When a child has severe difficulty stabilizing the paper during writing, a blotter or large sheet of construction paper taped to the desk may provide just enough friction to keep the paper from slipping.

Uncertain Hand Dominance

If a student has not clearly demonstrated a preferred hand by 1st grade, the decision should be made for the student based on observations of which hand is better coordinated. If teachers and parents feel unclear about which is the more skilled hand, it is probably wise to request consultation from an occupational therapist or other motor skills specialist before encouraging the use of either hand. Once a preferred hand is identified, teachers may reinforce the student's awareness by placing jewelry or a ribbon on that wrist.

Children with delayed hand dominance or hesitancy in crossing the midline of the body will tend to reach for objects with whichever hand happens to be the closest. Most school-aged children will retain the object in the grasping hand, even if its use requires reaching across the midline. For this reason, the student's work area should be organized so that materials are located on the same side of the desk as the preferred hand.

Difficulty Copying from the Chalkboard

Problems in this area can result from a variety of factors, including poor short-term visual memory, poor visual perception (especially figure-ground separation), or poor eye-muscle control. Students with this type of difficulty should be seated as close to the chalkboard as possible.

They may benefit from having the teacher write only small amounts on the chalkboard at any one time or use different colored chalk to write different portions of the material. When older students are required to copy large amounts of material from the chalkboard, teachers may consider offering them a copy of the teacher's plan to copy from near point.

Problems with Spatial Organization

For students who have difficulty with spacing, prompts such as placing a finger between words may serve as a helpful reminder. If the student has trouble remembering to write from left to right, the teacher may run a length of green tape for *Go* along the left side of the desk, and red tape for *Stop* along the right side. For the student who forgets to leave left or right margins on the page, a clear strip of tape run along the side of the paper may serve as an effective marker. The slickness of the tape adds a tactile cue that is often more reinforcing than simply drawing a margin line. Students who have difficulty placing long or short letters on the appropriate line may benefit from having the lines highlighted with a colored marker. Students with severe difficulty in this skill may benefit from using a cardboard frame that forces the pencil to stop when it hits either the top or bottom line.

> Use of multi-sensory (visual-auditory-kinesthetic-tactile) strategies may be most helpful in teaching children the correct letter formations.

Students with spatial confusion often have particular difficulty organizing their work in math. Graph paper may help to teach them how to organize work simultaneously in horizontal and vertical planes.

Students with visual perception problems frequently reverse letters beyond the developmentally appropriate age. It is common for children to have more difficulty *drawing* letters in the correct orientation than *recognizing* letters that have been reversed or inverted. Use of multi-sensory (visual-auditory-kinesthetic-tactile) strategies may be most helpful in teaching children the correct letter formations.

Outside the Classroom

While many of the suggestions presented here can be readily incorporated into the classroom routine, others require the student to spend a considerable amount of time in supervised practice of specific skills. Parents or other family members should be encouraged to supervise students in practice outside the school environment and to include assignments in motivating nonacademic formats. Examples might include copying the weekly grocery list from a parent's dictation or scanning the television guide to select and write a schedule of programs to watch during the week.

References

Benbow, M. (1988). *Loops and other groups: A kinesthetic writing system.* Randolph, NJ: O.T. Ideas.

Oliver, C.E. (1989). A sensorimotor program for improving writing readiness skills in elementary-age children. *American Journal of Occupational Therapy, 44* (2), 111-116.

PEANUTS

PEANUTS reprinted by permission of United Feature Syndicate, Inc.

Handwriting Success for All

Kama Einhorn

Instructor, January/February 2001, ©Scholastic, Inc.

Row upon row of wobbly, cursive lowercase w's were spread across Matty's paper, like pointy waves in an ocean of blue lines. The rips and smears of repeated erasing were all too visible. As I looked over his work, I made notes on his progress: "Matty responds well to an active, hands-on approach. He is a tactile learner who seems to enjoy experiencing new things in the classroom."

What Matty clearly did not enjoy was practicing the new cursive letter forms. Laboring to fill his page with "perfect" letters left him restless, frustrated, and unsuccessful. He needed a different approach.

> **Attention to all styles of learning is, as in every area of the curriculum, a necessary part of handwriting instruction.**

How can we simultaneously teach children to copy from a model, while at the same time honoring their individual learning styles? Visual learners, for instance, may respond well to copying from a model, but tactile learners respond well to incorporating their sense of touch, exploring letters through texture and shape. Auditory learners need to hear descriptions of letter formation. Physical learners can better remember letter forms if they experience letters using gross motor movements. Attention to all styles of learning is, as in every area of the curriculum, a necessary part of handwriting instruction.

Easy Ways to Handwriting—Practice Success

When you begin handwriting practice, you'll want to teach to children's strengths, keep children creatively engaged, and not overwhelm reluctant writers. The teaching of handwriting varies depending on the grade level, but a step-by-step initial lesson might proceed as follows:

1) Preview the letter you'll be teaching by writing it on the board.

2) Demonstrate its formation on the board as you verbally describe it.

3) Have students "air trace" the letter with their fingers in the air.

4) Have students pick up their pencils and try the letter once on their paper. Monitor, checking to see if they have understood the

basic strokes. If not, take the student's hand in yours and guide him or her through the strokes one by one.

5) Invite students to complete one row of the letter and then circle their "best" in the row.

Regardless of the children's grade level, there are certain helpful guidelines to follow whenever you teach handwriting skills. Adapt your lessons to incorporate the following suggestions, which will give learners of all styles a better grasp of the art of handwriting.

Combine modalities. Visual learners will respond to copying from a model, but auditory learners will benefit from "talking through" a letter's formation, tactile learners from tracing it in sand, and physical learners from having the letter traced on their back or palm by a partner.

Bring it together. Children learn letter formation by actively exploring letter names, the sounds the letters stand for, each letter's arrangement of curves and lines, and the movements used in its formation. (See Further Resources, Bear et al.) As you introduce letters, refer to their names and sounds. Use physical descriptions such as, "b has a bat that goes down, and a round ball at the bottom."

Put practice rows in their place. Practicing rows of letters certainly serves its purpose, but so does experiencing the sheer fun of letters. Balance rote letter practice with engaging and meaningful activities that integrate all the senses.

Guide self-assessment. Help children learn to critique their own handwriting ("My t is not tall enough") by either comparing it with a model or having an assessment checklist to read against.

Provide media other than pencil and paper. Writing on or with easily erasable materials such as sand, rice, clay, or finger paint takes away the need to erase, and therefore frees up reluctant writers. It also reaches children who learn kinesthetically. Writing on a chalkboard allows children to use gross motor movements and see letters at eye level; and practicing on dry erase boards takes away the need to erase mistakes on paper.

> Children learn letter formation by actively exploring letter names, the sounds the letters stand for, each letter's arrangement of curves and lines, and the movements used in its formation.

Write for a purpose. After children finish their practice rows, have them use writing for a real-life purpose. If they've just learned W, have them address an envelope to a friend whose name begins with W.

Introduce letters according to similarity of formation. Most handwriting programs order the letters so that children can organize their visual perceptions; for instance, l, b, h, and k all begin with the same first downward stroke. Pointing out similarities and differences between letters is helpful.

Make time for independent practice. Explicitly teaching a letter's formation to the whole group takes a short time; children can then work independently or practice at the writing center as you focus on other areas of the curriculum. You might also send worksheets home with students for extra practice in trouble areas.

Assessment Strategies

Do you know anyone whose writing looks like the samples in the handwriting books? Of course not! When guiding children's letter-formation practice, consistency and legibility are the goals. Do children make the same letters the same way each time? Are all the tall letters tall, and all the small letters small? And most important, can you or another child read what the child has written?

Especially with older children who are refining their techniques, it is helpful to remember the "five S's": size, slant, shape, spacing, and smoothness. (See Further Resources, Zaner-Bloser.)

Five Quick and Easy Activities for Manuscript or Cursive

Glitter Templates. Help tactile learners reinforce letter shapes by writing a letter on a large index card. Include guiding horizontal lines (top, bottom, and dotted middle). Children can glue yarn on the top and bottom lines, glue short pieces of plastic straw to the dotted lines, and squeeze glue along the letter's lines and cover in glitter. When the work is dry, children can close their eyes and feel the orientation of the letter within the lines.

> Help children learn to critique their own handwriting

Sidewalk Chalk. Take letter practice outdoors! Invite children to use sidewalk chalk to decorate the sidewalk or playground surface with letters. They might make a giant letter and take turns walking on it in the directions the letter is formed; or the whole class might stand on the lines to make a human letter.

Calligraphy Demonstrations. Invite a calligrapher to visit and demonstrate "fancy" letters, and let children try their hand at forming them. Children might also write with quills: Use craft feathers from a craft-supply store and dip (either end) into tempura paint. In addition, you might invite a parent whose first language does not use the Roman alphabet to demonstrate how letters are formed in his or her native language.

Letter Café. Spread out foil or wax paper and let children practice letters with various foods: squeeze cheese or cake frosting, licorice strings, cooked and raw spaghetti, and so on. Or, spread pudding, yogurt, or whipped cream in a thin layer on wax paper and let children trace letters onto the surface with their fingers. Melt chocolate chips, and use a thick paintbrush to "paint" chocolate letters onto wax paper. Refrigerate, peel, and eat the letters!

> Introduce letters according to similarity of formation.

Invisible Ink. Use lemon or grapefruit juice and cotton swabs to paint invisible letters onto plain white paper. Let the paper dry, then sandwich it between two sheets of newspaper and iron with a medium-hot iron. Watch the secret letters appear!

Added Material

Kama Einhorn is the author of *Cursive Writing Made Easy & Fun!* (Scholastic, 2000), and two other Scholastic books on teaching manuscript to children in grades K–1 (illustrations by Michael Moran).

Size: Letters are the right height and rest neatly on the line.

Slant: Letters all slant in one consistent direction, usually forward or straight up. A backward slant is also fine.

Shape: Letters are closed where they should be; they are not too narrow or wide.

Spacing: Spaces between letters, words, and sentences are even.

Smoothness: Line quality is even, not too light or heavy, or inconsistent.

What's the Difference?

- Cursive comes from the Latin currere, which means "to run." It is usually taught in second or third grade and perfected in fourth.

- Script, as cursive is often called, comes from the Latin scribere, "to write," and can be used to describe any system of writing.

- Print refers to the stick-and-ball formation of letters that students learn before cursive. Many kindergartners know how to print uppercase letters, while lowercase letters are commonly introduced in first grade.

• Manuscript is the technical name for print.

Handwriting Instruction: It Makes Sense

Even in the age of computers, handwriting is still an important skill. If our ideas aren't expressed legibly on paper, we lose ground in a main form of social communication. Also, practicing single letters leads to faster letter recognition, which allows for more cognitive energy to be spent on higher-level thinking. Being able to read our own writing gives us quick and easy access to our own thoughts. And on many of the new language-arts tests, children must respond in essay form to open-ended questions, which requires competent, quick, and legible handwriting.

Research has shown that learning about letters and their shapes often turns into interest in their sounds and how they are used in words. In practicing letter forms, children develop and strengthen fine motor skills. In addition, many learners will "imprint" the letter model and use it for forming their own letters—by writing the same letter over several times, children help to seal it in their visual and physical memory.

Further Resources

• *Handwriting: A Way to Self-Expression,* Zaner-Bloser
www.zaner-bloser.com

• *D'Nealian,* ScottForesman
www.scottforesman.com/language/dnealian.html

• *Handwriting Without* Tears www.hwtears.com

• *Beginning to Read: Thinking and Learning About Print,* by Marilyn Adams (The MIT Press, 1994).

• *Words Their Way: Word Study for Phonics, Vocabulary & Spelling,* by Donald R. Bear, Marcia Invernizzi, and Francine Johnston (Prentice Hall, 1995).

Teaching the Left-Handed Writer

Clinton S. Hackney and William Hendricks

In the average classroom, there are two to four "lefties" who have special needs that must be considered by the teacher.

Approximately ten percent of all people are left-handed. This often-overlooked minority includes United States Presidents Ronald Reagan, George H. W. Bush, Bill Clinton, and Barack Obama, as well as many other famous and gifted people, such as Prince Charles, Norman Schwarzkopf, Oprah Winfrey, Benjamin Franklin, and Henry Ford. In the average classroom, there are two to four "lefties" who have special needs that must be considered by the teacher. Yet many right-handed teachers are unaware of the subtle ways in which classroom tools and activities can be biased. Pencil sharpeners face the wrong way, notebook spirals dig into the hand, the cutting edge of scissors is upside down, and tight seating at tables causes elbows to bump. Right-handed teachers may practice the left-handed position themselves to better understand the needs of left-handed writers.

Determining Hand Dominance

Early childhood teachers may encounter children who have not yet developed a clear preference for one hand or the other. If the child is definitely left-handed, it is better to teach him or her to use that hand in writing. If, however, there is some doubt as to which is the dominant hand, there are several simple ways of determining which will be the hand to train. Working with one child at a time, observe the student in the following situations. Be careful to let the child pick up the testing materials; do not hand them to the child. Keep a record of the results; if a child is truly ambidextrous, it is probably better to train the right hand.

> ...many right-handed teachers are unaware of the subtle ways in which classroom tools and activities can be biased.

Hand puppet—Place a puppet on the table and observe which hand the child puts the puppet on.

Key and lock—Padlock a cupboard and place the key on a table. Ask the child to take the key, unlock the padlock, and bring you an object from the cupboard. Observe hand preference.

Hammering nails—Observe the child's hand preference as he or she hammers pegs with a toy hammer or places pegs in a pegboard.

Screwing lids on jars—Place several jars of different sizes in one pile and the matching lids in another. Observe handedness as the child matches the lids to the jars.

Throwing a ball—On the playground, ask the child to pick up a ball and throw it to you.

Discouraging the "Hooked" Writing Position

Handwriting can be an especially difficult area for left-handers. Without good instruction, left-handers may develop bad writing habits, including the tendency to "hook" the wrist in order to see what they are writing. Emphasize the correct pencil and paper positions for left-handed writers, shown below, to help students develop good habits.

Paper Position for Left-Handed Writers

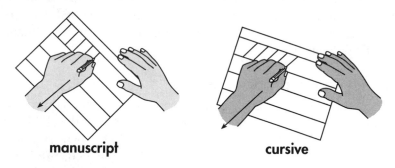

manuscript   **cursive**

Pencil Position for Left-Handed Writers

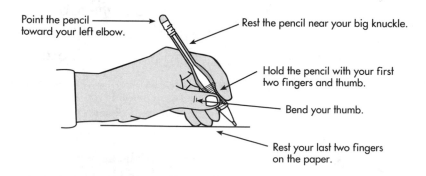

Point the pencil toward your left elbow.

Rest the pencil near your big knuckle.

Hold the pencil with your first two fingers and thumb.

Bend your thumb.

Rest your last two fingers on the paper.

Hints for Handwriting

Although teachers may find that left-handed students in their classrooms have already developed awkward handwriting, it is not necessary to lower expectations for these students. The suggestions that follow will help left-handed students write as well as right-handed students.

- Emphasize correct paper position to help left-handed writers resist twisting or "hooking" their hands and wrists in order to see what they are writing.

- Suggest that left-handed students hold their pencils slightly farther back than right-handed students. This allows them to see what they are writing.

- Seat left-handed writers to the left of the board for better visibility.

- Encourage left-handed writers to practice writing at the board for full, free arm movement.

- Occasionally, group left-handed students together for handwriting instruction.

- If table and arm chairs are used, make sure left-handed students are not seated at desks designed for right-handed students.

- If possible, provide left-handed scissors and other left-handed tools.

- Be aware that reversing letters is a common problem for the left-handed child. Most errors result from confusion between manuscript **d** and **b** and **p** and **q**. To help, concentrate on formally teaching left-to-right progression and the correct formation of forward and backward circles before introducing these letters.

Teachers should be aware of the left-handers in their classrooms and plan support for them. Care should be taken, however, to avoid attention that will make left-handers self-conscious. Showing sensitivity to the needs of these students can build self-esteem and make left-handers a bit more comfortable in a "right-handed world."